WITHDRAWN

READINGS IN THE APPLIED ECONOMICS OF AFRICA

VOLUME 2: MACRO-ECONOMICS

READINGS IN THE APPLIED ECONOMICS OF AFRICA

Edited by
EDITH H. WHETHAM
*Sometime Visiting Professor in Agricultural Economics
at Ahmadu Bello University, Northern Nigeria*

and
JEAN I. CURRIE
*Sometime Lecturer in Economics at
Ahmadu Bello University*

VOLUME 2: MACRO-ECONOMICS

CAMBRIDGE
AT THE UNIVERSITY PRESS
1967

CARL A. RUDISILL LIBRARY
LENOIR RHYNE COLLEGE

Published by the Syndics of the Cambridge University Press
Bentley House, 200 Euston Road, London, N.W.1
American Branch: 32 East 57th Street, New York, N.Y. 10022

© Cambridge University Press 1967

330.96
W57r
79937
Sept 1972

Printed in Great Britain
by Billing & Sons Limited, Guildford and London

PREFACE

This two-volume collection of *Readings in the Applied Economics of Africa* is designed to supplement courses in economics given in African universities. The purpose of teaching economics is to help students to understand the working of the countries in which they will eventually become business men, lawyers, advisers, civil servants and politicians. But the 'principles of economics' are too often memorized for reproduction at examinations, and are too seldom used to illuminate the current problems of rapid change, which are discussed mainly in journals and official reports. Students in the early stages of university courses cannot be expected to consult a variety of journals, even if available in their libraries, which may not be the case in new universities; further, librarians are finding difficulty in obtaining information about other African countries. There is therefore a need for a selection of papers illustrating the economy of African countries, papers which can be used in conjunction with standard text-books.

In Volume 1—Micro-economics, the use of resources is considered from the angle of the firm or the farm. Parts I and II deal respectively with agriculture and with industry, and Part III considers prices and markets, through which goods and services are exchanged and incomes are earned.

Volume 2—Macro-economics, contains papers concerned with the framing and implementation of economic policy. Part IV illustrates the problems encountered in compiling and using the national accounts of African countries. Part V is devoted to public finance, banking and the balance of payments; Part VI, dealing with economic development, includes papers on population, export trades and import-saving industries, employment and inflation.

The selection made by the editors from the mass of material now published has been determined by many factors, including topic, length, suitability for student discussion, geographical coverage and ease of access; they express their thanks to those authors who have allowed their work to be reprinted here, and to the editors of the journals concerned. For each paper, only those references have been included which are mentioned in the extracts printed. It has not been thought necessary to provide an index, but the scope of each paper has been indicated briefly in the List of Contents.

v

Preface

The editors have in preparation a companion text-book which will be published shortly by the Cambridge University Press under the title *The Economics of African Countries*.

E. H. W.

December 1966   J. I. C.

ACKNOWLEDGEMENTS

We should like to thank the following for their permission to reproduce copyright material: the author, Bowes and Bowes (Publishers), the International Association for Research in Income and Wealth, North-Western University Press and Longmans, Green for P. Okigbo's articles; the authors and David and Helen Kimble for the articles by R. H. Green and H. L. Engberg; the author and the Royal Economic Society for G. J. Helleiner's article; the author, the Economic Society of Ghana and Allen and Unwin for A. J. Killick's articles; the author and the Overseas Development Institute for P. William's article; the authors and Professor P. Robson for the articles by J. F. Due, B. van Arkadie and D. M. Etherington; the author, Macmillan and the F.A.O. for G. Blau's article; the International Labour Office.

Precise details of the original form of publication are to be found in the List of Contents.

CONTENTS

Contents

CONTENTS OF VOLUME 1

PART IV

NATIONAL ACCOUNTS

---

19. NIGERIAN NATIONAL ACCOUNTS, 1950-7

P. OKIGBO*

The structure of the accounts

1. *Interdependence of the output and expenditure estimates*

... The Nigerian national accounts refer to the gross domestic product obtained from two methods which were highly interdependent. Our estimates of the national expenditure on product are obtained substantially from our output estimates. Some independent estimates of expenditure, for instance on food, could be obtained from household budget studies available for several large townships for single years, and from cost of living studies available for Lagos for several years. On the whole, however, the budget studies were for different places at different points of time—Enugu 1954, Ibadan 1955—and for very few places at that in a country as large as Nigeria. We did not, therefore, feel justified in using them to build up a series except where we had no alternative. We relied on our figures of output valued at retail market prices to obtain expenditure on food and used the budget studies to cross-check our estimates on particular items.

We thus have in reality only one set of tables, because of the interdependence of our output and expenditure estimates and the absence of income estimates. Our output tables are partially based on expenditure estimates and our expenditure estimates are derived for the most part from output tables. It is to be hoped that as refinements are made in the series we have produced the two accounts will be more independent of each other, so that one can truly be used as a check on the other.

The estimates measure gross domestic product as well as gross national product. The former measure gives the value of production within Nigeria, including the activity of Nigerians temporarily resident abroad as well as that of foreigners temporarily resident in

---

* In the preparation of this paper I had the assistance of Mr. Bisi Adu of the Nigerian Institute of Social and Economic Research, Ibadan.

1

Nigeria. It excludes, however, net income from abroad which enters into the gross national product. A further distinction is often drawn between these two measures already referred to and the territorial (or geographical) product. This last is defined by reference to the value of production within Nigeria plus income of foreigners resident in Nigeria *less* income of Nigerians resident abroad. Our procedure in defining our gross domestic product makes it evident that we have adopted the territorial or geographical concept. As we made estimates of depreciation for only 1956 and 1957, the net domestic (geographic) and net national product are given for these two years only.

2. *Regional estimates in a Federal territory*

One feature of the Nigerian accounts was the necessity to provide estimates for each of the political regions which make up the Federation. We found it convenient for statistical reasons to merge Lagos Federal territory with Western Nigeria and Southern Cameroons with Eastern Nigeria, because in many branches of activity it is impossible to maintain the division. On the output side, we built up our national figures in most branches of activity from regional data, whilst in other branches it was easy to split the national figures between the regions, except in the case of value added by trade, to which we shall refer later. We were therefore able to show the output of Northern Nigeria (including Northern Cameroons), Western Nigeria (including Lagos), and Eastern Nigeria (including, wherever it was convenient to do so, Southern Cameroons). We could not show the expenditure on product by region, because we could not identify the extent of interregional trade in foodstuffs. However, we were able to show regional expenditure on a number of sub-aggregates and specific items: domestic fixed investment, drink, tobacco, fuel and light, clothing and other non-durable goods, durable goods, travel, education and miscellaneous services.

3. *Summary tables for the Federation of Nigeria, 1950–7*

Tables 1 and 2 show the gross domestic (geographic) product of Nigeria, 1950–7, at current and at 1957 (factor) cost; Tables 3 and 4 show respectively the expenditure on product at current and at 1957 market prices. We cannot enter here into the details of the estimation or into an interpretation of our findings. A note of warning is, however, in order. In Table 4 we have left the row of net income

Table 1. *Gross domestic product by branch of activity at current prices (£ million)*

	1950	1951	1952	1953	1954	1955	1956	1957
Agriculture	285·7	323·8	327·0	365·6	427·3	455·8	450·9	471·4
Livestock	37·9	44·3	39·2	42·9	48·7	52·5	57·2	57·7
Fishing	6·3	6·7	6·4	6·3	7·4	9·8	12·8	13·3
Forest products	7·5	10·8	8·8	10·3	11·4	12·2	13·8	14·6
Mining and oil exploration	5·5	10·7	11·4	11·2	11·0	10·2	8·2	9·4
Manufacturing and public utilities	3·3	3·5	4·9	6·4	7·1	8·4	12·2	13·1
Communications	1·9	2·0	2·2	2·4	2·3	2·1	2·9	3·1
Building and civil engineering	8·1	12·2	16·8	17·6	28·0	31·4	36·5	43·0
Ownership of buildings	5·9	6·2	6·4	7·1	7·5	8·8	8·2	10·3
Transport	22·8	26·9	29·3	40·5	45·9	54·2	65·2	74·6
Crafts	15·8	15·9	16·0	16·1	16·2	16·4	16·5	16·7
Missions	3·4	4·0	4·6	5·3	6·0	9·0	12·7	15·9
Government	10·8	11·8	14·3	15·0	16·0	21·3	28·7	30·5
Marketing boards	35·5	19·5	36·5	36·2	51·2	16·3	41·0	11·7
Banking, insurance and the professions	0·7	0·7	0·9	1·1	1·4	1·8	2·1	2·5
Domestic services	2·6	2·6	3·0	3·5	3·9	4·4	5·4	5·5
Miscellaneous services	0·7	0·7	0·7	1·0	1·0	1·2	1·8	2·0
Land development	3·5	3·5	4·0	4·7	5·2	5·9	7·0	8·2
Distribution, residual error, etc.	54·2	67·4	82·1	71·8	76·7	105·8	87·5	106·5
Gross domestic product at factor cost	512·1	573·2	614·5	665·0	774·2	827·5	870·6	910·0
Indirect taxes *less* subsidies	12·2	13·8	16·3	17·9	20·6	23·7	29·4	28·7
Gross domestic product at market prices	524·3	587·0	630·8	682·9	794·8	851·2	900·0	938·7
Net income from abroad	−3·3	−4·5	−3·0	−3·2	−1·4	−0·6	0·9	4·2
Gross national product at market prices	521·0	582·5	627·8	679·7	793·4	850·6	900·9	942·9

Table 2. Gross domestic product by branch of activity at 1957 prices (£ million)

	1950	1951	1952	1953	1954	1955	1956	1957
Agriculture	377·6	415·0	430·5	446·0	471·3	483·9	459·8	471·4
Livestock	60·1	57·7	52·5	53·5	55·7	56·5	57·6	57·7
Fishing	9·7	9·8	9·9	10·0	10·2	10·3	12·6	13·3
Forest products	9·4	12·0	10·1	11·9	12·3	13·4	13·6	14·6
Mining and oil exploration	7·6	7·6	8·2	7·9	8·1	9·0	9·6	9·4
Manufacturing and public utilities	3·9	4·0	5·8	6·3	7·9	8·7	12·0	13·1
Communications	2·7	2·7	3·0	2·9	2·6	2·4	2·6	3·1
Building and civil engineering	20·3	25·4	19·4	25·9	37·8	38·3	36·5	43·0
Ownership of buildings	8·9	9·1	9·2	9·4	9·6	9·7	9·8	10·3
Transport	28·6	34·0	35·3	45·4	50·9	60·2	65·1	74·6
Crafts	15·8	15·9	16·0	16·1	16·2	16·4	16·5	16·7
Missions	6·9	7·0	7·6	7·8	8·7	11·4	12·7	15·9
Government	15·0	16·4	19·9	16·5	17·6	23·4	28·7	30·5
Marketing boards	41·0	10·5	28·0	28·8	42·7	25·0	44·9	11·7
Banking, insurance and the professions	1·5	1·2	1·3	1·7	1·7	2·1	2·2	2·5
Domestic services	4·4	4·4	4·4	4·7	4·8	5·0	5·7	5·5
Miscellaneous services	0·9	1·0	1·1	1·1	1·2	1·5	1·9	2·0
Land development	8·2	8·2	8·2	8·2	8·2	8·2	8·2	8·2
Distribution, residual error, etc.	64·6	98·3	122·6	105·7	104·7	112·7	74·1	106·5
Gross domestic product at factor cost	687·1	740·2	793·0	809·8	872·2	898·1	874·1	910·0

4

Table 3. *Gross national product by category of expenditure at current prices (£ million)*

	1950	1951	1952	1953	1954	1955	1956	1957
Consumers' expenditure	457·1	514·9	536·5	580·3	673·3	743·1	792·7	815·5
Government expenditure on goods and services	17·3	19·3	24·1	27·2	28·4	41·4	43·8	47·6
Gross fixed investment in Nigeria	30·8	37·8	54·0	58·8	71·5	85·7	101·2	113·0
Increase in marketing boards' stocks	−3·8	4·3	0·3	−0·2	−6·8	5·1	−4·3	9·1
Plus exports of goods and services	88·9	114·2	126·3	128·6	154·3	128·2	135·7	129·1
Final expenditure	590·3	690·5	741·2	794·7	920·7	1003·5	1069·1	1114·3
Less imports of goods and services	66·0	103·5	110·4	111·8	125·9	152·3	169·1	175·6
Gross domestic product at market prices	524·3	587·0	630·8	682·9	794·8	851·2	900·0	938·7
Plus net income from abroad	−3·3	−4·5	−3·0	−3·2	−1·4	−0·6	0·9	4·2
Gross national product at market prices	521·0	582·5	627·8	679·7	793·4	850·6	900·9	942·9

Table 4. *Gross domestic product by category of expenditure at 1957 prices (£ million)*

	1950	1951	1952	1953	1954	1955	1956	1957
Consumers' expenditure	609·4	650·2	695·9	717·3	774·6	805·5	798·9	815·5
Government expenditure on goods and services	24·0	26·8	33·5	29·9	31·2	45·5	43·8	47·6
Gross fixed investment in Nigeria	48·4	59·7	75·0	79·9	92·9	102·6	108·0	113·0
Increase in marketing boards' stocks	−7·3	6·3	1·5	−0·1	−6·2	4·6	−4·8	9·1
Plus exports of goods and services	99·9	93·6	111·7	114·8	131·9	126·9	138·5	129·1
Final expenditure	774·4	836·6	917·6	941·8	1024·4	1085·1	1084·4	1114·3
Less imports of goods and services	75·1	82·6	108·3	114·1	131·6	163·3	180·9	175·6
Gross domestic product at market prices	699·3	754·0	809·3	827·7	892·8	921·8	903·5	938·7

Table 5. Gross fixed investment by type of assets at current prices (£ million)

	1950	1951	1952	1953	1954	1955	1956	1957
New buildings:								
Dwellings		13·4	18·8	19·5	23·7	27·7	35·3	41·9
Other		3·0	4·7	6·0	9·7	9·3	10·0	12·6
Total		16·4	23·5	25·5	33·4	37·0	45·3	54·5
Civil Engineering works								
Roads		0·4	0·5	0·8	3·3	4·5	1·7	2·5
Bridges		0·2	0·5	0·3	0·8	0·6	0·5	0·3
Maintenance of roads and bridges		0·9	1·0	1·3	1·6	1·8	2·0	2·3
Railways		1·7	2·1	2·0	2·3	2·5	2·5	2·7
Ports, harbours and rivers		0·1	0·1	0·2	0·3	0·5	6·0	1·0
Waterworks and wells		0·8	1·0	1·0	1·0	1·3	1·6	1·6
Other		1·2	2·2	1·7	1·4	2·8	1·0	3·1
Total		5·3	7·4	7·3	10·7	14·0	15·3	13·5
Vehicles								
Road		2·8	4·6	5·0	5·0	6·8	9·7	8·1
Rail		0·7	0·4	0·6	1·4	2·6	1·6	2·1
Water		0·8	0·8	0·9	0·6	0·5	0·5	1·3
Air		0·1	0·5	0·4	0·3	0·9	0·5	0·6
Total		4·4	6·3	6·9	7·3	10·8	12·3	12·1
Plant, machinery and equipment		6·7	10·9	11·9	11·3	13·6	17·8	19·3
Plantations and mineral explorations		1·5	1·9	2·5	3·6	4·4	3·5	5·4
Total of above		34·3	50·0	54·1	66·3	79·8	94·2	104·8
Land clearance by peasants (imputed)	3·5	3·5	4·0	4·7	5·2	5·9	7·0	8·2
Total	30·8	37·8	54·0	58·8	71·5	85·7	101·2	113·0

6

Table 6. *Gross fixed investment by type of assets at 1957 prices (£ million)*

	1950	1951	1952	1953	1954	1955	1956	1957
New buildings:								
Dwellings		17·5	23·3	25·5	29·4	32·3	36·9	41·9
Other		4·5	6·6	7·4	11·3	10·3	10·5	12·6
Total		22·0	29·9	32·9	40·7	42·6	47·4	54·5
Civil engineering works:								
Roads		1·1	1·5	1·8	5·2	6·6	2·0	2·5
Bridges		0·4	0·8	0·5	0·9	0·6	0·5	0·3
Maintenance of roads and bridges		1·8	1·8	2·2	2·4	2·2	2·2	2·3
Railways		5·0	5·8	4·3	3·8	3·7	3·0	2·7
Ports, harbours and rivers		0·2	0·2	0·3	0·4	0·6	6·4	1·0
Waterworks and wells		1·4	1·4	1·3	1·2	1·5	1·7	1·6
Other		1·6	2·6	2·1	1·7	3·1	1·0	3·1
Total		11·5	14·1	12·5	15·6	18·3	16·8	13·5
Vehicles:								
Road		3·7	5·2	5·8	6·0	7·8	9·9	8·1
Rail		0·9	0·4	0·7	1·7	2·9	1·7	2·1
Water		1·0	0·9	1·1	0·7	0·6	0·5	1·3
Air		0·1	0·5	0·5	0·4	1·0	0·5	0·6
Total		5·7	7·0	8·1	8·8	12·3	12·6	12·1
Plant, machinery and equipment		8·6	12·0	14·0	13·6	14·9	19·1	19·3
Plantations and mineral exploration		3·7	3·8	4·2	6·0	6·3	3·9	5·4
Total of above		51·5	66·8	71·7	84·7	94·4	99·8	104·8
Land clearance by peasants (imputed)	8·2	8·2	8·2	8·2	8·2	8·2	8·2	8·2
Total		59·7	75·0	79·9	92·9	102·6	108·0	113·0

7

from abroad undeflated. It would be evident that the entries in this row are sufficiently small not to cause us any anxiety. Tables 5 and 6 show the gross domestic fixed investment by types of assets.

From Tables 2 and 4 we see that the gross domestic product in real terms increased by 32 per cent between 1950 and 1957. Some branches of activity grew faster than the economy as a whole—manufacturing, public utilities, transport and communications, building and civil engineering construction, and Government each stood in 1957 at over 200 per cent of the 1950 output measured at 1957 prices. By contrast, some of the large sectors, particularly agriculture and livestock, grew at a much slower rate than the economy.

Special problems: Methodology

We now turn to the special problems with which we had to deal in our exercise. Discussion of our project with the potential users of our results in Government showed that almost invariably interest was centred on the following sets of questions: What is the national income per head? How does Nigeria compare with Ghana and other African territories? How much higher is our current standard of living than it was ten years ago? Which region in the country is least well off? In short, in the minds of government officials the use of national income figures was to be dominated by welfare considerations, i.e., by international and intertemporal comparisons of welfare.

The definition of product

The design of national accounts depends to a large extent on how much we focus on measuring welfare or how much on providing a consistent time series. For measuring welfare we may have to define production in its widest sense to cover all output produced by members of the household whether for themselves or for other households. Prest and Stewart's estimates referred to a single year.* In the absence of any figures for other years, their estimates for 1950–1 could not be expected to show the movement of the Nigerian economy. It did not, therefore, matter a great deal how large their estimate of the gross domestic product turned out to be. In our view, their focus on measuring welfare led them to the amusing but dubious exercise of measuring intra-household services by reference to the

* A. R. Prest and I. G. Stewart, *The National Income of Nigeria, 1950–51* (*Editors*).

8

number of wives and the average bride price. We decided not to be unduly concerned with welfare questions, because we believed that an articulated and consistent time series would be more meaningful in Nigeria. We therefore defined production much more narrowly in our effort to keep subjective estimates and imputations to a minimum. All identifiable product was thus counted in our gross domestic product, including intra-household activity yielding marketable product, but excluding intra-household services of a general nature. Thus we eliminated the output of drummers, beggars, praisers and housewives—and, for purely statistical reasons, prostitutes.

Valuation of agricultural production

In valuing agriculture output we came up against the same problem in another form. First, Prest and Stewart had chosen to weigh the output of farm crops by retail prices. Second, they chose to value food crops in their most processed form, not because these crops were sold in that form, but because it was considered desirable to extend the coverage of national income to include intra-household services. Third, they chose to use retail prices ruling in or near the place where the output was actually consumed.

Our decisions followed different lines. First, since we wished to focus on constructing a time series of agricultural output we decided that weighting by 'producer' prices was preferable to weighting by retail prices. Second, we had chosen to exclude intra-household services of a general nature and there was, therefore, no question of valuing farm output in its most processed form. Food crops were, therefore, accounted for in their natural state, except cassava, which is sold as 'gari' (grated and baked cassava) in Lagos and Western Nigeria and as 'akpu' (fermented and strained cassava) in Eastern and Northern Nigeria. Third, it became evident to us that in the absence of firm figures of interregional trade in these commodities it would be unreasonable to weight farm output by prices ruling in or near the place where the output was actually consumed. We therefore valued the farm output of each region at a single price ruling in the producing region.

We were still left with the problem of selecting the prices to represent 'producer' prices. Ex-farm prices were non-existent and we had to resort to the more manageable expedient of taking for each crop for each year a simple average of the unweighted average of prices ruling over the year in representative markets in the main producing

9

areas of each region. This procedure, it must be explained, introduced a certain downward bias in our figures. We were convinced that the value added by agricultural production is somewhere between our valuation at 'producer' prices and valuation at retail market prices. The former is too low because it treats all output as if it were sold in rural markets, and the latter too high because it assumes that all output is sold in urban markets. However, it is arguable that even if price data were better it was preferable to keep down imputations to a minimum by adopting our procedure of single price valuation and by weighting, wherever possible, by rural farm prices ruling in the main producing areas of each region.

There is a distinction between marketed, marketable and non-marketable output. The first category would cover output in the cash economy: the second would cover output mainly in the agricultural sector, where a part of the output of each crop is sold and a part is withheld for domestic use; the third would consist predominantly of general services within the household. Prest adopted a definition wide enough to include the third category; we have been more ambivalent by counting marketable output in the agricultural sector, but only marketed output in all branches of activity.

Take as another example our procedure in another branch of activity—forest products. If we used Prest's definition we would treat all firewood as part of the gross domestic product. We know, however, that in the rural areas firewood was there to be collected by anyone who wished, and that no further effort was spent beyond that of collection. We decided to count only urban consumption of firewood as part of the gross domestic product. We were fully aware of the suggestion that this procedure would appear inconsistent with our treating the output of wild palm groves as part of the national income. We took the position that the two situations were not strictly analogous. We treated rural firewood as a free good because it was, in fact, free to any villager who cared to collect it from any bush; palm fruit, whether from wild groves or from plantations, is not free to anyone but to the owner of the land on which the trees stand.

Transfer payments

Some transactions are excluded from national accounts because they are regarded as transfer payments, for example purchase of old houses and gifts to beggars. Prest observed in 1957 that in Nigeria

10

'it is a recognized social necessity to hand money over to beggars',*
and concluded that it is not indubitably true that this should be
excluded from productive activity. Our judgment was that the so-
called 'social necessity' is no stronger and no more necessary in
Nigeria than elsewhere and that the Nigerian economy did not offer
any special reason either in 1950 or 1960 for the position taken by
Prest.

Capital formation

Our estimates of gross fixed capital formation cover expenditures
on new construction (excluding repair and maintenance), civil engineering works—roads, bridges, harbours, airfields, railroads and
waterways, vehicles—road vehicles (excluding bicycles and mopeds
and personal cars), railway vehicles and rolling stock, aircraft and
rivercraft, plant, machinery and equipment (including farm implements and sewing machines), mining (including oil), land development—plantations and peasant investment in agriculture. In the
more mature economies the classification of goods into capital or
consumer durables has been conventionally determined. In the final
analysis the decision to treat them one way or the other must be
arbitrary. The usual criteria—capital assets are expected to last for
more than a year, to yield an income, or to be used for production
—can be satisfied by a number of goods conventionally treated as
durable consumer goods in the more advanced countries. We have,
therefore, drawn the line arbitrarily to exclude from our capital
formation estimates expenditure on bicycles and personal motor-
cars (the proportion of expenditure on motor-cars which we treated
as personal was derived from vehicle registration data). In our view
what is important is that whatever convention is adopted the figures
should be so displayed that any one who wants to should be able
to rearrange them to suit his own convention.

In Table 7 we show the Federal Department of Statistics' series
for three years, 1955, 1956 and 1957, side by side with our new series.
It will be seen from this table that the main differences between the
official series and the new series occur in respect of vehicles, plant,
machinery and equipment. These differences are due mainly to con-
ceptual differences—our estimate of investment in vehicles is consistently lower than the official series, because we excluded bicycles and

* A. R. Prest, *The Investigation of National Income in British Tropical Dependen-
cies* (Commonwealth Papers, No. IV, London, 1957), p. 20.

P. Okigbo

personal cars. Similarly, our estimate of investment in plant, machinery and equipment is higher because we have counted items of equipment, e.g. imported farm implements, which were omitted from the official series. We shall refer later to the method we adopted to measure investment in buildings, which yielded results strikingly close to the official figures.

Table 7. *Gross fixed capital formation by type of assets at current prices (in £ million)*

	1955		1956		1957	
Assets	Official series	New series	Official series	New series	Official series	New series
Vehicles	17·6	10·8	21·2	12·3	21·3	12·1
Plant, machinery and equipment	7·8	13·6	10·5	17·8	18·0	19·3
Buildings and other construction	48·8	51·0	62·0	60·6	62·6	68·0
Mining and plantation development	4·4	4·4	3·5	3·5	5·1	5·4
Total of above	79·3	79·8	97·3	94·2	107·1	104·8
Peasant investment in agriculture (imputed)	—	5·9	—	7·0	—	8·2
Total	79·3	85·7	97·3	101·2	107·1	113·0

Special problems: statistical

There were problems which one could describe as purely statistical rather than methodological. Our estimates of the output of agriculture were, to say the least, quite shaky; those of livestock sheer guesses. Difficulties arose from paucity of records, and from the strange attitude within ministries that if exact figures did not exist no attempt should be made to estimate.

Estimation of output of agriculture

We can illustrate our problem by reference to two branches of activity: agriculture and construction. On agriculture there were the following sets of data: for 1950 we had the Report on the Census of Agriculture; for 1957 we had only the results of a sample survey

12

carried out in Northern Nigeria for different groups of provinces from 1955 to 1957, but such that a different group was surveyed each year and no province was surveyed more than once; there was also the result of a limited sample of villages in Western Nigeria in 1958 and, of much more doubtful usefulness for our purpose, of villages in Eastern Nigeria in 1959. Within the limits imposed by these difficulties we were able to estimate from the data on acreages and yields the output of each crop in 1950 and 1957.

Table 8. *Crops grown primarily for domestic use: comparison with Prest's estimates for 1950*

	Quantities (million tons)		Prices (£ per ton)		Values (£ million)	
	Prest	Revised estimates	Prest	Revised estimates	Prest	Revised estimates
Root crops:						
Yams	15·2[1]	6·63	4·6[1]	16·8	70·6	111·5
Cassava	19·7[1]	3·61	4·7[1]	6·8	93·2	24·5
Cocoyams	0·78	0·60	8·4	8·4	6·4	5·1
Total					170·2	141·1
Cereals:						
Guinea-corn	1·81	1·38	20·5	19·6	37·1	27·1
Millet	0·93	0·92	19·5	18·7	18·1	17·2
Maize	0·62	0·47	20·5	20·5	12·7	9·6
Rice	0·19	0·19	47·4	44·8	9·3	8·7
Total					77·2	62·6
Kolanuts		0·08		46·0 ·	4·7	3·9
Beans	0·29	0·07	23·3	27·1	6·7	2·0
Other food crops					15·4	18·5
Total					274·2	228·1

[1] The quantities of yam flour and gari given in Prest, *National Income of Nigeria* (H.M.S.O., 1953), Table 2, have been re-calculated so as to refer to the natural products, yams and cassava. The prices shown are the result of dividing the values by the adjusted quantities.

For the intervening years it was obvious that interpolation on the basis of the 1950 and 1957 figures was out of the question. In agricultural production interpolation is reasonable only if it is based on detailed and reliable information on weather conditions or information on yields and changes in acreages under different crops. We found that the Regional Ministries of Agriculture kept records of crop and weather prospects prepared every quarter in respect of each agricultural province by field agricultural officers. However, these reports were highly subjective and did not lend themselves easily to quantification. We had no choice but to use them to quantify changes in output in the period 1951–6. Since foodcrop production dominates the accounts, it would be clear that in the national accounts for 1951–6 one of the softest series refers to the most important branch of activity.

It would be of interest to compare our figures for 1950 with those of Prest and Stewart in this branch of activity. Table 8 shows that our estimate is some £36·1 million lower than the Prest–Stewart figures.

This is explained by the differences in our estimates of quantities and in the prices used for valuation. Take rootcrops as an example. Our figures refer to the natural products—yams and cassava—rather than to their most processed equivalents—yam flour and gari. We have adjusted Prest's quantities to conform to our procedure. Second, our quantities differ from Prest's also because we have had access to data which were not available to him and his colleague. It should be recalled that they completed their fieldwork before the Report of the Census of Agriculture (1950) was published and that although they had some of the preliminary Census data they did not have the benefit of the later criticism of the Census Report which became available after their work was published. Third, what we have shown in Table 8 as Prest's prices are obtained as a result of dividing Prest's values by the adjusted quantities.

Investment in building and construction

When we came to estimate gross investment our methods were generally similar to those used by the Federal Department of Statistics to produce the official series. The major point of departure was in respect of building and construction. The official series estimated investment in building from the supply side—investment in new construction was obtained from a presumed ratio between imports of cement and the gross output of the building and construction industry. The global estimates obtained by this method could not, however, be broken down by class or type of building. We decided to estimate from the demand side and soon discovered that the sources available were not uniform throughout the country—a problem which is, however, not unique to Nigeria.

14

New construction can be measured by reference to work done or paid for, contract awards, building permits, or other sources. In Nigeria, government records show work done or paid for by Government, so that public buildings can be estimated from government accounts. Contract awards are not a helpful guide, because the records are scanty and are available only in the public sector. The coverage of permit-issuing localities varied from region to region. In Lagos, the coverage is almost complete and, aided by supplementary information from the Government Valuation Unit's records, we were able to estimate the gross investment in private residential construction. In Western Nigeria, although permits were not issued prior to the start of building, there was a widespread system of control through the requirement that each prospective home builder was to submit a building plan or sketch. These plans were available for many local authority areas. Adjustments had to be made for coverage, for the lag between submission of plan and completion of building and for contravention of the plan. In Eastern Nigeria there were five permit-issuing townships, only three of which maintained usable records. It was, therefore, necessary to conduct a census of private dwellings with the help of the Ministry of Local Government. In Northern Nigeria we abandoned the attack from the demand side and reverted to the cement calculation for a global estimate of investment in buildings using cement, but we estimated mud buildings by reference to population.

Census of private buildings in Eastern Nigeria, 1957

It would be of interest to describe briefly how we tackled the problem of tabulating investment in private dwellings in Eastern Nigeria. This represented a first attempt to estimate the stock of private capital in the form of buildings. We were assisted by local government authorities—there were about a hundred of them. Each District Council was requested to tabulate on our behalf on forms supplied by us the following information in respect of each building in each ward: year of completion, year of commencement if this is known, materials used for walls, materials used for roof, and number of rooms. Churches, schools, hospitals, halls and buildings owned by major firms, missions, local authorities, regional and federal governments were excluded.

There were complete returns—i.e. certified as complete by secretaries of councils—from sixty of the one hundred district council

15

areas in the Region; incomplete returns were received from six areas; and no returns were submitted for thirty-five areas. We then tabulated the returns to show the number of buildings completed each year, the number of rooms, and type of building classified by type of materials used for walls and roof.

We then made imputations for the areas for which no returns were submitted and for the wards for which we had incomplete returns. In each case we relied on the advice of the local authorities and on our estimates for neighbouring areas or areas which in our view had similar experience of building activity. As a result we had a quantity series for the Region as a whole.

We must point to the dangers which one must expect in an enumeration of this kind. It was impossible to check the accuracy of the enumerators' records; the enumerators had no previous experience of this type of work—this was the first major exercise of this kind in Nigeria. Finally, house-owners had to rely on their memory to recall when the building was completed. We believe that the estimates have a downward bias for the earlier years and an upward bias for the later years.

Value added by trade

How to measure the contribution of trade presented us with an almost insoluble problem. In a country in which everyone engages in some petty trade,* this might assume quite a large significance. The value added by trade is made up of the following elements: value added by trade in exports, value added by trade in imports, and value added by trade in goods produced and consumed in Nigeria. Of these three components, trade in exports presents no serious problem. For goods handled by the marketing boards the value added by trade is represented by the difference between marketing-board receipts and payments for produce. Other exports which represent a very small fraction of the total can be estimated from the export values (f.o.b.) and identifiable expenses—transport, and payment to producers.

The problem with trade in imports is to determine the margins between c.i.f. values and retail values, bearing in mind the long chain of distribution between the wholesaler and the final consumer. We could not follow this chain to its ultimate end nor could we tell the

---

* Cf. P. T. Bauer, *West African Trade* (Cambridge University Press, 1954), chapter 2.

16

quantities which moved from port to retail points in the country. There is still much room for improvement, and our figures shown in the rows of national expenditure on particular imports beg this question. In respect of commodities produced and consumed in Nigeria we can separate trade in local manufactures, e.g. beer and cigarettes, from trade in agricultural foodcrops. The former presented no difficulty, as factory records offered us detailed information. In respect of foodcrops we had no estimates of total quantities traded—in the absence of estimates of home consumption—nor had we firm estimates of movement of crops from region to region. We adopted the simple device of valuing all such output as if they were all purchased in the producing region. In the end our estimate of trade was obtained as a residual figure incorporating within it the errors in all other estimates.

Inventories

One serious omission—again for purely statistical reasons—was that we did not include any estimate of inventory changes except the changes in marketing-board stocks. Changes in stocks of imported merchandise and foodcrops (this latter can be taken to be quite negligible because of the high degree of perishability and lack of adequate storage facilities) were therefore left out of account. It is quite clear that in a country apparently growing as fast as Nigeria, inventory changes would constitute a significant element of capital accumulation. It is to be hoped that future workers in this field will fill this gap in our work.

Peasant investment in agriculture

There is one more problem to which we wish to refer. After the publication of Prest and Stewart's estimates for 1950–1 and of the International Bank Mission's Report on Nigeria, Peter Bauer raised the criticism that substantial peasant investment in agriculture had been left out of account in both works.* We had tried to accommodate Bauer's criticism. Peasant investment takes the form of new seedlings, clearing and preparing new land, purchase of new farm implements, and inventory accumulation. We have already referred to our inability to estimate changes in inventories of farm crops except for the changes in stocks held by marketing boards; our

* P. T. Bauer, 'Economic Development of Nigeria', *J. of Political Economy*, vol. 63, October 1955.

allowance for farm implements was taken from our estimates of the output of blacksmiths. With regard to new farm land, our method was to estimate peasant investment by reference to yearly increases in the total cultivated acreage and to the average cost of clearing and preparing an acre of new farm land.

Calculation of real national income

When we came to derive estimates of real income a new crop of problems emerged. First, what should we use as our base year, 1950 or 1957 (our terminal point) or some year in between? We finally settled on using 1957 as the base year for two reasons:

(a) price data were much better for the last year than for any other year in the series; and

(b) if the series was to be continued, it seemed desirable to use 1957 so that with the continuation of the series our base year would become more central.

Second, we were quite eclectic in our choice of deflators, our guiding principle being what could be continued easily in future years. We switched quite frequently from quantity to price deflators depending on which was the more manageable. In some cases we were prepared to adopt very crude devices in the interest of simplicity. Take, for example, government expenditure. Much of this is on wages and salaries, but a not inconsiderable part is on goods (some imported) and other services. We were confronted with a choice of deflating the components separately or of deflating the aggregate sum by reference to either a simple index or a composite index. For the sake of simplicity we deflated the aggregate government expenditure by means of an index of wages paid to general labour. Again, take exports and imports. Here we found it possible to strive for elegance. If we agree that the real value of exports is the amount of imports we can buy with it, then we should deflate exports by means of an index of import prices. There is much to commend this view, since what enters into the expenditure on gross domestic product is the difference between exports and imports. Although it was easier to deflate both exports and imports (or merely the difference) by reference to the same import index, we chose the more laborious method of deflating them independently.

Third, it was not always easy to find homogeneous units for our quantity indices. What, for instance, should we use to construct an

18

index of the quantity of vehicles purchased—horsepower, cylinder capacity, tare weight, or number? We tried the following pairs of quantity indices: one in which we assigned an equal weight to each vehicle, one in which we used average cylinder capacity to weight vehicles of each make, and one in which we used the tare weight to weight vehicles of each class. The results were so similar that there is no reason why a simple index of the number of vehicles purchased should not suffice in the future. When we came to roads and bridges we had to get around the fact that not all roads of uniform surface or bridges of uniform structure have the same breadth of carriageway. We therefore reduced all roads of given surface to units of foot-miles (a foot-mile being a road one foot wide and one mile long) and all bridges of given specification to units of foot-runs (a foot-run being a bridge one foot long and twelve feet wide). In most branches of activity, however, we were able to construct quantity indices without resorting to such esoteric units.

Conclusions

There is already a shift in many African countries from calculating national accounts for a single year to compiling a time series. This development has been accompanied by a similar shift of emphasis from measurement of welfare to a presentation of the dynamics of the economy. There is therefore very little justification for defining production so extensively that we are obliged to make very large imputations.

We have not faced directly the question of measuring the so-called subsistence output. In agriculture, for instance, the real value of output may be rising over time because increasing proportions of the output are brought to the market although the total output may not have risen. It is then argued that without an estimate of subsistence output we would confuse increased monetization of activity with increased physical output. This argument is untenable, because we can get at total production directly through acreage and yield figures. Once we have reasonable figures of total output, the only virtue in measuring subsistence production is to determine what prices to use in valuing output—what weights to assign to ex-farm prices, rural and urban market prices.

We have attempted three new exercises which should be improved upon in future years. First, our series at constant prices should be

19

kept up. The Federal Department of Statistics has built up unusually good price data; additional work would be required to maintain a usable quantity series in some branches of activity. Second, our census of industrial production should be extended—we covered all manufacturing establishments employing ten or more persons. Third, our census of private residential construction in Eastern Nigeria and our tabulation of building-permit data in Lagos and Western Nigeria should be carried forward. We failed, however, to provide reliable estimates of internal trade, because with the resources available to us we could not undertake a detailed survey of the movement of merchandise (imports and homegrown crops) within and across regional boundaries. We believe that this shortcoming in our work can be rectified. If these facets of the work are strengthened, sufficiently detailed and useful information will become available to the planning agencies in the country.

20. FOUR AFRICAN DEVELOPMENT PLANS: GHANA, KENYA, NIGERIA, AND TANZANIA

R. H. GREEN

... The Ghana *Seven Year Development Plan* (1963/64–1969/70) is an explicit attempt to build an economic framework for the attainment of the Convention Peoples Party's basic socio-political goals as set out in their 1962 programme, which contains nearly 200 fairly specific objectives, perhaps half of which had direct implications for economic policy. The plan makes concrete proposals for advance towards these goals, in quantitative terms where possible—as for employment, consumption, and industrial output—and in specific policy form for others, for example the expansion of state economic activity and control over the private sector. The Ghana plan also explicitly relates the economic means to the socio-political ends. The plan is unusual; it is virtually a text of applied economic analysis and policy for the concerned and intelligent non-economist, as well as a detailed blueprint of policies, projects, and their implementation. (For some selected data, see Table 1.)

The clear expression of economic programmes as a function of national aspirations is matched by a sober—if perhaps optimistic—calculation of what can be achieved and what are the real resource constraints on development. As a result the plan *is* a serious force both in the political drive behind its implementation and in the fact that its fulfilment—at least to, say, 80 per cent of output and 80–90 per cent of input targets—is attainable, barring radically unfavourable foreign-sector influences.

In the case of Tanzania's *Five Year Plan for Economic and Social Development* (1964–9), the planning process was somewhat different. The Tanganyika African National Union did not provide a body of detailed proposals and did not develop a prior set of firm socio-political ideological commitments. As a result the planning secretariat had a far broader and less specific set of goals to translate into economic policy. They proceeded by offering basic alternative choices

21

to the Government, first on a general and later on a more specific level. This led to the simultaneous creation of a set of detailed socio-political aims and an economic plan for their attainment. (For details, see Table 2.)

In terms of government commitment to the plan, which is now a central element in an over-all policy, this approach appears to have been highly satisfactory. However, the socio-political programme thus developed still lacks the broad understanding and commitment that would have been present had it pre-dated the plan and sprung from a party ideology. As a result, there appears to be a dangerously low level of national consciousness of the plan and of its relevance to national aspirations, for example in the lower ranks of the civil service, the party, and the party-related mass movements.*

The Tanzania plan is realistic in its internal calculations; but the level of national effort demanded and of external financing needed appear highly optimistic, and their full achievement doubtful.

Nigeria's *National Development Plan* (1962–8) evolved in an almost diametrically opposite manner. For one thing it is actually four (now five) plans, one for each Regional Government and one for the Federation. These are not fully co-ordinated even on paper, and far less so in actual organization and implementation.

Even more basic, neither the planning process nor the resultant plan shows evidence of any serious attempt to make the economic targets and policies represent national goals in more than the vaguest sense. For all practical purposes the federal plan was drawn up by a limited number of expatriate economists, working virtually in a vacuum so far as detailed direction or consultation with political leaders went, and with only peripheral advisory contact with Nigerian civil servants and planners. The social and political preferences of the plan, as was inevitable given this method of preparation, represent what the planners preferred or felt Nigerians ought to prefer, rather than any expressed Nigerian preferences.†

The Nigerian political system contributed substantially to this

* Cf. H. Bienen, 'The Role of T.A.N.U. and the Five Year Plan in Tanganyika', East African Institute of Social Research Conference paper, Makerere University College, 1964.

† Comments on the Federal plan are largely applicable to the Northern as well. The Eastern and Western Regional plans had substantially greater Nigerian involvement, both technical and political. In the Western Region the post-plan Akintola Government has shown little concern with economic policy, so that only in the Eastern Region does there appear to be any serious commitment to the stated plan.

Table 1. *Selected plan data: Ghana, 1963/4–1969/70*

1. Investment sources	£m.	
Current budget surplus	81·0	
State corporation profits (less losses)	23·0	
Domestic borrowing (long-term)	26·0	
Domestic deficit finance (Treasury bills)	106·0	
Foreign loans and grants	239·0	
Public sector	475·0	
Communal and private direct labour	100·0	
Private capital inflow	100·0	
Domestic savings: Ghanaian	250·0	
foreign firms (reinvested profits)	150·0	
Capital repayment—margin	(59·0)	
Private sector	440·0	
Total	1,015·0	

2. Investment allocation (public and private)	£m.	%
Agriculture	176·6	17·4
Industry	206·4	20·3
Mining	41·7	4·7
Unallocated private	75·2	7·4
Directly productive	499·9	49·8
Transport equipment	62·9	6·2
Other physical infrastructure	109·4	10·7
Physical infrastructure	172·3	16·9
Education	61·3	6·1
Health	20·4	22·1
Housing	76·2	7·5
Social services	23·4	2·3
Human and social infrastructure	101·3	19·8
Administration	22·8	2·2
Renewal of fixed assets	140·2	13·8
Total	1,015·0	100·0

3. Composition of domestic output

Sector	1960–2		1964–60		1969–70 Index
	£m.	%	£m.	%	1960–62 = 100
Agriculture	249	49·1	381	47·9	153
Direct-labour investment	10	2·0	18	2·3	180
Mining	25	5·0	38	4·8	152
Industry[1]	120	23·6	219	27·5	183
Tertiary	103	20·3	140	17·5	136
G.D.P.	507	100·0	796	100·0	157

[1] Includes manufacturing, construction, public utilities, transport, and communications.

Table 2. *Selected plan data: Tanzania (excluding Zanzibar), 1964–9*

1. Investment sources

	£m.
Recurrent budget and state corporation surpluses	13·0
Domestic public borrowing	24·5
Foreign public loans	100·2
Foreign public grants	8·0
Self-help	4·0
Public sector	149·7
Domestic savings	76·0
Private capital inflow	16·9
Private foreign grants	3·4
Private sector	96·3
Total	246·0

2. Investment allocation (public and private)

	£m.	%
Agriculture	36·9	15·0
Industry	54·1	22·0
Mining	4·9	2·0
Commerce	33·1	13·4
Directly productive	129·0	52·4
Roads	13·4	5·5
Railroads and harbours	15·4	6·2
Power	4·4	1·8
Other physical infrastructure	6·2	2·5
Physical infrastructure	39·3	16·0
Housing	41·8	17·0
Education	18·1	7·2
Health, welfare, community development	10·0	4·1
Human and social infrastructure	69·9	28·3
Administration	7·8	3·2
Total	246·0	100·0

3. Composition of domestic output

Sector	1960–2 £m.	1960–2 %	1970 £m.	1970 %	1980 £m.	1980 %
Agriculture	105·9	57·4	158·6	47·8	237·5	37·3
Mining	5·2	2·9	7·5	2·2	10·3	1·6
Industrial	23·7	12·8	64·4	19·4	169·7	26·7
Tertiary	49·6	26·9	101·4	30·6	218·5	34·4
G.D.P.	184·4	100·0	331·9	100·0	636·1	100·0

4. Growth rates of domestic output by sector

Sector	1960–2/1970	1970/1980
Agriculture	4·7	4·2
Mining	4·7	3·2
Industry	11·8	10·6
Tertiary	8·1	7·9
G.D.P.	6·7	6·7

Table 3. *Selected plan data: Nigeria, 1962–8*

	£m.	
1. Investment sources		
Investment in recurrent votes	149·4	
Current corporation surpluses	263·0	
Foreign aid	327·1	
Estimated underspending	23·0	
Unallocated public-sector gap	63·7	
Public sector	793·8	
Foreign private capital inflow	200·0	
Domestic private savings	189·5	
Private sector	389·5	
Total	1,183·5	
2. Investment allocation (public sector only)	£m.	%
Primary production	91·8	13·6
Trade and industry	90·3	13·4
Directly productive	192·0	27·0
Electricity	101·7	15·1
Transport	143·8	21·3
Communication	30·0	4·4
Infrastructure	275·5	40·8
Water (except irrigation)	24·3	3·6
Education	69·8	10·3
Health	17·1	2·5
Other social welfare	50·4	7·5
Total 'Social Welfare'	161·6	24·9
Administration	56·6	8·3
Total	676·8	100·0

3. Composition of domestic output[1]

Sector	1958–59		1962–63	
	£m.	%	£m.	%
Agriculture	619·9	68·9	694·1	64·7
Mining	7·0	·8	18·2	1·7
Industry	100·7	11·2	138·3	12·9
Tertiary	172·4	19·2	221·7	20·7
G.D.P.	900·0	100·0	1072·3	100·0

[1] There is no official target for 1967–8.

25

Table 4. *Selected plan data: Kenya 1964–70*

1. Investment sources	£m.	
Public sector	129	
Private Sector	188	
Total	317	

2. Sources of public sector development expenditure (1964–7 only)

	£m.
Recurrent surplus	1·0
Local borrowing	2·8
External loans/grants	34·4
External: incl. E.A.C.S.O. ⎱ Internal: incl. local government ⎰	26·9
Gap	4·5
Total	69·6

3. Investment allocation (public sector only)

	£m.	%
Agriculture, lands, natural resources	21·7	16·8
Commerce and industry	4·8	3·8
Tourism	1·0	0·8
Directly productive	27·5	21·4
Power	20·5	15·5
Railways and harbours	14·2	11·0
Roads	6·8	5·8
Other physical infrastructure	2·6	2·0
Physical infrastructure	44·1	34·3
Education	9·7	7·7
Health	3·8	2·8
Housing	2·4	1·8
Other social services	0·2	0·2
Social services	16·1	12·5
Administration and security	11·9	9·3
Unallocable: mainly admin. and infrastructure	29·0	22·5
Total	128·7	100·0

4. Composition of domestic output

Sector	1962		1970		Growth rate
	£m.	%	£m.	%	%
Agriculture	102·9	42·3	150·5	41·4	4·9
Mining and quarrying	0·8	0·3	1·0	0·3	3·0
Industry	55·0	22·6	88·0	24·1	6·0
Tertiary	84·7	34·8	124·9	34·3	5·0
G.D.P.	243·3	100·0	364·4	100·0	5·2

process. The Government had no detailed set of socio-political goals and, at best, a vague and ill-defined commitment to national economic welfare (as opposed to that of the narrow political class which has dominated Nigerian governmental and para-governmental structures mainly for its own power, prestige, and enrichment). There was little sense of urgency or political insistence on rapid development for planners to interpret in economic terms.

The plan is equally isolated from economic policy as a whole. Although there is a brief and sketchy discussion of all-over targets and economic policies, the detailed proposals are basically limited to an integrated programme of capital expenditure for the public sector. While this did, indeed, mean a lack of interference by planners in economic policy, it also meant a lack of co-ordination and a complete isolation of state physical investment goals from current fiscal and monetary policy, from manpower development, and from incentives and controls for the private sector.

The Nigerian plan, while superficially modest in its targets, is rather unrealistic in its assumptions. The plan concentrates on allocations of government expenditure in such a way that it is basically a proposal for growth within the existing economic and socio-political structure; it is *not* a call for development through structural change. The modesty of the proposals so limits the possibility of mobilizing resources that even the stated growth goals—the lowest of any of the plans here considered—appear unrealistic. (For details, see Table 3.)

The preparation of Kenya's *Development Plan* (1964–70) was in principle somewhat similar to that of Tanzania, but in practice partially reminiscent of Nigeria. The inherent difficulty confronting the planners and economic ministers was that of timing. A plan was needed by mid-1964, but political developments had allowed the Kenya Africa National Union no time either to work out a detailed socio-political goal programme like the C.P.P., or to engage in a dialogue in some depth with the planners, as in Tanzania.

As a result, the Kenya plan (see Table 4) is by far the most uneven and least internally integrated of the four. Where national socio-political objectives were clearly spelled out and there had been previous attempts to formulate them in economic policy terms, the plan clearly represents an expression of socio-economic commitment. This is particularly true concerning agricultural development, which is the best formulated sector of the Kenya plan, both technically and

27

in its relevance to national aspirations, while it is weak in both respects in the other three plans. Elsewhere, the plan either relies very heavily on the World Bank proposals—which in no way represented and only peripherally took account of Kenya desires—or, as in the case of the industrial sector and of private activity in general, is both technically vague and only loosely linked to any probable government policy.

However, the Kenya plan was published in full awareness of these limitations. A process of continuing re-evaluation and refinement is built in to the planning system for sectoral and policy goals as well as the adjustment of individual projects. New governmental aims have been expressed, for example in President Kenyatta's speech of October 1964 on industrial development and state participation in industry, and in the agreements and plans made between July 1964 and January 1965 concerning East African industrial location. If these are incorporated, the Kenya plan will offer an increasingly complete and coherent economic policy. . . .

In both the Ghana and Tanzania plans, priority attention is given to manpower planning, in terms of employment totals, detailed requirements and stocks of high-level manpower, and an educational programme to provide the necessary human resources. In practice, Ghana is finding this part of the plan harder to implement than the physical investment programme, and productive efficiency has been increasingly hampered over at least the past four years by a growing shortage of technicians, managers, specialist civil servants such as statisticians, and secondary-school and university teachers. Similar problems appear likely to confront East Africa, at least on the graduate level, even if the University of East Africa's expansion targets are achieved. Kenya's manpower policy remains on a very general macro-level, which is not satisfactory for determining specific bottlenecks or policy priorities. (For some details from the Ghana and Kenya plans, see Table 6.) Nigeria's investment programme lacks projections of manpower needs and supplies; the section on education consists solely of capital expenditure targets without even clear enrolment and output figures.*

Although Ghana is the only one of the four countries which has had the benefit of a serious study of input-output relationships or of

---

* Nigeria has a set of manpower studies, including those in the widely known Ashby Report: *Investment in Education* (Lagos, 1960); but the relationship between these and investment in educational plant is not made clear in the plan.

the national production function,* these were not used to any substantial extent in the original drafting of the plan, and the modifications based on them after the 1963 conference of experts appear
rather superficial. No over-all check on project and sectoral consistency has been applied, and no 1970 input-output table has been
attempted.†

Table 5. 1. *Ghana seven-year development plan: employment figures*

	1963		1970 Projections		Increase
	'000's	%	'000's	%	%
Administrative/managerial	13		16		23
Professional	19		24		26
Sub-professional/technical	7		19		171
Skilled craftsmen	36		52		44
Teachers	34		75		112
High level	109	4	186	7	70
Clerical	43		65		51
Organized trade	46		69		50
Mining	33		42		27
Transport/communication	63		105·5		67
Semi-skilled workers	156		237		51
Service	54		80		48
Middle level	395	16	598·5	18	51
Petty traders	300		330		10
Tailors, etc.	75		82·5		10
Bakers, etc.	45		68		51
Unskilled labour	80		144·5		80
Non-farm unskilled	500	20	625	21	25
Self-employed farmers	1,300		1,337·5		3
Hired farm employees	200		250		25
Farm semi- and unskilled	1,500	60	1,587·5	54	5
Total	2,504	100	2,997	100	19

* See R. Szereszewski, 'The Inter-Sectoral Structure of the Economy of Ghana
1960', in *Economic Bulletin of Ghana* (Accra), 2, 1963; and 'Capital and Output
in Ghana, 1955–61', *ibid.*, 4, 1963.
† For a possible approach to such a formulation, see A. Bryant, 'Use of an Inter-
Industry (Input-Output) Table as Long-Run Planning Device to Aid in
Economic Development', *ibid.*, 1, 1965.

There is an even more striking lack of consistency tests for Kenya's and Nigeria's plans, with their larger and very vaguely defined projections for the private sector. Tanzania's planners, on the other hand, did make rough estimates of sectoral outputs, intersectoral flows, final demand patterns, and technical coefficients, and they concluded that the plan was basically internally consistent. Some of these calculations were published; indeed, the Tanzania plan and the U.N.E.C.A. advisory report on Zambian planning appear to be the only African publications to include a set of sectoral-flow and consistency projections.

Table 5.   2. *Kenya development plan: wage-earning employment*

	1962		1970 Projections		Increase
	'000's	%	'000's	%	%
Agriculture, forestry, fisheries	245·5		316·6		3·2
Mining	3·5		4·2		2·4
	249	42·8	320·8	44·2	
Manufacturing	45·4		51·9		1·5
Transport/communication	16		23·8		5·1
Construction	12·6		15·9		3.0
Public utilities	2·1		2·6		3.0
	76·2	13·1	94·2	13.0	
Trade	36·7		43·2		2·1
Financial	5·9		8·8		5.0
Government	168·5		200·3		2·2
Services	45		58·3		3·3
	256·1	44·1	310·6	42·8	
Total	581·3	100·0	725·6	100·0	2·8

Problems of implementation

A major weakness in many plans—in Asia as well as in Africa— has been an implicit belief that the planning process and the responsibility of the planning commission end on the adoption of the plan. In extreme cases, for example Ceylon, it would be reasonable to contend that economic planning has served as a substitute for, not a prelude to, implementation. Continuing discussion and publicity on what was to be done masked how little was being accomplished. A more common situation is one in which the plan remains a somewhat isolated account programme which is amended *ad hoc* by the Treasury and by operational ministries and treated as one of a number of more or less equal priorities, along with fiscal stability and increases in current welfare expenditure, for example. Under these conditions the plan soon becomes diffused and inconsistent; important projects and inter-relationships are dropped without re-estimating the over-all impact; policies crucial to development are modified or dropped for inadequate reasons. . . .

A different, but equally crucial, question, is that of the size of the plan's output and input targets. This is not simply a question of whether too much is being attempted, but equally, and perhaps even more, of whether the total effort and results are large enough to be attainable.

If a plan has too low a set of goals it will prove difficult to generate any great enthusiasm or drive for its fulfilment, and certainly well-nigh impossible to impose sacrifices to that end. On the quantitative side, a low rate of growth will drastically limit the possible increases in personal consumption and the investable surplus for maintaining or stimulating growth. On balance, growth rates of 5 per cent for national product, 2·5 per cent for output per head, and 1–1·5 per cent for personal consumption per head appear to be the minimum that a plan can safely assume under African conditions. The target rates of growth for these three variables are 6·7 per cent, 4·5 per cent, and 2·5–3 per cent respectively for Tanzania; 5·5 per cent, 2·9 per cent, and 1 per cent for Ghana; 5·2 per cent, 2·19 per cent, and 1·5 per cent for Kenya; and 4 per cent, 1·49 per cent, and 1 per cent for Nigeria.

The estimated increase in the annual level of gross investment as compared with recent years shows a similar pattern; it is about 70 per cent for Tanzania, 50 per cent for Ghana, 33 per cent for Kenya, and 25 per cent for Nigeria. These aggregates somewhat cloud the public-sector increases required: 200 per cent in Tanzania, 60 per cent in Ghana, and 50 per cent in Kenya and Nigeria. Tanzania has a very low initial ratio of public to total investment, which is expected to rise radically during the plan period, so that in 1970 the proposed ratio of public to total investment will be 60 per cent in Tanzania, Ghana, and Nigeria, and 40 per cent in Kenya.

The projected increases in private-sector investment are relatively low: zero for Nigeria, 20 per cent for Tanzania, 25 per cent for Kenya, and 50 per cent for Ghana. Oddly enough, the two most optimistic are Ghana and Nigeria; Ghana because of the high target

31

rate, and Nigeria because during 1958–60 private investment included substantial petroleum development, which will taper off sharply.

The public sector still depends to a considerable extent on foreign government long-term loans and grants and/or shorter-term supplier credit (including five- to eight-year project credits from socialist countries); these make up approximately 50 per cent of the public-sector total in Ghana and Nigeria, nearly 80 per cent in Tanzania, and over 90 per cent in Kenya. The latter two figures appear to be unreasonably optimistic, even in theory, while in practice Nigeria has been unable to attain the planned level of foreign assistance, and Ghana has made very heavy use of short- to medium-term supplier credit, which is already posing severe repayment problems. . . .

PART V

PUBLIC FINANCE AND BANKING

---

21. THE REFORM OF EAST AFRICAN TAXATION*

J. F. DUE

This paper is designed to offer general outlines for reform of taxation in East Africa. The suggestions are based upon the author's observations in two visits to the three East African countries, in 1962 and 1964, a review of the literature on the question, and a study of taxation in developing economies elsewhere. It does not seek to provide final answers or to give detailed provisions for reform measures, a task which requires substantially more intensive study of the tax systems. Rather, it seeks to suggest directions of reform which warrant consideration. There have been several studies of the tax structures in recent years, including the rather superficial ones in the three International Bank Reports,† and the more detailed ones of the Uganda and Kenya Fiscal Commissions.‡ A study sponsored by the Uganda Government is now under way. But the studies have had rather limited objectives and have not considered the tax structure of East Africa as a whole.

The goals

Tax structures and reform measures can be evaluated only in terms of certain goals which cannot be derived by scientific analysis, but

* The author is indebted to officials of the three governments and EACSO who discussed questions of taxation and tax reform; to various university faculty members in East Africa, and particularly Professor Peter Robson and Mr. Dharam Ghai, for their assistance, and to the Social Science Research Council and to the Columbia University International Economic Integration Programme for the travel grants which made it possible to visit Africa in 1962 and 1964. The points of view expressed are strictly those of the author.

† See International Bank for Reconstruction and Development, *The Economic Development of Tanganyika* (1961); *The Economic Development of Uganda* (1961), and *The Economic Development of Kenya* (1963), Baltimore: Johns Hopkins University Press.

‡ See *Report of the Uganda Fiscal Commission* (Entebbe: Government Printer, 1962), and Government of Kenya, *Report of the Fiscal Commission* (Nairobi: 1963). A review of the tax structure is also found in the unpublished University of Illinois M.A. dissertation by Azarius Baryaruha, *Public Finance as it Affects Growth and Economic Development—East Africa, A Case Study*, 1964.

33

must be selected in terms of the wishes of contemporary society. For the purpose of this paper the following goals are assumed:

1. The tax structure should facilitate economic development to the maximum extent possible. The primary goal of the East African countries is rapid economic growth which will raise the level of *per capita* income towards that of the developed economies. Rather than retarding this growth, the tax structure should facilitate it to the maximum extent. The tax structure will aid economic growth to the extent to which it—

(a) Restricts consumption expenditures without impairing total output, and thus increases the potential rate of capital formation.

(b) Encourages investment in new capital goods. A higher rate of savings permits a higher rate of capital formation but does not ensure it; adequate investment is necessary as well.

(c) Channels investment into the avenues which contribute the most to economic development.

(d) Increases total factor supply or factor unit efficiency, for example, by encouraging persons to enter the labour market, to work longer hours, to use more efficient techniques, and the like.

2. The tax structure should provide continuing maximum revenue productivity consistent with the optimum growth rate. This requires a tax structure that is automatically adaptive to a developing economy, and thus has a high degree of income elasticity of tax revenue. This is especially true in East Africa, where the need for negotiation and agreement among the three countries for major tax changes delays upward adjustments in taxes. It is imperative that the time lag between the occurrence of the taxable event and the payment of tax be as short as possible.

3. The tax structure should be feasible of effective administration with a minimum use of scarce resources for compliance on the part of the taxpayer and enforcement on the part of the government. Simplicity in tax structure and clarity of information are imperative.

4. The structure must accord with accepted standards of equity in contemporary East Africa. It is difficult to define these; presumably, under the general philosophy of the governments, the principles of ability to pay and progressivity of tax structure should be accepted. Matters of equity among individuals must, of course,

be considered in terms of East African conditions, not those of the United States or the United Kingdom.

There are, of course, serious conflicts among these objectives, and the overall tax structure must reflect a compromise among conflicting considerations. Thus income taxation which is most equitable by usual standards, and most responsive in revenue to expansion of the economy, is the most likely, if raised too high, to have adverse incentive effects. Consumption taxes are most likely to stimulate saving, but they are less likely to conform with accepted standards of equity. A Kaldor-type expenditure tax is probably the most effective possible tax for encouraging saving, but it is among the most difficult of all taxes to administer. Customs duties are simple to administer, but decline in revenue potential as domestic production expands. A balance must be sought among the various considerations; there can be no 'perfect' solution.

The East African tax structure

A brief summary of the East African tax structure will suffice for present purposes. Table 1 summarizes the revenues from major sources for both central and local governments. Key features of the tax structure include:

1. Heavy reliance on customs duties, as is typical of newly developing countries, and considerable use of excises. There are no general sales taxes. Customs and excises combined yield about 54 per cent of total central government tax revenues.

2. A well-developed and rather sophisticated income tax structure, the tax on individuals, however, applying only to a very small percentage of the population. The corporate tax structure includes major provisions to lessen adverse effects on incentives for investment, but the tax holiday system of West Africa is not employed. Income taxes yield about 25 per cent of central government revenue, corporations and individuals each yielding roughly half of the figure.

3. General use of the graduated personal tax (GPT), an elementary form of direct taxation, well adapted to the circumstances. The tax has from all indications reached its highest level of development in Uganda. The use of the tax establishes the principle of direct taxation for virtually all persons. The tax yields over half of local government revenue; only Tanganyika employs the tax at both central and local levels.

4. In the last two years a sharp increase in the importance of

35

export taxes, levies which had not previously been significant except in Uganda. In Uganda currently the taxes yield more than the customs duties.

5. Emphasis on the site value tax in urban property taxation.

6. A very high degree of harmonization of taxation among the three countries, with common administration of most major taxes (customs, excise; individual and company income and profits taxes), and a uniform tax policy.

The structure as a whole has several very major advantages:

1. The uniform customs system, the high degree of tax harmonization, and joint tax administration of the major taxes offer significant advantages for economic development, although admittedly giving rise to certain problems. This issue has been discussed extensively elsewhere, and will not be reconsidered in detail in this paper.*

2. The use of direct taxation affecting all income levels is firmly established. The individual income tax reaches persons in the higher income groups, the personal tax those in the lower levels. Direct taxation has many inherent advantages including tax consciousness, and offers a high degree of income elasticity of revenue; it is a tax which automatically grows in importance as the economy develops. The basic income tax structure, while not perfectly adapted to East African conditions, has many merits. The personal taxes reflect the adaptation of the principle of income taxation to the environment.

3. Extensive reliance is placed on consumption based taxes, thus avoiding the dangers of excessively high income taxation.

4. Relatively high standards of tax administration have been developed, compared to many countries in similar stages of economic development.

5. Taxes which are impossible of effective administration in the circumstances have been avoided, as well as ones giving rise to strong popular resistance.

6. Land taxation has been established in urban areas.

The system however, suffers from several major limitations as well:

1. Tax system rigidity. The very high degree of tax harmonization among the three countries may prove to be increasingly unsatisfactory as revenue needs of the countries commence to vary. Somewhat

---

* See B. F. Massell, *East African Economic Union* (Santa Monica: RAND, 1964); D. Ghai, 'Territorial Distribution of Benefits and Costs of the East African Common Market', *East African Economic Review*, vol. 2 (June 1964), pp. 29–40.

greater deviation from the existing degree of harmonization should be possible without loss of the advantages which the present system gives.

2. The very heavy reliance on customs duties. Such taxes, while perhaps according in a rough way with the accepted standards of equity, leave much to be desired on equity grounds. The income

Table 1. *Estimated tax revenue, East Africa, 1964–65 (Millions of £s)*

	Kenya	Uganda	Tanganyika	Total
Central Governments, Budget Estimates				
Collected by EACSO:				
Income Tax	13·0	4·0	7·1	24·1
Customs	14·2	9·6	11·7	35·5
Excises	6·4	4·2	4·4	15·0
Total	33·6	17·8	23·2	74·6
Collected by Governments:				
Personal Taxes	—	—	1·1	1·1
Export Taxes	0·7	10·0	3·4	14·1
Other	1·4	0·5	1·8	3·7
Total	2·1	10·5	6·3	18·9
Total	35·7	28·3	29·5	93·5
Local Governments, Estimates				
Personal Taxes	3·6	4·2	3·7	11·5
Cesses	0·3	—	0·7	1·0
Property Taxes	2·1	0·4	0·8	3·3
Other	0·2	0·6	0·5	1·3
Total	6·2	5·2	5·7	17·1
Overall Total	41·9	33·5	35·2	110·6

Source: Budget documents of the three countries; Lee, E. C., *Local Taxation in Tanganyika* (Dar-es-Salaam: Institute of Public Administration, 1964); information supplied by the governments of the three countries. The figures for the local governments should be regarded only as rough estimates, since complete current data are not available.

elasticity of tax revenue is low, particularly with the specific rate duties. But most significantly, the customs duties constitute a 'declining' revenue source, one which will inevitably fall in importance as domestic production expands. Already substantial import substitution has occurred.

3. Certain deficiencies in the income tax: its very limited coverage, the high tax rates in the upper brackets, the unnecessarily complex

allowance system, the long time lag between receipt of income and payment of tax.

4. Lack of integration of the income and graduated personal taxes, and defects in structure and operation of the latter.

5. The absence of rural land 'tax' or 'rental' payment.

6. The structure of export duties.

7. The overall inelasticity of tax revenue relative to changes in national income.*

Tax reform

The individual income tax

The individual income tax provides an exemption of £225 for single persons, £700 for a married couple, and from £75 to £250 for children, depending on age and education. As a consequence (the annual *per capita* income in East Africa is roughly £26) only a very small percentage of the population is covered; 1963 data (for 1961 taxable year) show 55,513 taxpayers in Kenya, 18,069 in Tanganyika, 12,397 in Uganda. These figures constitute about 0·6 per cent of the population in Kenya and 0·2 per cent in Tanganyika and Uganda. A high percentage of the taxpayers are non-African. The rates, on the other hand, are relatively high, ranging from 10 per cent to 75 per cent. No PAYE† is employed, and the time lag between the end of the taxable year and the payment of tax is very long, up to fifteen months. Only East African income is taxable.

While the tax is not excessively complicated, particularly since changes in 1962, some additional simplification is warranted:

1. Elimination of the special deduction for passages to or from East Africa, a carryover from colonial days, and for insurance—a deduction not particularly objectionable, but not sufficiently warranted to justify the additional complexity.

2. Simplification of the system of personal allowances, which is unnecessarily refined and not particularly suitable to East African conditions. A single basic allowance regardless of size of family should be considered, as in Ghana and Northern Nigeria. The family system in East Africa is such that the sharp line drawn in western countries between dependants and non-dependants is not suitable.

---

* Note the paper by Dharam Ghai, 'Growth and Structure of Central Government Tax Revenue in Uganda', Economic Development Research Project, Makerere University College, 1964.

† Pay As You Earn—taxes on wages and salaries deducted by employers (*Editors*).

Most persons, married or not, parents or not, have others dependent upon them, and the usual structure of allowances for dependants is not appropriate. If this drastic change is not made, the allowance figure should be made uniform for all children regardless of age.

3. In conjunction with the elimination of the deductions for children, one special deduction should be re-established: for costs of education of dependants up to a specified amount per dependant. This complication is warranted, in view of the tremendous importance attached to education, and in order to mitigate somewhat the tax burden on large families.

4. Substantial reduction in the allowance figure, so as to bring within the scope of the tax all persons receiving regular wages and salaries, or operating a business.

The exact figure should be selected in terms of studies of present-day incomes; a figure of £100 or £150 might be appropriate.

5. A reduction in rates, particularly at the top level. The top marginal rate, now 75 per cent, should not exceed perhaps 50 per cent, and the speed of the progression should be reduced accordingly. The present high rates (which apply to very few taxpayers) offer potential dangers to incentives out of all proportion to the revenue obtained. East Africa does not have a small, very high income landlord or other class which warrants heavy taxation, as do some developing countries. At the beginning levels, covering the large numbers of additional taxpayers that would be encompassed by change (4), a figure of perhaps 5 per cent would be most appropriate.

6. Establishment of PAYE, coupled with a declaration system to place other taxpayers on to a current basis. PAYE is used widely in other countries, many of which are less capable of administering it than East Africa. In fact it is used to some extent with the graduated personal taxes in the East African countries. Current payment not only reduces evasion, but establishes concurrency of tax payment with the earning of income, and is extremely important for income elasticity of tax revenue. The lack of PAYE is one of the most serious defects in the East African tax structure.

The tasks created for employers by PAYE would not be serious; various stamped card systems, as now used in Kenya for personal tax, would facilitate application of tax to lower income workers. The transition problem could be solved by requiring that in the transitional year the taxpayer pay whichever amount is higher—that owed for the previous year, or that determined for the present year.

For persons other than wage earners, the declaration system is not entirely satisfactory, but is workable and greatly accelerates the speed of payment.

7. Shift to the self-assessment system, whereby the taxpayer would calculate his tax when filling out his tax return and remit the tax due with the return, subject to subsequent review and possible additional assessment upon examination. This procedure will speed the timing of payment significantly.

8. Elimination of exemption of income earned outside of East Africa, a feature which encourages expatriation of capital, particularly to low-income-tax countries. Double taxation should be avoided by tax treaties.

Personal taxes

The personal tax systems have important advantages, in firmly establishing the principle of direct taxation for persons in all income levels, and encouraging subsistence farmers to produce for the market or look for outside work. The taxes are admittedly somewhat crude, and assessment and enforcement are by no means perfect. Every effort should be made to improve the standards of operation, and some reconsideration of rate schedules is desirable. Many of the Tanganyika local rates are not graduated, and a change toward graduation in these areas is highly desirable. Likewise in Tanganyika, merger of the local produce cesses with the personal tax would ensure more uniformity of burden on farmers and wage earners.

Even with a high level of perfection, however, the personal taxes are inferior to income taxation, in terms of equity (particularly the fixed tax in each rate bracket, instead of a percentage rate) and responsiveness to changes in income. Thus as recommended above, the coverage of the income tax should be greatly increased by reducing the exemptions. If this is done without change in the personal taxes, larger numbers of persons—all except those in the lowest graduated personal tax brackets—will pay both income and personal taxes. This is not necessarily objectionable, although it does involve some wasted administrative and compliance effort. In Tanganyika the central government personal tax applies only to persons with incomes over £100; this tax should thus be eliminated once the income tax exemptions are lowered, with a supplement to the income tax collected by EACSO if desired.

For the local personal rates in Tanganyika and the local graduated personal taxes in the other two countries, merger of the personal and income taxes (along the lines of the Eastern Nigeria policy) would have merit, but is complicated by the fact that these levies provide the major source of local revenue. Furthermore it is desirable that taxes be collected from the lowest income groups (who comprise most of the population) by local administrations rather than by EACSO. The number of persons required to pay two taxes will remain relatively small for some time. It is therefore suggested that the local graduated personal taxes remain as they are for the present; over a longer period of time the portion collected from the persons subject to income tax can be shifted to become an income tax supplement, and personal tax collected only from those not subject to income tax.

Company and corporation tax

The *company* tax is applied as a form of withholding of the individual income tax; the *corporate* tax is a separate levy. The combined rate is 42½ per cent, a figure in line with those in many other countries. Liberal depreciation and investment allowances reduce the potential adverse effects on investment. It is recommended that the rates of these taxes not be increased, because of dangers of check upon investment. Like the individual income tax, these levies automatically grow in importance as the economy grows.

The investment allowance system as employed has the advantage of minimizing the adverse effects of the tax upon investment. It also offers significant possibilities of directing investment along lines consistent with overall economic planning. This has been done thus far only in a rough way. But significant differences in allowances for various industries can be introduced to encourage certain fields and discourage others, or to aid the growth of certain regions. The success of such a policy depends in large measure upon the quality of the overall planning of economic development. But the allowance offers a significant tool for this purpose.

Unfortunately, however, an investment allowance is likely to increase the degree of capital intensity in industry. To many—but not all—students of economic development, such a policy is unfortunate in a situation in which under-employment (and even unemployment) is widespread and thus the labour supply is highly elastic, and the optimum capital-labour ratio may be very different from what it is in a developed economy. It is important to devise a system of

41

income tax concessions that relates the amount of tax reduction to the rate of increase in output rather than to the volume of investment. It is doubtful that such a system will provide direct incentive to increase in output (as proposed by the Knorr-Baumol plan* and attempted in Canada), but it will minimize adverse incentive effects without providing artificial incentive toward capital intensification.

Customs, excises, and sales taxes

Customs duties remain the chief source of revenue, accounting for about 35 per cent of the total national government revenue, a situation typical of developing economies generally. In the earliest stages of economic development, extensive use of customs for revenue is not without merit. The duties can be concentrated upon non-necessities, and particularly upon items primarily consumed in the upper income levels. Administration in East Africa is highly effective. However, customs constitute a deteriorating revenue source as the economy develops: use of tariffs for protection cuts revenue, and as more and more of the total of consumption consists of domestic goods, the base for customs revenue falls. Furthermore, inequity becomes more serious, since the tax burden varies with the preference between imported and domestic goods. But the most serious problem is the decline in the potential revenue base—yet tax capacity is not falling.

At the same time, it is widely agreed that a developing economy must not rely too heavily on income taxation, or, more correctly, it can raise a greater total revenue with a given rate of economic growth if it makes extensive use of commodity taxation than if it concentrates almost wholly on direct taxes, as developed economies may do if they wish. Thus a system must be developed in East Africa to continue to tap on a consumption basis the tax capacity now reached by customs duties. To a limited extent, in the fields of traditionally heavy sumptuary taxation, particularly liquor and tobacco, this can best be accomplished with excise taxes on the manufacturers. But as broader coverage is desired, the excises become less satisfactory; to extend them to large numbers of items, one by one, creates disturbances in the markets, and increases administrative and compliance problems and inequity among the consumers of various goods.

* K. Knorr and W. S. Baumol, *What Price Economic Growth?*, Englewood Cliffs, N.J.: Prentice Hall, 1961.

The ideal solution, were it administratively feasible, would be a retail sales tax on all commodities except those specifically exempted, as for example, basic foods. But, given the nature of East African retailing at the present time, it is doubtful if adequate compliance could be attained without excessive cost and use of scarce personnel. The next best alternative, and the one recommended, is a general wholesale sales tax, levied on the last wholesale transaction, that is, the purchase by the retailer. The taxable vendors would include wholesale firms, manufacturers selling directly to retailers or final consumers, and importers selling to retailers; on direct importation by retailers or consumers tax would apply at the time of importation. The tax would apply equally to imported and domestic goods while protection would continue to be applied where desired by customs duties. Otherwise, purely revenue customs duties would be reduced to avoid an excessive combined tax burden. This is the form of sales tax used for many years by Australia. For simplicity and effectiveness of operation, it is strongly recommended that the tax rate be uniform (unlike that in Australia), and that exemptions be confined to basic foodstuffs, medicines, and a few other items. Producers' goods would not be taxed. If all 'necessities' were exempted, the base of the tax would be seriously reduced. It is not desirable to exempt processed foods (except perhaps a few particular items), since the income elasticity of consumption of processed food appears to be very high in East Africa. To gain partial advantage of the retail form, it would be possible to follow the Swiss tradition of allowing larger retailers to register for tax purposes, buy goods tax free, and apply the tax to their sales at a rate sufficiently lower to reflect retail margins. By this means more and more of the tax could be collected at the retail level, with the advantages of broader base, simpler definition of taxable price, and greater possibility of inter-country variation which this tax affords.

Control of the tax would rest upon examination of the accounts of manufacturers and wholesalers. On imported goods control would be linked with the importation documents. While control might not be completely effective, the leakage should be minor. The tax should be administered by the EACSO Commissioner of Customs and Excise.

Like the income tax, revenue of a levy of this sort would expand automatically with the growth of the East African economy. The tax likewise would offer one other major advantage: the yield would

43

accrue to the country of consumption, and thus some of the advantage which Kenya gains with the income tax because of the possession of a large portion of industry would be lessened. Furthermore, while a uniform rate throughout East Africa would have merit, some deviation in rate among the three countries would not create impossible problems. Such deviation would be least objectionable with a retail sales tax, but feasible with the wholesale tax.

In the author's opinion, a broad based consumption tax at a relatively low rate is preferable to very high 'purchase taxes' on selected luxury items. Such taxes are inevitably discriminatory, selection of items for tax on any logical basis is not possible, and the high rates increase evasion. But most significantly, such taxes are likely to encounter widespread popular opposition, as experience in Ghana, British Guiana, and elsewhere has demonstrated. Tax structures must meet general acceptance on the part of the public if they are to function satisfactorily and avoid adverse incentive effects. Very high taxes on consumption items which, while luxuries in the usual sense, are widely sought by many people as their incomes rise can have adverse effects on incentives as serious as those of excessive income taxation.

Export duties

Export duties are presumably direct taxes, in the sense that they reduce the incomes of the producers of the products subject to tax selling in the world markets. The disadvantages of export duties are well known, and need not be repeated. But the blanket indictment frequently made of them ignores the potentiality of their use when the prices of the products rise sharply. The export crops of East Africa are subject to severe fluctuations in price; increases lasting a few years do not serve a useful function in reallocating resources, and in fact may produce undesirable readjustments. The very high incomes of the primary producers in the high-price years are likely to contribute more to inflation than to economic growth. Thus the essentially windfall gain can justifiably be taken by the government with very little harm to the economy. The export duties cannot be relied upon as a regular source of government revenue if used in this manner, but they can provide substantial funds for development programmes in high-price years.

Thus the export duty system should be reconsidered, to convert those which have flat rates unrelated to prices of the products into the forms based upon the prices, with no tax applying when product prices are low, and rates sharply progressive with higher prices.

Property taxation

The principle of taxation of urban land, with the tax entirely or primarily on site value, is generally accepted in East Africa, and the tax has significant merit as a source of local government finance. While the site value basis is advantageous in terms of encouraging building, the direct relationship of many local government activities to building construction suggests that some levy on improvements is also desirable. This procedure will allow greater total revenue than the site value basis alone.

Rural land taxation is virtually unknown, except to a limited extent in Buganda and portions of Kenya. This situation is, of course, in part a product of communal ownership of land in many areas, the lack of clearly defined titles and land surveys and other considerations. In large measure, the graduated personal taxes take the place of land taxation. While no overnight changes are feasible, consideration should be given over a longer period to gradual introduction of rural land taxes or land rental charges. Such levies should encourage, rather than discourage, efficient use of land.

Tax harmonization

Since this paper is concerned only with tax structure as such, it will not seek to review the broader question of the desirability of the continuation of the common market. The assumption is made that the common market and other elements of economic integration will continue. Given the general structure, the high degree of tax harmonization and common administration have important advantages, in increasing the effectiveness of tax administration, lessening the need for fiscal frontiers, simplifying the task of tax compliance, avoiding the possible effects of tax differentials on industry location, and avoiding competitive undercutting of taxes on the part of the various countries to lure industry and business.

It is highly important that the principle of a common approach to taxation and common administration of taxation be retained, with overall tax policy determined as a part of co-ordinated economic planning. However, somewhat greater deviation from the present degree of uniformity is possible without loss of the major advantages of the system; it is important, however, that the departure from

45

uniformity be developed through agreements among the three countries rather than by unilateral action, which can quickly lead to tax competition. There are two major types of deviations which may be acceptable: (1) special tax concessions, perhaps through differences in investment allowances, to aid the growth of the less developed areas, (2) higher tax rates in countries wishing additional revenue. Some variation in individual income tax rates (but not tax structure) would be feasible, and some variation in excise rates, or in the wholesale sales tax outlined above, or in special purchase taxes. Such deviations inevitably give rise to problems, and they are not recommended, *per se*; it is merely suggested that limited deviation from the present degree of uniformity is feasible if regarded as desirable for development purposes.

Conclusion

To what extent would the suggested changes increase the extent to which the tax structure attains the goals outlined early in the paper?

First, by improving the long-range quality of consumption-based taxation, and by reducing the higher-bracket income taxes, the structure should be more conducive to economic growth, by encouraging savings and expansion in business investment.

Secondly, through change in the investment allowance system, investment could be directed more effectively along desired lines, and the incentive to capital intensification removed.

Thirdly, the revenue potential, and particularly the income elasticity of revenue and the long range automatic adaptation of the tax structure to economic growth, would be greatly improved by establishing a general wholesale sales tax to supplement and ultimately in large measure replace the customs duties, by the establishment of PAYE for income tax collection, and by reduction in personal allowances under the income tax.

Fourthly, administration would be improved by the use of PAYE and by simplification of the income tax structure; the other changes suggested should not seriously complicate administration and compliance.

Fifthly, the overall equity would be increased somewhat by partial substitution of a sales tax for customs duty revenue, and by the extension of the scope of the income tax. While the recommended changes in income tax allowances would lessen equity as among some families, especially in the non-African groups, on the whole they would adapt the system much more satisfactorily to the East African environment.

At the same time, the principle of direct taxation would be retained, as well as the high (if slightly reduced) degree of harmonization of income taxation among the three countries, and common administration. No tax structure can meet all objectives perfectly; the changes, however, should improve the overall operation of the structure.

On the other hand it is strongly recommended:

1. That the income tax allowance not be increased, thus reducing the coverage. The important advantages of the income tax from a long range point of view are so great that no shift away from it should be made for administrative considerations of a temporary nature.

2. That the 'tax holiday' system not be used. The gains are doubtful and the administrative problems so great that the net effect may be disadvantageous.

3. That 'nuisance' taxes be avoided. There is a tendency for newly developing countries to levy a number of minor taxes, such as ones on bank cheques, which yield little revenue, constitute a general nuisance, and impede the enforcement of major levies. Likewise any sort of gross receipts or turnover tax on all business firms is highly objectionable in terms of its effects on the business community and violates all usual standards of taxation.

22. COMMERCIAL BANKING IN EAST AFRICA

H. L. ENGBERG

Foreign transactions, domestic income, and the money supply

...In order to understand the monetary economy of East Africa and the conditions under which the banking system is working it is essential to emphasize the role of foreign transactions in the determination of domestic income. The money economy of the three countries of the East African Common Market is oriented in the direction of world markets, and has consequently been described as 'economically dependent'. This concept needs to be briefly clarified, since it has considerable implication for the banking system and for economic policy.

Economic dependence refers to both exports and imports,* and implies three basic conditions: first, the ratio of export revenues to national income is relatively high; second, a relatively large proportion of any increment to national income is spent on imported goods and services; and third, export revenues are largely determined by conditions which prevail in the world markets and over which the economically dependent country has little or no control.

A relatively high ratio of exports to national income means that a large proportion of aggregate income is generated directly and indirectly by the export sector. Activities in the export sector create income directly; but in addition there are secondary effects, as part of the income received by those engaged in the production of exports

---

* The discussion is conducted in terms of exports and imports, but it should be noticed that invisible items in the East African balance of international payments represent a growing proportion of the current account. Thus a substantial amount of foreign exchange has been earned in connection with the presence of British military forces, and interest and dividend payments abroad constitute an important use of foreign exchange. The behaviour of the capital accounts, including foreign aid, should also be taken into consideration. See East African Statistical Department, *Estimate of Payments 1959, 1960, and 1961* (Nairobi, 1962), and later figures published in the quarterly *Economic and Statistical Review* (Nairobi).

48

will be spent and thereby create a second round of income. The size of the secondary effects is influenced by the proportion of any increase in income that will be spent on domestically produced goods and services, such as food, clothing, housing, and other consumption goods, as well as certain capital goods and services produced locally. The smaller this proportion is, either because people choose to hold a large fraction of an increase in their income as inactive liquid balances, or because they prefer imported to domestic goods, the smaller the ultimate impact on aggregate income of expanded sales abroad. The higher the proportion of the extra income that is spent on home products, the greater will be the 'multiplier' effect which increases total income at home.

The dimension of this so-called multiplier* is crucial, since the stimulus imparted by export production to domestic economic activity will be limited if it is small. Unfortunately, a relatively low multiplier is typical of an economically dependent and less developed country. The supply of domestically produced goods and services is limited in range and quality, and cannot be quickly expanded to meet increased demand, which will therefore be directed towards imports. This propensity to import may be strengthened by an uneven income distribution where a substantial proportion of national income is earned and spent by a comparatively small number of spending units. Such an income distribution in a developing country will usually result in transfers abroad of interest and capital, and may be accompanied by a relatively persistent, or inelastic, demand for higher-quality imported goods. This may be offset, at times more than offset, by an inflow of capital funds from abroad, particularly if the developed market economy is dominated by expatriate enterprise which attracts foreign investment.

Export proceeds, capital imports, private domestic investment, and government expenditure all represent 'injections' into the income stream, while expenditure on imports, transfers abroad, hoarding of currency, and government taxation are 'leakages' from the point of view of national income determination. Commercial banks are obviously affected by changes in these 'injections' and 'leakages' and may in turn affect the 'multiplier' process. For example, an increase in exports will usually expand the banks' holdings of foreign

---

* The multiplier can for our purpose be defined as the reciprocal of the sum of the marginal savings ratio and the marginal ratio of imports to income. The higher the marginal savings and import ratios, the lower the multiplier.

exchange. Local bank reserves may be further augmented by attracting the spare cash holdings of people who do not ordinarily use banks, and by offering profitable openings for the use of temporarily idle cash balances of business firms, which might otherwise be invested in foreign money markets. The final effect on domestic income of the increased bank resources will depend on the direction of bank lending and investment. Thus, increased lending to agriculture and to businesses producing for the domestic market may accentuate the impact on national income without a proportionate increase in imports (depending on the level of employment), while an expansion of lending to the commercial sector may result in a second round of imports and consequently a smaller ultimate impact on the domestic economy.

The relationships between the gross domestic product, foreign transactions, and the money supply for East Africa are indicated in Table 1.* In the first place, the figures illustrate the significance of foreign transactions to the East African economy. The average ratio of imports to gross domestic product for the period 1950–63 was 40 per cent, with a range between 32 per cent (1959) and 48 per cent (1952). This compares with an average of 5 per cent for the United States, 10 per cent for Japan, 23 per cent for the United Kingdom, and 27 per cent for Sweden.† The average ratio of exports to gross domestic product in East Africa was 35 per cent, ranging from a low of 33 per cent (1957) to a high of 50 per cent (1951–2). The relative importance of exports in East Africa can again be compared with the corresponding figures for the United States, (5 per cent), Japan (12 per cent), the United Kingdom (24 per cent), and Sweden (27 per cent).

Secondly, the data in Table 1 show a relatively high average correlation between changes in the rate of increase or decrease of all four series. For example, from 1960 to 1961 the annual rate of growth of the gross domestic product declined from 6 to 1 per cent; at the same time there was a change in the rate of increase for imports from 10 to 1 per cent, while exports changed from an 8 per

---

* The data should be used with caution, particularly for the gross domestic product, which is essentially an estimate. It would have been desirable to have used net national income in the table, but it is not yet possible to make allowance for fixed capital consumed during each period on the basis of the East African national accounts.

† Hal B. Lary, *Problems of the United States as World Trader and Banker* (New York, 1963), p. 104.

Table 1. *East African gross domestic product, foreign trade, and money supply, 1950–63*[1]

Year	Gross domestic product[2] £m.	Annual change %	Imports £m.	Annual change %	Exports[3] £m.	Annual change %	Money supply[4] £m.	Annual change %
1950	186·9	—	71·3	—	72·9	—	70·5	—
1951	232·1	24	104·1	46	115·2	58	91·7	30
1952	251·9	9	121·1	16	124·8	8	104·7	14
1953	252·7	(—)	105·8	−13	92·2	−26	108·0	3
1954	282·3	12	117·5	11	101·6	10	116·8	8
1955	318·5	13	149·0	27	107·7	6	124·4	7
1956	337·3	6	133·8	−10	120·8	12	122·5	−2
1957	356·5	6	140·1	5	119·1	−1	122·6	(−1)
1958	359·8	1	121·4	−13	123·4	4	113·9	−7
1959	377·1	5	121·5	(—)	128·8	4	116·2	2
1960	399·6	6	133·9	10	139·7	8	117·7	(−1)
1961	402·1	1	135·2	1	133·6	−4	117·1	(−1)
1962	409·7	2	135·5	(—)	139·7	5	123·3	5
1963	443·8	8	145·0	7	170·6	22	140·3	14

[1] Figures for the gross domestic product, imports, and exports represent annual flows; money supply figures refer to 30 June each year. (−) denotes a change of less than 1 per cent. Sources: East African Statistical Department, *Quarterly Economic and Statistical Review* (until 1961), and *Economic and Statistical Review* (quarterly, since 1961). Also, East African Currency Board, *Annual Reports* (Nairobi).

[2] G. D. P. of the monetary economy at factor cost, and at current prices.   [3] Exports include re-exports and gold exports.

[4] Money supply is defined as the sum of cash with the public (currency in circulation *minus* cash in vault at banks) and demand deposits of banks in East Africa.

cent annual rate of increase in 1960 to a 4 per cent decline in export earnings in 1961. In both years there was practically no change in the money supply. This connection between, on one hand, changes in the gross domestic product, and, on the other, changes in imports, exports, and the stock of money is of course to be expected in a dependent economy.

Thirdly, the high correlation between the gross domestic product and imports is indicative of the relatively large proportion of any increment in income that will be spent on imported goods and services.* In only two of the eleven pairs of data for the two series did the changes take place in opposite directions. The looser connection between exports and the money supply implies that foreign transactions are only one, albeit an important one, of several determinants of changes in the money stock.

These observations lead to the conclusion that the comparatively close interrelation between the balance of payments and the gross domestic product in East Africa gives rise to a significant and relatively quick response of the domestic economy, through income changes, to deficits and surpluses in current external transactions. Likewise, changes in domestic economic activity unrelated to foreign transactions, but brought about, for instance, by an autonomous increase in public or private investment, will quickly be reflected in the balance of payments. This means that a deficit in the balance of payments in a sense is symptomatic of economic development, since it reflects an excess of domestic investment over domestic savings and is caused by the high ratio of changes in imports to changes in income. Domestic stability and growth must therefore in the long run, at least to some extent, be subjugated to the dictates of the balance of payments, which inevitably will continue in the future to represent an important restraint on any independent monetary and fiscal measures to influence the domestic economy, such as credit expansion and government-budget deficits.

The composition of the money supply

The changes in the composition of the East African money supply are shown in Table 2. It can be seen that the currency component,

* This 'marginal propensity to import' averaged about 0·36 for East Africa over the period 1950–63. This means that, on the average, an increase in national income of £100 would result in an increase in imports of £36. However, such an average figure is not very useful for policy-makers, since it disguises substantial year-to-year shifts.

or cash with the public, rose faster than demand deposits, leading to an almost uninterrupted increase in the ratio of currency to money stock. This upward trend in currency is not surprising and has been noticed in other developing countries, where the monetization of the non-monetary economy has typically progressed faster than the extension of banking facilities and has therefore raised the ratio of currency to deposits.* In East Africa the growing proportion of indigenous agricultural produce sold for cash as well as the substantial migration from rural to urban areas have contributed to an increasing use of currency for transaction purposes.†

Table 2. *Composition of the money supply in East Africa, 1950–63*[1]

30 June	Cash with public[2]	Demand deposits[3]	Money supply	Proportion of cash to total
	£m.	£m.	£m.	%
1950	19·4	51·1	70·5	27·5
1955	42·8	81·6	124·4	34·4
1960	46·7	70·0	116·7	40·0
1961	47·2	69·9	117·1	40·3
1962	48·3	75·0	123·3	39·2
1963	57·1	83·2	140·3	40·7

[1] Kenya, Uganda, and Tanzania, excluding currency circulating in certain occupied territories and in Ethiopia (1950–1), and in Aden. Sources: as for Table 1.
[2] Cash with the public is currency in circulation *minus* cash in vault at banks.
[3] Banks in East Africa only; government deposits included.

It is also to be expected that the currency component in East Africa is relatively high compared to such mature economies as the United States and the United Kingdom, but, on the other hand, it is a smaller element of the stock of money than in several other developing countries. For example, the ratio of currency to the money supply in India is about 73 per cent, in Nigeria 62 per cent, in the Philippines

* India, for example, has followed a pattern similar to East Africa. See J. D. Sethi, *Problems of Monetary Policy in an Underdeveloped Country* (New York, Asia Publishing House, 1961), chapter 1.
† Regional redistribution of income favouring the low-income, high-currency-using areas was also found to be a major factor in the increased use of currency in the United States from 1939 to the early 1950s. See Stephen L. McDonald, 'Some Factors Affecting the Increased Relative Use of Currency Since 1939', in the *J. of Finance* (New York), vol. 11, 3, September 1956. Also Phillip D. Cagan, 'The Demand for Currency Relative to the Total Money Supply', in the *J. of Political Economy* (Chicago), vol. 66, 4, August 1958.

48 per cent, and in Argentina about 60 per cent.* Little significance, however, should be attached to the composition of the money supply as a measure of the degree of economic development.† Thus, the relative use of currency has been consistently large in several highly developed countries, such as France, Western Germany, and Sweden, even if various payments techniques operated by the postal system, the savings banks, and the rural and urban credit co-operatives are taken into consideration. In contrast, it has been consistently low in many Latin American countries, such as Venezuela and Uruguay. The flow of payments, i.e. the volume of transactions carried out in currency compared to deposits, would be a more useful measure of the degree of monetary development. Available information is usually too meagre to make such a comparison, but an attempt is made by the use of debit statistics in Table 3, below.

A large currency component is significant in another respect, however. Wide seasonal and cyclical changes in the public's demand for cash affect commercial bank reserves, and thereby the total stock of money. While the monetary authority has partial control over fluctuations in demand deposits through its ability to vary bank reserves, a central bank has no direct means to influence changes in the relative use of cash. These changes may be offset by open-market operations of the central bank, but even in countries with relatively well-developed money and capital markets this is not always effective.‡

It was indicated in Table 1 that changes in exports and imports have important effects on the money supply. Exporters sell part of their earnings of foreign exchange to the banks and receive in return claims on the banks in the form of deposits. Rising export earnings will therefore tend to expand the volume of demand deposits, which is likely to be accompanied by an increase in the use of currency, as the demand for goods and services of those engaged in the export sector expands and requires a larger amount of cash for transaction

---

* International Monetary Fund, *International Financial Statistics* (Washington), vol. 17, 11, November 1964, and Central Bank of Nigeria, *Economic and Financial Review* (Lagos), vol. 2, 1, June 1964. Figures represent four-year averages.

† Edward Nevin, *Capital Funds in Underdeveloped Countries* (New York, 1961), p. 2, argues to the contrary.

‡ See, for example, Robert V. Roosa, *Federal Reserve Operations in the Money and Government Securities Markets* (Federal Reserve Bank of New York, 1956), pp. 70–1. See also Erin E. Jucker-Fleetwood, *Money and Finance in Africa* (London, 1964), pp. 71–83 and 200–10.

purposes. However, the process may be slowed down by the propensity to spend a relatively large fraction of any net addition to current income on imports. The resulting use of foreign exchange—to purchase abroad tools, machinery, and other equipment as a result of the growth in exports, and to increase imports of consumer goods—tends to reduce bank deposits, thereby reducing the stock of money and the liquid assets of the banking sector.

Table 3. *Turnover rates of money supply and demand deposits in East Africa, 1950–63*[1]

Year	Debits to current account[2]	Demand deposits[3]	Turnover of demand deposits[4]	Turnover of money supply[5]
	£m.	£m.	ratio	ratio
1950	213·9	52·4	4·1	2·7
1955	530·5	84·0	6·3	2·6
1960	660·9	68·7	9·6	3·4
1961	671·7	73·5	9·1	3·4
1962	750·8	78·1	9·6	3·3
1963	827·8	83·8	9·9	3·2

[1] Sources: East African Statistical Department, *Quarterly Economic and Statistical Review* (until 1961), and *Economic and Statistical Review* (quarterly, since 1960).

[2] Annual averages of quarterly figures computed on the basis of index numbers published by the East African Statistical Department.

[3] Annual averages of quarterly figures.

[4] Debits to demand deposits divided by the volume of demand deposits.

[5] Gross domestic product (see Table 1) divided by the money supply.

The net effect of these opposite forces may be that business firms, households, and the government sector end up holding a larger amount of money in the form of demand deposits and currency than before, and that the banks may have larger reserves on the basis of which a multiple expansion of bank credit and deposit can take place. But the close relationship between bank liquidity, foreign transactions, and the stock of money also implies that an autonomous increase in bank lending and investment, not matched by an increase in export earnings of foreign exchange, is likely to reduce not only the liquidity of the banking system but also the external currency reserves of the economy.

Much the same applies to an expansion of the fiduciary issue of

currency by the East African Currency Board.* By purchasing local
government securities the Board creates extra currency against local
assets and thereby adds to the money supply. Likewise, the power to
rediscount and to make advances against three-month agricultural
paper also adds to the stock of money, when used. The purchase of
local assets in either form tends to increase bank reserves directly,
and the proceeds derived by the Government from the sale of its
public securities to the Currency Board may, when spent by the
Government, return to the banks for a while in the form of deposits.
Such an expansion of the money supply may or may not be a
powerful stimulant to the economy, depending on the use made of
the funds.† But if it creates new demand for goods and services it is
inevitable that part of it should spill over into increased imports.
In that case the monetary expansion, resulting from the Board's
purchase of local assets, amounts to a drawing on sterling assets,
and the ratio of external currency reserves to local currency liabilities
of the Board will consequently decline. In the event that the entire
increase in the money supply is used to purchase sterling assets from
the Currency Board, then the demand liabilities of the Board remain
approximately the same as before the acquisition of local securities,
but it now holds a correspondingly lower reserve of sterling assets;
i.e. external currency reserves have been replaced by local reserves
in the form of government obligations or agricultural paper.‡ This

---

* The fiduciary issue represents that part of the local currency which is not
backed in full by sterling assets, i.e. currency and (usually U.K.) government
securities. Under the original currency-board system all local currency was
issued only in exchange for sterling. The East African Currency Board was
granted authority to purchase local government securities in 1955 (see the
Board's *Report for 1955*, p. 11 and Appendix 2), and the limit of £10m. was
extended to £25m. in May 1963. The Board was moreover given power to
rediscount agricultural paper for the banks and to make advances against
promissory notes secured by agricultural paper in November 1960 (see the
Board's *Report for 1961*, p. 7, *Report for 1962*, pp. 4–5, and *Report for 1963*,
pp. 11–12, 14–15 and 17–18). The fiduciary issue for crop finance is limited to
£10m. Thus the potential expansion of the Board's currency liabilities, based
upon East African assets, is £35m., or about one-quarter of the stock of
money in 1963. At that time the Board held £13·5m. of local assets, compared
to £64m. of sterling assets.

† What usually happens is that a particular project in the development plans of
the three countries is financed by currency from the East African Currency
Board, issued in exchange for long-term fiduciary securities purchased directly
from the governments.

‡ Indeed, this was the idea behind the creation of a fiduciary issue: to free part
of the external reserves held in London and to make them available for capital

puts an effective limit to the stimulus of the domestic economy that can be achieved through the expansion of the fiduciary issue.*

The money supply in East Africa has finally been characterized by an upward trend in its rate of turnover over the period from 1950 to 1963; i.e. the available stock of money has been used more intensively from year to year. Although the money supply virtually doubled between 1950 and 1963, the gross domestic product of the monetary economy (at current prices) grew at an even faster rate. Comparison of the two figures gives an estimate of the rate of turnover (or velocity of circulation) of the money supply. The turnover of demand deposits can also be estimated by relating their volume to the total debits against current account. The data for East Africa are presented in Table 3, on page 55.

The ratio of gross domestic product to the stock of money indicates the average number of times each money unit would have to be spent to purchase the total annual output, and the turnover of demand deposits suggests the average number of times each unit deposited on current account with the banks is used by the depositor for some purpose within a period of a year.† There is an upward trend in both series, particularly pronounced for the turnover rate of demand deposits; this might be expected in a growing economy, although

---

expenditure in East Africa. It should be noted at this point that changes in the fiduciary issue are not the same thing as 'open-market operations', i.e. the purchase and sale of local government securities by a central bank. In the first place, the Currency Board has been run much as a government department, rather than a bank; and secondly, it has not attempted deliberately to influence the banks' liquidity, primarily because the absence of a developed money and capital market and the existence of three separate borrowing governments present considerable obstacles to such an initiative.

* The question of what constitutes an adequate volume of external reserves for the domestic currency has been discussed at some length by, among others, W. T. Newlyn and D. C. Rowan, *Money & Banking in British Colonial Africa* (Oxford, 1954), pp. 201–5 and 258–61; and Edward Nevin, *op. cit.*, chapter 1. The actual problem has been faced by several countries formerly served by a currency board; see, for example, the 'Nigerian Budget Speech 1962 by the Federal Minister of Finance' (Lagos, April 1962), p. 7. Also Erin E. Jucker-Fleetwood, *op. cit.*, chapter 20.

† Both types of velocity should be considered an index rather than a true measure of the rates of turnover of demand deposits and of the money supply. The gross domestic product is at best a relatively crude estimate, and debits to current account also involve a certain amount of estimation. Moreover, debits to current account and gross domestic product represent flows of values, while demand deposits and money supply are stocks, although annual averages of quarterly figures for demand deposits have been used in Table 3.

there is considerable disagreement on this point.* In the long run the level of demand-deposit turnover is largely determined by the banking and payments habits, as well as the wealth or income level, of the community. The increasing velocity of demand deposits in East Africa reflects the growing use of cheques in effecting payments and the increased ease of acquiring income-earning money substitutes and of borrowing. The existence of an elastic and accessible supply of earning assets with a high degree of liquidity, such as savings deposits, savings bonds,† Treasury bills, and shares of building societies, has lessened the need to hold currency and, in particular, demand deposits, and has led to a better utilization of deposits and hence a higher rate of turnover. The rise in turnover probably also reflects the substantial expansion of bank offices since the early 1950s, through which the three large banks have made banking services available even at places remote from urban centres. Finally, the growth in the gross domestic product of the monetary economy in East Africa is not only an indication of growth in the volume of goods and services produced, but also suggests that a greater amount of the national output is coming into the money economy, which in itself tends to increase the rate of turnover of the money supply.

The debit figures are by themselves of considerable interest (Table 3). Debits to current account include cash payments of cheques presented over the counter or received by the banks through the mail, telegraphic and telephonic transfers of funds, and withdrawals of currency by depositors in return for debits on their current account.‡ They show a high positive correlation with the monetary gross

---

* See, for example, George Garvy, *Debits and Clearing Statistics and Their Use* (Washington, Board of Governors of the Federal Reserve System, 1959), pp. 96–9, and by the same author, 'Structural Aspects of Money Velocity', in *Quarterly J. of Economics* (Cambridge, Mass.), vol. 73, 3, August 1959. Also Richard T. Selden, 'Monetary Velocity in the United States', in *Studies in the Quantity Theory of Money*, ed. by Milton Friedman (Chicago, 1952). The behaviour of income velocity of money in Germany from 1890 to 1931 is analysed by the present author in *Mixed Banking and Economic Growth in Germany* (Ann Arbor, Michigan, 1964), pp. 160–6. With special reference to under-developed countries, see Erin E. Jucker-Fleetwood, 'The Money Supply in Mature and Developing Countries', in *Basle Centre Publication Series A*, No. 38 (Basle, 1961).

† M. D. McWilliam, 'A Savings Experiment in Kenya', in *East African Economics Review*, vol. 8, 2, December 1961.

‡ The East African debit statistics also include debits to government accounts, which tend to represent an irregular factor not directly related to economic activity.

domestic product at current prices, which is not surprising, since a growing monetary economy is associated with greater diversification and involves a larger amount of payments by cash and cheques.* As the aggregate volume of payments made through banks depends on the total number of transactions and purchases of all kinds and on the methods of effecting payment, total debits may be used as an approximate index of the degree to which the money economy has been diffused in a developing country. Debits to current account are typically several times larger than the money value of the gross national product in a highly developed economy. For example, in the United States, total debits were almost six and a half times the gross national product,† in the United Kingdom close to ten times, in Western Germany five and a half times, and in France about five times.‡ In East Africa total debits were less than twice the gross domestic product for the monetary economy. However, it should also be noticed that debits to current account almost quadrupled from 1950 to 1963, while the gross domestic product at current prices increased by less than one and a half times. This significant increase in the volume of payments by cheque is another indication of the growth and diversification of the exchange economy in East Africa. ...

The sources and uses of bank funds

Turning now to the financial resources of the commercial banks, it may be seen from Table 4 that total bank deposits in East Africa almost doubled between 1950 and 1963, and that the growth in time§ and savings deposits was considerably faster than in demand deposits. As a result the ratio of time and savings deposits to demand deposits rose from 11 per cent in 1950 to almost 39 per cent at the end of 1963.

Total deposits grew at a slower rate, however, than that of the monetary gross domestic product at current prices. Thus, if the relation of bank deposits to gross domestic product in 1963 were to be restored to the level of 1950, the banks would carry about £35

* Moreover, both series are expressed in current money units, and changes in the price level will therefore tend to affect both series roughly in the same way.
† Board of Governors of the Federal Reserve System, *Federal Reserve Bulletin* (Washington, D.C.), November 1964.
‡ These are estimates based on the International Monetary Fund, *International Financial Statistics*, *op. cit.*, for the individual countries.
§ Demand deposits may be withdrawn on demand; time (or fixed) deposits are left in the bank for a certain length of time, during which they earn interest, but are not negotiable.

million more of deposits, or a deposit volume close to 40 per cent higher than at the end of 1963. There is of course no reason to suppose that the position of the banks in the monetary economy was 'right' or 'normal' in 1950; and, moreover, the banks were still in 1963 recovering from the heavy outflow of funds from Kenya subsequent to the Lancaster House meeting. But the trend has been so pronounced—and it resembles the pattern in many other countries, including the United Kingdom—as to warrant a few comments.

The decline in the relative importance of the commercial banking system in the East African monetary economy, measured by the growth of deposits compared to the growth of the domestic product, is apparently not a result of any reduction in the volume of bank payments needed to support the level of economic activity. It was shown earlier that the bank debits almost quadrupled from 1950 to 1963, while the gross domestic product at current prices increased less than one and a half times. However, the banks have, particularly in Kenya, in recent years been facing a growing competition for idle funds from non-bank financial institutions, such as building societies and life insurance companies;* also Treasury bills are now issued by all three countries. It is to be expected that this competition for deposits will continue to grow, as the financial structure becomes more diversified and as government borrowing needs increase, leading to a larger supply of Treasury bills.

It is of course impossible to determine precisely to what extent the competition from the non-bank financial sector so far has reduced the growth in bank deposits. Some of the deposits so 'withdrawn' from the banks because of the availability of alternative, higher-yielding, local money substitutes have returned to the same banks as credits to other deposit accounts. But another part has undoubtedly been placed abroad. For example, companies in East Africa with pronounced seasonal swings in their sales are known to remit at certain times of the year large cash balances to the London money market, where there is an elastic supply of high-quality liquid assets.

* Building societies have actively developed their deposit business by offering higher interest rates than the banks, and by making deposits withdrawable on demand.

Life insurance premiums have grown from £4·8m. in 1957 to £6·5m. in 1962. Total assets held locally and in London by all 130 insurance companies operating in East Africa stood at £32·2m. in 1961, compared to £25·6m. at the end of 1959. See East African Statistical Department, *East African Insurance Statistics, 1960*, May 1962, p. 16, and *Economic and Statistical Review*, June 1964, p. 85.

Commercial Banking in East Africa

To the extent that these funds otherwise might have been channelled into local investments through the banks, this represents a loss to the East African economy.

The major banks in East Africa have made little effort to compete for business deposits in general or to bid for particular kinds of

Table 4. *Distribution of deposits in East Africa by type, 1950–63*[1]

End of year	Demand deposits	Time deposits	Savings deposits	Total deposits	Proportion of time and savings to demand deposits
	£m.	£m.	£m.	£m.	%
1950	57·6	4·3	1·8	63·7	10·6
1955	85·8	6·8	6·0	98·6	14·9
1960	67·7	8·3	11·3	87·3	29·0
1961	77·0	10·3	13·4	110·7	30·8
1962	83·8	13·1	16·1	113·0	34·8
1963	87·5	15·0	18·9	121·4	38·7

Table 5. *Earning and liquid assets of banks in East Africa, 1950–63*[1]

End of year	Local earning assets[3]	Percentage of total deposits	Loans and advances[4]	Percentage of total deposits	Liquid assets[5]	Percentage of total deposits
	£m.	%	£m.	%	£m.	%
1950	22·3	35·0	16·8	26·4	43·7	68·7
1955	69·6	70·6	59·8	60·5	35·0	35·5
1960	78·4	99·8	69·3	79·4	16·8	19·2
1961	81·9	81·3	72·8	72·3	20·0	20·0
1962	88·9	78·7	79·2	70·1	25·1	22·2
1963	104·5	86·1	92·8	76·5	19·4	16·0

[1] Sources: as for Table 3.
[2] Individual figures may not add up to totals because of rounding off.
[3] Bills discounted, loans, advances, and investments in East Africa.
[4] Loans and advances to industry, agriculture, and 'other' (see Table 7).
[5] Here defined as cash + net balance due from banks in East Africa and abroad + bills discounted. Bills discounted are computed as total loans and advances *minus* the sum of industrial, agricultural, and other loans.

deposits. In an attempt to counter the non-bank competition, a few of the smaller banks have been willing to accept limited amounts of business funds as savings deposits, which yield a higher interest than the rate on time deposits with a comparable degree of liquidity.

There are confidential banking agreements regulating interest rates and other matters pertaining to bank deposit and lending business which some of these banks accept and follow only with reluctance.* It is apparent that they, and in particular future indigenous banks, may become less willing in the coming years to concert their policies and to abstain from direct competition for business deposits.

Traditionally, it is argued that there is nothing to be gained from competing for deposits, because the volume of deposits is fixed by the cash and liquid assets made available through exports, the inflow of foreign capital, and by the Currency Board. This means that competition would merely result in paying more on funds shifted from existing deposits. Such an attitude is characteristic of a system where the banks are few in number and share an identity of interest; but, as implied above, it ignores the possibility that the commercial banks themselves can influence not only their share but also the total amount of business deposits, since part of the funds invested in money markets abroad undoubtedly would be placed with the East African banks, were liquid and negotiable bank instruments available.

That the banks can increase the total volume of deposits in the economy as well as their share of the available liquid assets is illustrated by the remarkable growth in savings deposits from 1950 to 1963 (Table 4). The annual growth in savings deposits averaged 21 per cent over this period, which was considerably more than for time and demand deposits, and greater than could be expected on account of rising prices. Moreover, the rate of growth was increasing throughout the period, except in 1959, when it slowed down, and in 1960, when the volume of savings deposits actually declined. It can of course be anticipated that the volume of savings deposits will grow as a larger part of the population is drawn into the monetary economy. But the substantial growth over the past fifteen years undoubtedly also reflects the expansion of bank offices since the early 1950s which has brought banking facilities to places where previously little systematic monetary saving had been possible, and illustrates what can be done by the banks in activating domestic saving potentials.

The dramatic change that has taken place in the nature of banking in East Africa since the war is most readily illustrated by the substantial increase in the relative importance of local earning assets

---

* These cartel-type agreements would in many countries constitute a violation of anti-trust laws.

and the simultaneous decline in bank liquidity (Table 5). Bills discounted, loans and advances, and investments in East Africa, all of which are considered local assets, increased from 35 per cent of total deposits in 1950 to 86 per cent in 1963. The ratio of loans and advances to deposits followed the same pattern and was accompanied by a sharp reduction in bank liquidity (the ratio of liquid assets to total deposits) from more than 68 per cent in 1950 to a mere 16 per cent at the end of 1963. It should be noticed that the volume of loans and advances in relation to deposits in recent years has far exceeded the conventional level accepted in Britain, and that the banks in East Africa are operating on very narrow reserves, compared to the banking systems of other British Commonwealth countries.

The significant growth in local earning assets, relative to total bank resources, undoubtedly reflects partly an increasing tendency of the large overseas banks to identify themselves more closely than in the past with the countries in which they operate, and partly the increase in profitable local investment opportunities.* The regional managers have also been given greater discretion to manage the local loan portfolio and actively to explore local earnings opportunities. However, it remains to be seen to what extent this has altered local bank lending policies. So far there seems to have been little correlation between changes in loans and advances and changes in the banks' local reserves. On the contrary, when the banks experienced a very substantial drop in their liquid assets during 1960, and again in 1963, loans and advances continued the steady growth which had started in 1958. This could not have taken place unless the banks were able to meet the heavy withdrawal of deposits, induced by political uncertainties, by moving funds from their headquarters in London.†

The high proportion of bank resources invested in local earning assets becomes even more pronounced when the overall figures are broken down on a quarterly basis for the three countries of the regional economy (Table 6). There is a distinct seasonal pattern in

---

* For an inside view on this point, see Geoffrey Tyson, *100 Years of Banking in Asia and Africa* (London, National and Grindlays Bank, 1963), chapter 16; also J. A. Henry, *The First Hundred Years of the Standard Bank* (London, 1963), chapter 24.

† The determinants of local lending policies have implications for the desirability as well as the potential effectiveness of monetary policy in East Africa. See Donald C. Mead, *op. cit.*, pp. 60–6. For a discussion with reference to developing countries in general, see Ida Greaves, *op. cit.*, pp. 46–7, and W. T. Newlyn and D. C. Rowan, *op. cit.*, chapter 9.

the demand for credit, particularly in Uganda and Tanzania, which is related to the marketing of the major crops, cotton, coffee, and sisal. The seasonal pattern varies from country to country, which enables the regional banks to economize in the use of reserves by inter-territorial transfers of funds via the Currency Board. For example, the buying of cotton from African growers in Uganda starts in December and generally finishes in April (although the processing and sale of this cotton to the Lint Marketing Board may well continue until July). During this period there is also a very heavy demand for credit to assist in the harvesting and marketing of African-grown Robusta coffee, and funds have to be moved in from Kenya and Tanzania. By April or May reserves are flowing back to the banks in Uganda and can be made available for meeting credit requirements in the two other countries. In this way a strong seasonal demand for credit in one place can be met readily and swiftly by moving funds from banks in another, thus ensuring smooth financing of the major cash crops. It also implies that the regional nature of bank operations has made the local reserve ratio for each of the three countries rather meaningless.

The distribution of loans and advances as between industry, agriculture, and 'other loans and advances' indicates that the greatest growth has taken place in the third group, consisting mainly of commercial loans to finance crop movements and the import trade* (Table 7). Practically all these credits are short-term and come close to the 'self-liquidating' ideal so vigorously striven for, yet seldom achieved, by British bankers. They are extended primarily to the Europeans and Asians who dominate the commercial sector. Table 7 also shows the relatively limited engagement of the banks in the finance of agriculture, in spite of the overwhelming importance of the agricultural sector in the East African economy. Farm credits represent only 20 to 25 per cent of total loans and advances, and most are for a maximum of twelve months.

The number of seasonal crop loans to Africans has increased significantly since 1958–9, and the large banks in Kenya and Tanzania have also made some advances of up to three years to Africans for the purchase of coffee trees and tea plants, and for the development of sisal growing by African co-operatives. But the aggregate amount of loans and advances to indigenous agriculture

* Most exports, from the moment of arriving on board ship at an East African port, are financed from London.

Table 6. *Local earning assets[1] as a percentage of deposits, 1962–3[2]*

End of quarter	Kenya	Uganda	Tanganyika[3]	East Africa
June 1962	79·1	98·7	79·6	82·6
September 1962	77·7	94·5	94·0	84·8
December 1962	74·7	101·2	74·8	78·7
March 1963	76·5	116·2	63·9	79·7
June 1963	80·6	109·0	76·7	83·9
September 1963	82·4	115·9	81·6	87·0
December 1963	84·7	121·6	70·7	86·1

Table 7. *Composition of loans and advances in East Africa, 1950–63[1]*

End of year	Industry		Agriculture		Other[4]		Total[5]	
	£m.	%	£m.	%	£m.	%	£m.	%
1950	3·9	23·0	3·8	22·8	9·1	54·2	16·8	100·0
1951	7·6	24·5	5·8	18·7	17·6	56·8	30·9	100·0
1952	7·0	24·4	5·7	20·0	15·9	55·6	28·7	100·0
1953	8·1	25·6	8·6	27·3	14·9	47·1	31·5	100·0
1954	10·0	22·2	11·0	24·3	24·2	53·5	45·2	100·0
1955	10·4	17·4	12·9	21·6	36·5	61·0	59·8	100·0
1956	11·7	22·5	10·7	20·6	29·5	56·9	51·8	100·0
1957	13·7	22·7	14·7	24·4	31·9	52·9	60·3	100·0
1958	11·3	21·2	13·8	25·7	28·4	53·1	53·4	100·0
1959	13·8	22·4	15·4	24·9	32·6	52·7	61·8	100·0
1960	13·3	19·2	16·7	24·1	39·3	56·7	69·3	100·0
1961	12·9	17·8	16·8	23·1	43·1	59·1	72·8	100·0
1962	19·3	24·3	11·8	14·9	48·1	60·8	79·2	100·0
1963	14·8	16·0	20·7	22·3	57·3	61·7	92·8	100·0

[1] Bills discounted, loans, advances, and investments in East Africa.
[2] Sources: as for Table 3.
[3] I.e. Tanzania excluding Zanzibar.
[4] Mostly commercial loans, but including in recent years a growing proportion of loans and advances to governments.
[5] Figures may not add to totals because of rounding off.

is very small, except in Uganda, where a significant proportion of the banks' outstanding farm loans are made to Africans.* However, it should also be noted that some important changes in the relative importance of loans to indigenous agriculture may occur in connection with the financing of land settlement under the schemes now in operation or planned.

* This unfortunately, cannot be quantified since no statistics are available on the distribution of loans and advances according to size. The statements are based on discussions with bankers and government economists in East Africa.

One major difficulty in granting credits to Africans has been to find credit-worthy customers, according to traditional banking standards, and many Africans have yet to understand the nature of a debt obligation. Another difficulty is the lack of acceptable collateral. Titles to land ownership are far from settled in many parts of East Africa, and settlement is made particularly intricate by the multitude of tribal laws. For example, the usefulness of land as security for loans is seriously limited in Uganda by the Mailo system, under which land ownership can be transferred only to Africans. Still another problem in expanding the volume of credit to African farmers is the relatively small loan amounts needed in most cases. They are costly to administer, which tends to increase further the high interest rate that is necessary to compensate for the high risk.*

Faced with these difficulties, and with the almost constant decline in their liquidity, the banks have chosen to accommodate the commercial sector, in need of short-term credits to finance 'self-liquidating' transactions, at the expense of the more uncertain and inevitably less liquid agricultural advances to African farmers.

Some conclusions

In the previous four sections an attempt has been made to draw a picture of the monetary and banking situation in East Africa today, and the developments since 1950. Certain structural patterns seem to emerge as particularly relevant for an inquiry into the future role of money and finance in the East African economy.

1. The growth in the stock of money, coupled with the rise in the ratio of currency to deposits and in the turnover of demand deposits, reflects the increasing dissemination of money-using habits and the diversification of the East African exchange economy. In this the commercial banks have played a major role, principally through the expansion of bank offices in all three countries and the remarkable growth in their local earning assets. There may now be a period during which the number of bank offices may actually decline and the rise in the loan-to-deposit ratio may level out. Many of the small bank agencies in rural areas are undoubtedly unprofitable at the present time and will remain so for many years, and there is obviously a limit, set by the requirements of liquidity and safety, to the increase

---

* See Anthony Bottomley, 'The Premium for Risk as a Determinant of Interest Rates in Underdeveloped Rural Areas', in the *Quarterly J. of Economics*, vol. 77, 4, November 1963, pp. 637–47.

in local earning assets, particularly in the absence of an East African central bank.

2. Although bank deposits nearly doubled between 1950 and 1963, the rate of increase was less than for the gross domestic product. There seems to be evidence that the commercial banks have lost ground, in terms of deposits, due to the increasing competition from financial intermediaries, such as building societies, insurance companies, and Treasury bills. While the three big banks have apparently become increasingly interested in attracting small savings and, perhaps, in cultivating future indigenous lending business, they have traditionally been reluctant to bid for large time deposits.

It seems now to be widely recognized that the commercial banks in East Africa will have to make greater efforts if they are to retain their share of the available volume of deposits. The problem for the banks is to what extent they can profitably expand their lending activities by bidding more actively for deposits. One procedure would be to make the fixed deposit receipts of the banks negotiable for larger amounts along the lines of the American system of negotiable certificates of deposit, and to offer rates of yield comparable to the money market rates in London.* Thereby the banks would avoid paying higher rates across-the-board and yet offer profitable opportunities for the local placement of business funds. The volume of negotiable fixed deposit receipts is likely to be modest in the beginning, but it is not unreasonable to expect that a secondary market would eventually develop *pari passu* as the Treasury bill market developed. Indeed, the stimulus of a high-quality, liquid bank paper may greatly hasten the advent of a local money market, without which an effective monetary policy is not possible.

3. The nature of the East African banks gives the credit system a high degree of flexibility through the regional and international mobility of funds, since most of them operate in all three countries. This has made possible a smoother financing of the harvesting, storage, and transport of export commodities than could have been achieved by banks limited in their operation to national 'compounds'. The banks have also been able to meet strong cyclical demands for

---

* Time certificates of deposit in the United States are evidence that a depositor, usually a business firm, will leave his funds for a specified length of time in return for a specific rate of interest. They are negotiable and are in most cases readily marketable in a secondary market, which is their most attractive feature. See 'Negotiable Time Certificates of Deposit', in *Federal Reserve Bulletin*, April 1963, pp. 458–68.

credit in East Africa as a whole through their access to head-office balances in London, derived from the accumulation of excess reserves in other countries in which the banks operate. This international mobility of funds, for which the free convertibility of the East African shilling into sterling at a fixed rate of exchange is a pre-requisite, means that the international banks have performed some of the essential functions of a central bank; when a strong aggregate demand for credit arose in East Africa, or large withdrawals of deposits took place, as in 1955, 1960, and 1963, the banks used the 'discount window' at their London head office.

However, there are signs that the banks in recent years have attempted to become regionally self-contained. Such a regional 'fragmentation' may be expected to follow political independence, as monetary areas become more clearly defined. This may limit their access to overseas reserves and hence will lead to an increasingly close connection between local lending policies and the banks' East African reserves. To the extent that this happens there may be wider fluctuations in bank loans and advances than there have been in the past. This further emphasizes the need for an East African central bank to counteract unnecessarily sharp adjustments of bank credit to changes in bank reserves.

4. The major emphasis of East African banking business is still on activities more closely related to trade and commercial payments than to the savings-investment process, in spite of the considerable extension of bank agencies and the significant increases in local earning assets and in the number of small loans to indigenous farmers. East African bankers continue to regard themselves as predominantly engaged in meeting seasonal credit needs and financing the working capital requirements of commercial enterprise. This has to some extent caused the borrowing needs of certain sectors, in particular agriculture, to be neglected.

A main reason for the banks' less than venturesome exploration of profitable business outside the commercial sector is to be found in their inclination to apply the traditional standards and conventions of their head offices to the different, and largely under-developed, countries in which they are operating. They have tended to insist on credit standards which few indigenous enterprises—agricultural, commercial, or industrial—are able to reach, and to demand collateral which is often non-existent. By ordinary banking criteria it may be justifiable to maintain the same high standards for lending in overseas territories as in the banks' home country, but it is unquestionable that traditional conventions are inadequate, if the banks are to make a more positive contribution to economic development.

They may in future find it necessary to place more emphasis on the capacity of the borrower to repay, rather than on his ability to offer the tangible collateral traditionally demanded by commercial bankers. It is undoubtedly true that the mere pledging of property as security for a loan exercises a restraining influence on the borrower, but the effectiveness of the restraint is probably influenced more by the intangible value of the property to the borrower than its market value to the lender. Institutions financing consumers in industrialized countries, such as the personal loan companies in the United States and the credit co-operatives in continental Europe, have long been aware of this, and the total of small personal loans often far exceeds the market value of pledged security. This has some analogy to the agricultural sector of economically under-developed countries: the major asset of the farmer is his labour and that of his relatives, and the major source of repayment is the money that he earns from selling his products. The solution of the problems of agricultural credit is consequently related to efforts to increase the repayment capacity or productivity of the farmer.*

However, it should be emphasized that the agricultural credit gaps can only be partially closed by the banks establishing special terms and security arrangements. The problem of financing the farmer is not merely a banking issue but invokes social and political, as well as technical, considerations which make it distinctly different from that of meeting credit needs in other sectors of the economy. The contribution of the existing banks in East Africa to the finance of agriculture will most likely continue to be a modest one. Government intervention in one form or another is inevitable, as it appears to be in highly developed countries, and government assistance in the developing countries seems to be even more necessary in view of the political and social significance of agriculture and the high priority of farm credit in any development scheme.

* For a detailed analysis of the use of agricultural credit to promote economic development, see Horace Belshaw, *Agricultural Credit in Economically Under-developed Countries* (F.A.O., Rome, 1959). On risk and the nature of security, see pp. 98–111 and 128–31.

23. THE FISCAL ROLE OF THE MARKETING BOARDS IN NIGERIAN ECONOMIC DEVELOPMENT 1947–61

G. K. HELLEINER

I. The accumulation of the trading surpluses

...It is widely recognized that the period 1947–54 was one during which Nigeria's Marketing Boards acquired enormous reserves. Table 1

Table 1. *Accumulation by Nigerian Commodity Marketing Boards, 1947-54* (£ thousands)

	Cocoa	Palm oil	Palm kernels	Ground-nuts	Cotton	Total
Initial reserves	8,896·6[1]	11,457·0[2]		4,487·8[2]	250·0[3]	25,091·0
Net trading surplus[4]	33,797·4	2,269·7	18,790·8	22,483·6	6,968·6	84,310·1
Excess of other income over expenditures[5]	3,349·3		2,497·3	3,563·9	1,102·7	10,513·2
	46,043·3		35,014·8	30,535·3	8,321·3	119,914·7

Sources: Annual Reports of Nigerian Marketing Boards.

[1] Reserves accumulated in respect of Nigerian cocoa by West African Produce Control Board before 1947 and turned over to the Nigeria Cocoa Marketing Board upon its creation in 1947.

[2] Reserves accumulated in respect of Nigerian produce by West African Produce Control Board in 1947–9 period and turned over to the Nigeria Oil Palm Produce Marketing Board and the Nigeria Groundnut Marketing Board upon their creation in 1949.

[3] Grant from U.K. Raw Cotton Commission to the Nigeria Cotton Marketing Board in compensation for previous underpayments to Nigerian cotton producers upon its creation in 1949.

[4] Cocoa: 1947–8 to 1953–4 inclusive; palm oil and palm kernels: 1949–54 inclusive; groundnuts and cotton: 1949–50 to 1953–4 inclusive. Calculated from the original accounts of the Marketing Boards as follows: sales at f.o.b. prices less export duties, value of purchases, total expenses and decrease in stocks. The resulting figures for trading surpluses sometimes differ from those stated in the accounts.

[5] Calculated from the original accounts of the Marketing Boards. Primarily interest on reserves held in U.K. securities. The figure for groundnuts includes trading surpluses earned on other minor commodities under the jurisdiction and control of the Nigeria Groundnut Marketing Board (benniseed, sunflower seed, soya beans, groundnut oil and groundnut cake); that for cotton includes development premium paid by the U.K. Raw Cotton Commission.

shows the total accumulations of the four Nigerian Commodity Boards until their dissolution in 1954. By 1954 nearly £120 million had been mobilized by these four Boards, over £100 million (net) of which* had been realized as 'trading profits' during this seven-year period alone. (For comparative purposes it may be worth observing that the two principal sources of government tax revenue at this time each earned less over the same seven-year period. Between 1947–8 and 1953–4 import duties accounted for a total of only £93·5 million, whereas export duties totalled only £56·7 million of revenues.)

The largest trading surpluses had been realized by the Cocoa Marketing Board, but all four had piled up substantial reserves. Only palm-oil producers, who received over £6·9 million in subsidies in 1953 and 1954, received any stabilization benefits, in the form of price supports in lean years, during this period; and even these substantial subsidies could not alter the fact that they had already contributed far larger amounts to the Oil Palm Produce Marketing Board's reserves.

These accumulations were a not inconsiderable share of the total earnings on exported produce which could have been distributed to Nigerian peasant producers or what I have called 'potential producer income.'† Nor were they the only levy on this potential producer income. Further amounts were withheld in the form of export duties and, from 1953 on, Regional produce sales taxes, which were levied as specific duties upon each ton of produce sold to a Marketing Board. Table 2 summarizes these government withdrawals from the Marketing Board agricultural sector during this and the subsequent period.

It can be seen that during the 1947–54 period over 42 per cent of potential producer income earned from cotton, 40 per cent of that from groundnuts, over 39 per cent of that from cocoa, over 29 per cent of that from palm kernels and 17 per cent of that from palm oil were withheld by the Government through taxes and Marketing

---

* Including the accumulations in respect of Nigerian oil palm produce and groundnuts by the West African Produce Control Board during the 1947–9 period before the creation of the Nigerian Marketing Boards for these products.

† 'Potential producer income' is defined here as actual producer income plus export duties, Marketing Board trading surplus and produce sales tax. Strictly speaking, the potential for producer incomes is actually higher than this if, as is likely, there exists positive price-elasticity of supply and greater than unit elasticity of world demand for Nigerian produce.

Board trading surpluses. By far the greatest share of this total in each case except that of palm oil, in respect of which, as has been seen, substantial trading losses were incurred in 1953 and 1954, was made up of Marketing Board trading surpluses. In peak years individual Marketing Boards alone withheld over 40, 50, and even 66 per cent of potential incomes of producers of particular crops (see Appendix).

Less well known is the Nigerian Marketing Board experience since 1954. With the constitutional revisions of that year, which involved the devolution of considerable powers to the Regional governments, there came a reorganization of Marketing Board structure as well. Henceforth, instead of being organized on a nation-wide commodity basis, they conducted their operations on a regional cross-commodity basis. Each Regional Marketing Board handled all the relevant exportable produce of its region of jurisdiction. Effectively, this meant that the Eastern Region Marketing Board did the bulk of its business in palm oil and palm kernels, the Northern Region in groundnuts and cotton, and the Western Region in cocoa and palm kernels. These were not the only commodities handled by the Marketing Boards, but the remainder were of small relative importance. The Regional Marketing Boards took over the assets of the former commodity Marketing Boards, their distribution being determined by the Region of origin of the products on which the surpluses had been earned. As can be seen in Table 3, this meant that the Eastern Region, dependent upon palm produce, came off very poorly, whereas the cocoa-producing Western Region received close to half the redistributed unspent total of £87 million. This table also shows clearly the pattern of regional concentration in agricultural export production.

The year 1954, which divides Nigerian Marketing Board history into two separate periods distinguished by different institutional arrangements, also marks the end of a period of export prosperity and the beginning of a period of declining barter terms of trade.

No longer was a large trading surplus to be relied upon year after year simply by the holding of the producer price line as commodity prices followed their standard post-war upward course; for world primary product market conditions had by now changed significantly in character. The usual instability of Nigerian export prices continued as before, but the price fluctuations were now about a steady or even declining trend.

Table 2. *Government withdrawals from major components of the Marketing Board controlled agricultural export sector in Nigeria, 1947–62*

	Export duties		Marketing Board trading surplus		Produce purchase tax		Total withdrawals, £000s	Potential producer income, £000s	Total withdrawals as a % of potential producer income
	£000s	% of potential producer income	£000s	% of potential producer income	£000s	% of potential producer income			
Cocoa									
1947/48 to 1953/54	27,565	17·6	33,797	21·6	390	0·2	61,752	165,829	39·4
1954/55 to 1961/62	36,917	17·9	12,841	6·2	4,163	2·0	53,920	206,216	26·1
Total	64,481	17·8	46,638	12·8	4,553	1·3	115,672	363,046	31·9
Groundnuts									
1947/48 to 1953/54	11,329	11·5	27,797	28·1	425	0·4	39,549	98,776	40·0
1954/55 to 1960/61	20,825	14·0	−2,053	−1·4	3,574	2·4	22,346	149,660	14·9
Total	32,154	12·9	25,743	10·4	3,998	1·6	61,895	248,436	24·9
Palm Kernels									
1947–54	11,872	9·4	25,096	19·9	—	—	36,968	126,438	29·2
1955–61	15,125	13·1	11,883	10·3	4,327	3·7	31,335	116,558	27·1
Total	26,997	11·1	36,978	15·2	4,327	1·8	68,303	242,996	28·1
Palm Oil									
1947–54	7,356	9·0	6,544	8·0	—	—	13,899	81,608	17·0
1955–61	9,646	13·3	4,305	5·9	4,592	6·3	18,543	72,421	25·6
Total	17,002	11·0	10,849	7·0	4,592	3·0	32,442	154,028	21·0
Cotton									
1949/50 to 1953/54	2,687	11·7	6,969	30·3	70	0·3	9,726	23,014	42·3
1954/55 to 1960/61	5,771	13·5	−1,696	−4·0	722	1·7	4,796	42,753	11·2
Total	8,458	12·9	5,272	8·0	792	1·2	14,522	65,767	22·1

Sources: See Appendix.

73

Table 3. *Total transfer of assets from Nigerian Commodity Marketing Boards to Nigerian Regional Marketing Boards[1] (£ thousands)*

Marketing Board	Eastern Region	Northern Region	Western Region	Total[2]
Cocoa	176·1	135·5	32,625·1	32,936·7
Oil palm produce	11,248·4	484·5	10,199·0	21,931·9
Groundnut	39·6	24,722·6	—	24,762·2
Cotton	—	7,309·2[3]	73·0	7,382·2
	11,464·1	32,651·8	42,897·2	87,013·0

Sources: Annual Reports of the Marketing Boards.
[1] These transfers were not all made at the same time. The final allocations were not resolved for several years.
[2] Excluding Southern Cameroons.
[3] Including development premia from the liquidation of the U.K. Raw Cotton Commission of £803·1 thousands.

Given that Nigeria's Marketing Boards began the period apparently still pursuing stabilization as their principal objectives, it is noteworthy that they nevertheless continued, in the aggregate, to accumulate trading surpluses. Admittedly these accumulations were now much smaller in magnitude. Still, between 1954 and year-end of 1961, another £21·8 million was added to the Marketing Boards' resources through their trading activities. Although this amount is less than one-quarter the size of the aggregate trading profits of the previous seven years, it remains a sizeable sum. Earnings on the reserves accumulated earlier produced a net surplus on other operations of another £9·5 million (see Table 4).

Aggregation of Marketing Board data for this period conceals, however, important differences between the experiences of individual Marketing Boards. One of the Marketing Boards, that handling the produce of the Northern Region, actually ran a net deficit on its trading operations. Indeed, it ran a net overall deficit as well, in spite of its earnings on assets during this period. From 1954 until 1961 this Marketing Board paid to agricultural producers £3·2 million* more than it earned from the sales of their produce. Moreover, these subsidies were paid both in respect of groundnut and cotton production.

* Only groundnut and cotton trading are included in this figure. Rough calculations suggest that a further large deficit was encountered in groundnut trading during the 1961–2 season, but there are as yet no figures to confirm them.

The greatest trading surpluses over the 1954–61 period were earned by the Western Region Marketing Board, which, as was noted earlier, was already the wealthiest at the outset of the period. Over £14·3 million were withheld from Western Region producers, £9·7 million of which came from cocoa production. The remaining £4·6 million came from palm-kernel producers, who contributed in the East and West together over £10·7 million to total Marketing Board reserves. The Western Region Marketing Board's wealth also produced net income of another £5·3 million, mainly from interest on the securities held in its investment portfolio.

The proportions of Nigerian export producers' potential income which were withheld during the latter period were, in general, of course, rather smaller than they had been between 1947 and 1954. Palm oil was again the only exception to this rule. The most dramatic reductions in this proportion were those for groundnuts—from 40 to 14·9 per cent, and for cotton—from 42·3 to 11·2 per cent. (These percentages are still positive because of the withholding of export duties and produce sales taxes, which more than offset the Marketing Board trading losses.) These products are produced in the Northern Region, where the Marketing Board had not yet abandoned its policy of attempting to stabilize producer prices, and had therefore, as has been seen, actually incurred trading deficits. There was also a substantial drop in the share of cocoa producers' potential income which was withdrawn—from 39·4 to 26·1 per cent. Export duties, in all cases, now not only removed a larger proportion of potential producer income than previously but also withheld a larger share than did the Marketing Boards in the form of trading surpluses. The higher export duties were the result of the shift from specific to *ad valorem* duties at the end of 1950 and the introduction of a progressive rate, increasing with the world price, together with a higher base rate, a few months later. Produce purchase taxes on groundnuts and cotton obviously also withheld greater shares of potential producer income than did the Marketing Boards (which ran deficits). What is notable is that in the Eastern and Western Regions the governments were able to continue the withdrawal of over 25 per cent of total export producers' income even in a period of stagnant or deteriorating world export markets.

Some of the tax burden upon cocoa farmers was eased by the increasing productivity achieved through the use of insecticides during these years; but producers of palm oil and palm kernels

75

enjoyed no such improvements and, in fact, suffered from steadily declining real incomes from 1954 onwards. While Marketing Board trading surpluses were no longer at this time the most important means of withholding income from export producers, it is with them that this paper remains primarily concerned.

Table 4. *Total accumulation by Nigerian Regional Marketing Boards, 1954–61* (£ thousands)

	Eastern Region	Northern Region	Western Region	Total
Transfer from Commodity Marketing Boards	11,464·1	32,651·8	42,897·2	87,013·1
Net trading surplus[1,2]	10,736·2[3]	–3,202·7	14,303·9[5]	21,837·1
Excess of other income over expenditure[1,4]	1,718·9	2,451·2	5,349·1	9,519·2
Total	23,919·2	31,900·3	62,550·2	118,369·4

Sources: Annual Reports of the Marketing Boards.
[1] Eastern Region: 1955–61 inclusive; Northern Region: 1954–5 to 1960–1 inclusive; Western Region: 1954–5 to 1960–1 inclusive.
[2] Calculated in the same way as Table 1.
[3] Treatment of the produce sales tax has been altered so as to make the Eastern Region's trading results comparable with those of the other Regions.
[4] Calculated in the same way as in Table 1. Principally interest earned on reserves. Includes trading results in minor commodities.
[5] This figure incorporates corrected trading results for year 1960–1, which were furnished by the Western Region Marketing Board. The originally published accounts were incorrect.

II. The evolution of official attitudes towards trading surpluses

Why were these trading surpluses earned? Through consideration of policy statements over the entire post-war period one can trace a steady evolution of official attitudes towards the role of the Marketing Boards in development. Prior to regionalization the accumulation of large reserves was primarily fortuitous and unpremeditated. It was at that time sincerely intended by the governmental authorities that they should be used for stabilizing purposes. From 1954 onwards the earning of trading surpluses became, more and more, a matter of conscious design. The surpluses were now to be used for the intensified development effort. Only in Northern Nigeria has this change of attitude not quite been completed. . . .

Reserves of the size which had been accumulated by 1954 constituted a very great temptation to the Regional governments, which had been granted vastly increased responsibility for the promotion of economic development following the constitutional revisions of 1954. The World Bank Mission estimated that liquid reserves of £25 million were adequate for the fulfilment of the stabilization responsibility and recommended that the remaining surplus (or 'second line reserves') be 'loaned on a long-term basis to government for development purposes'.* At the same time it recommended that no further stabilization reserves be accumulated.

The World Bank was taken at its word—and considerably more than its word! But a further recommendation to the effect that the Marketing Boards henceforth confine themselves to the stabilization of producer prices and the improvement of quality it was found more convenient to ignore. Having seen, semi-accidentally, the enormous potential for the raising of revenues which the price-fixing function of the Marketing Board offers, first the Western Region, and then the Eastern Region as well, began consciously to take advantage of it for development purposes. Both the Western and the Eastern Region Marketing Boards continued to earn trading surpluses after 1954 which cannot reasonably be regarded as accidental or intended for stabilization.

The altered views of the Regional governments with respect to the primary functions of the Marketing Boards can be seen in their planning documents. The Western Region's 1955–60 development plan announced final abandonment of the '70–22$\frac{1}{2}$–7$\frac{1}{2}$' formula for distribution of the Western Board's trading surpluses, offered a strong defence of the Marketing Board's right to contribute to development, and provided for £20 million in loans and grants to come from the Board for the use of the Regional government during the plan. This was about two-thirds of the total capital funds expected and nearly 20 per cent of the total capital and current revenues anticipated for the planning period.† The 1960–65 Western Region plan called for a further contribution of £21 million from the Western Region Marketing Board over the course of the five-year period;‡ and, with over £14·5 million already having been granted

---

* International Bank for Reconstruction and Development, *The Economic Development of Nigeria* (1955), p. 88.
† Western Region of Nigeria, *Development of the Western Region of Nigeria, 1955–1960* (Sessional Paper No. 4 of 1955), p. 15.
‡ Government of Western Nigeria, *Western Region Development Plan 1960–1965* (Sessional Paper No. 17 of 1959).

under the former plan, another £10 million was called for in the 1962–68 plan. In the latter it is stated boldly that, 'In the public sector, the Marketing Board is the main source of savings for the improvement of agriculture and allied industries and the provision of social services'.* The Marketing Board's contribution is, in fact, 40 per cent of the total available domestic finance for the capital programme.† By this time these savings could no longer refer merely to the running down of previously acquired assets. It was now obviously intended to run trading surpluses to finance the Regional government's programme. The Western Region Marketing Board had by now become, apart from its other responsibilities, a fiscal arm of the Western Nigerian Government. This emphasis upon using the Board as a supplier of savings for development purposes has, incidentally, been very much underplayed by the Annual Reports of the Board itself; this seems to indicate that the Board is somewhat sensitive to producer complaints on the matter.

The operations of the Eastern Regional Marketing Board were evolving in much the same manner during this period, although the amounts which it now accumulated from trading surpluses were somewhat smaller than those piled up in the West. To be fair, an allowance should be made for the fact that the Eastern Region Marketing Board began with by far the lowest reserves; but it also had the smallest need for them—with respect both to working capital requirements and to stabilization reserves.

The Eastern Region's development programme for 1958–62 already showed that the Marketing Board was expected to contribute £5 million towards the construction of the new University of Nigeria at Nsukka, and a further £500,000 to the Eastern Region Development Corporation.‡ The current (1962–8) plan lists not only the Marketing Board reserves but also 'Marketing Board's earnings in the Plan period'§ as a source of finance. Altogether, the Marketing Board's contribution to the present plan is to be £13·6 million, a large share of total available domestic resources for the capital

---

* Government of Western Nigeria, *Western Nigeria Development Plan 1962–68* (Sessional Paper No. 8 of 1962), p. 12.

† *Ibid.*, p. 50.

‡ Eastern Region, Nigeria, *Development Programme, 1958–62* (Eastern Region Official Document No. 2 of 1959).

§ *Eastern Nigeria Development Plan, 1962–68* (Official Document No. 8 of 1962), p. 17.

programme. Thus, the Eastern Region Government is also employing the Marketing Board as a revenue raiser.

By 1962 even the Northern Region Government was consciously employing the Northern Nigeria Marketing Board as an important source of revenues for its development effort, though in a much modified fashion. That it was the Northern Regional Marketing Board which had formerly taken its stabilization responsibility most seriously and had consequently been the weakest accumulator of reserves is reflected in its aggregate trading losses and its policy statements. As late as 1958 it was still saying that 'the main object of establishing Marketing Boards was to ensure stable prices for produce'.* Subsequent Annual Reports modified this approach, emphasizing that stabilization constituted only 'one of the principal objects'† of the Board. By 1962, however, the Northern Nigerian Government had announced its intention of 'relieving the Board of its liability for subsidizing the producer prices of crops in lean years, and fixing producer prices annually at such a level in relation to world prices as to anticipate a surplus on the year's operation to cover operating costs'.‡ All of the Northern Nigeria Marketing Board's reserves above and beyond its needs for working capital (about £6 million) are to be mobilized for the use of its proposed 'Development Bank'. Even with the explicit abandonment of year-to-year stabilization, the Northern Nigeria Marketing Board remains the only one which has at no time stated its intention of running current trading surpluses for the purpose of contributing to regional economic development. Government attitudes in the Northern Region, in this as in most other matters, have been more conservative than those in the Eastern and Western Regions, where the Marketing Boards had abandoned their role as trustees for the farmers and assumed that of tax collector in the mid-1950s.

III. The disposal of the Marketing Board trading surpluses

How were the vast reserves accumulated by Nigeria's Marketing Boards ultimately employed? During the period before their regionalization, as has been seen, the Marketing Boards held the bulk of them as stabilization reserves in the form of United Kingdom

---

* *Fourth Annual Report of the Northern Regional Marketing Board*, p. 8.
† *Fifth Annual Report of the Northern Regional Marketing Board*, p. 7.
‡ Government of Northern Nigeria, Ministry of Economic Planning, *Development Plan, 1962–68*, p. 44.

and Commonwealth securities. Some of their profits, however, were spent upon or reserved for research and economic development. As has been seen, this was in keeping with announced policy.

By year-end of 1954 (see Table 5) over £23 million had been granted to the Regional Production Development Boards. With the final allocation of the dissolved Commodity Marketing Boards' assets, their total contribution to the Production Development Boards reached £24,666,700. The latter Boards were not able to spend these amounts as quickly as they were received, and therefore accumulated substantial reserves of United Kingdom securities themselves. The amounts which were spent or lent until the mid-1950s were concentrated in agricultural development projects (including government-owned plantations in the Eastern and Western Regions), small-scale processing of agricultural produce both for home consumption and for export, and roads.

In addition to these allocations, the Commodity Marketing Boards also spent nearly £6 million on their own research and development schemes. The largest items of this type were the support of the West African Institute for Oil Palm Research and the West Africa Cocoa Research Institute, grants in support of the Faculty of Agriculture at the University College, Ibadan, and expenditures on roads,

Table 5. *Disposal of funds of Nigerian Commodity Marketing Boards: cumulative grants, investments and loans outstanding, 1947–54[1]* (£000s)

	Cocoa (30 Sept. 1954)	Oil-palm produce (31 Dec. 1954)	Ground-nut (31 Oct. 1954)	Cotton (31 Oct. 1954)	Total (30 Sept.– 31 Dec. 1954)
Cumulative grants to Production Development Boards[2]	8,851·4	8,357·7	6,178·3	271·0	23,658·4
Cumulative research and development expenditure[2]	2,051·8	2,469·0	86·0	1,328·4	5,935·2
Loans outstanding to Government of Nigeria	2,494·0	—	—	—	2,494·0
United Kingdom securities	24,119·1	23,775·1	13,570·0	4,920·8	66,385·0

Sources: Annual Reports of the Marketing Boards.
[1] This is not a complete listing. Current assets and current liabilities are excluded.
[2] Further allocations were made from Commodity Marketing Board funds after this table's 1954 cut-off date, in the extended period during which their affairs were finally wound up.

distribution of improved seed, stores, etc., in connection with the development of cotton production in the Northern Region. Smaller sums were spent upon other research institutes, surveys, experiments and investigations, co-operative marketing schemes, and so forth.

A further commitment had been entered into by the Marketing Boards to lend £14 million to the Federal Government. By 1954 only £2·5 million had been lent (by the Cocoa Marketing Board), and the remaining obligations were assumed by the successor Regional Marketing Boards.

Table 6. *Disposal of Nigerian Regional Marketing Board Funds: cumulative grants, investments and loans outstanding, 1955–61[1] (£000s)*

	Eastern Region (31 Dec. 1961)	Northern Region (31 Oct. 1961)	Western Region (31 Sept. 1961)	Total (30 Sept.– 31 Dec. 1961)
Cumulative grants to Regional Government	7,500·0	—	25,589·1	33,089·1
Cumulative grants to regional development and finance corporations	2,800·0	1,883·2	—	4,683·2
Other cumulative grants and expenditures	212·1	3,226·7	5,717·4	9,156·2
Loans outstanding to Federal Government	1,816·9	3,323·6	—	5,140·5
Loans outstanding to Regional Government	—	6,811·2	10,000·0	16,811·2
Loans outstanding to regional development and finance corporations	500·0	—	4,200·0	4,700·0
Equity investment in Nigerian private companies	3,545·0	276·0	3,080·0	6,901·0
Loans outstanding to Nigerian private companies	—	800·0	6,288·2	7,088·2
United Kingdom Securities	3,202·2	6,578·0	1,721·6	11,501·8
Federation of Nigeria Securities	—	3,025·1	—	3,025·1

Sources: Annual Reports of the Marketing Boards.
[1] This is not a complete listing. Current assets and current liabilities are excluded.

A completely different pattern of disposition of Marketing Board funds emerged following their regionalization. Led by the Western Region Marketing Board, the Boards began to supply funds in the form of grants and loans to the Regional governments, directly to purchase equity in and offer loans to private companies, and to purchase Nigerian government securities. At the same time expenditures for research and development were continued and expanded in amount. Grants to the successors of the Regional Production Development Boards, now renamed Development Corporations, and to the similarly organized Regional Finance Corporations, on the other hand, were sharply curtailed. These Corporations sharply accelerated their own development expenditures, however, by running down their unspent reserves accumulated from earlier years' Marketing Board grants. By 1962, as a result of these new investments and expenditures, Nigerian Marketing Board holdings of United Kingdom securities had been all but eliminated (see Table 6). Nor was there much left in any other reasonably liquid form of investment which might be employed for stabilization. By 1961 even working capital requirements for one of the Boards were being supplied through the banking system rather than from the Marketing Boards' own reserves. . . .

IV. The cases for and against the fiscal role of the Marketing Boards

Given the need for revenues to finance the Government's development effort, is the earning of trading surpluses by monopsonistic Marketing Boards the optimal means of obtaining them? In the first place, the objections are frequently raised that the Nigerian Marketing Boards were originally established for the benefit of (or as trustees for) the producers, and that their activities should not, in any case, infringe upon the general revenue-raising and development-promoting responsibilities of the governments concerned. 'One cannot have it both ways: if an organization is to have taxation rights it should be integrated with the Government, and if it is not to be integrated it must not act so as to be a permanent instrument of taxation of the producer groups it is supposed to represent.'*

From the point of view of general principles and both administrative and intellectual tidiness, this cannot be disputed. Moreover, the present untidiness is easily remediable. Since both the largest share of trading surpluses and 100 per cent of export duties now return to the Regional governments, changes in export duty rates could quickly rectify the situation by converting trading surpluses into export taxes. But this is obviously not the central issue.

* A. R. Prest, *Public Finance in Under-Developed Countries* (1962), p. 71. See also International Bank for Reconstruction and Development, *The Economic Development of Nigeria* (1955), p. 88.

The main question concerns the general suitability of taxes, regardless of whether they are called 'trading surpluses' or 'export duties', levied upon export producers. The Marketing Board system of earning continual surpluses is institutionally different but does not, after all, alter the fact that an export tax is being collected; trading surpluses which are subsequently spent upon general development projects, as far as producers are concerned, are identical to export duties. The principal ground for heavy taxation of exports is its convenience. In a country where *per capita* income is very low, administrative personnel are scarce, modern accounting practices are non-existent and much of the population is self-employed or engaged in 'traditional' (and therefore unrecorded) economic activity, recourse must be had to maximum revenue collection in the few sectors where it is possible. In that it must pass through only a very few ports, foreign trade is easily measured, controlled and taxed.

From the point of view of equity, the case for heavy taxation of export production is a shaky one. One cannot, of course, adequately discuss the equity of one particular tax without considering its place within the whole tax structure. It is nevertheless clear that export taxation, in the Nigerian context, constitutes an extra burden for one type of productive activity which is not borne by others. The other principal sources of government revenues (import and excise duties, income taxes, property rates, etc.) are taxes which are levied upon all incomes, those of export producers as well as of others; but these export producers' incomes have already borne export tax. Export production is thus subject to double taxation. In some instances this may be quite fair, representing, among other things, a means of achieving some 'progressiveness' of the tax burden. It is altogether likely, for instance, that many of the highest incomes earned in Nigeria have always been attributable to export cropping. It is also true that the huge post-war export price increases involved a large element of windfall gain. But there can also be little question that many, if not most, export producers conduct operations on a tiny scale and can only be depicted as extremely poor. The burden of the tax on the latter seems unreasonably heavy when compared with that borne by non-export producers. It may also be considered unfair when compared with that borne by larger producers of the same export crop, for the tax is withheld to an equal extent on the sale of each individual ton of the export crop. The rich peasant who owns several acres and produces relatively large quantities has the same

83

proportion of his export crop income withheld, as does the poor one who sells very little. Export taxation may not therefore be the most equitable revenue earner imaginable.

Far more fundamental issues are involved in a consideration of the overall development effects of export taxes. There remains considerable disagreement as to the desirability, from a development point of view, of their imposition. The principal questions at issue are two: (1) the extent of supply elasticity with respect to prices on the part of the peasant producers; (2) the uses to which marginal increases in peasant incomes are put. Both are questions of fact, but neither have received a degree of empirical investigation sufficient to justify the making of very firm statements.

As soon as it is granted that there exists positive price-elasticity of supply, it must also be granted that the taxation of the sale of the commodity concerned reduces these sales, and therefore, given the elastic world demand curve facing Nigeria for all its principal exports, because of its small relative importance in world markets, reduces export proceeds and domestic product. In most less-developed countries lack of foreign exchange and the inadequacy of savings out of a very low domestic product are significant constraints upon the development effort. These effects cannot therefore be taken lightly.

Price-elasticity of supply is extremely difficult to establish in Nigeria, where disease, pests and weather are such important and largely uncontrollable variables, and where data are, in any case, so sparse and unreliable. As far as tree crops such as cocoa (and rubber, which is not sold through Marketing Boards in Nigeria) are concerned, it is clear that short-term supply elasticity must be very small, if not non-existent. Some such response may be possible through varying attention to disease and pest control and changing intensity of harvesting, but this is not likely to be very important. The important supply responses are longer-term ones, resulting in increased output only after a lag of several years. There is evidence that cocoa-tree planting in Nigeria has responded to changes in producer prices.* Thus, all other things being equal, export proceeds from cocoa will be greater in six or seven years' time in the absence of the export tax than they would have been with its imposition.

There do exist substantial opportunities for more immediate

* R. Galletti, K. D. S. Baldwin and I. O. Dina, *Nigerian Cocoa Farmers, An Economic Survey of Yoruba Cocoa Farming Facilities* (Oxford University Press, 1956), pp. 3–4.

supply responses on the parts of other peasant producers—those selling palm oil, palm kernels, groundnuts and cotton. Palm oil and palm kernels are obtained from wild trees which grow profusely in the southern parts of Nigeria without human involvement in plantings, cultivation, or care of any sort. It is unlikely that the harvest of palm fruit ever approaches the potential total available from the wild trees. One would therefore expect to observe substantial price-elasticity of supply of palm produce. Particularly is this so in the case of palm oil, which is consumed locally as a cooking fat, an illuminant and an input for soap-making, as well as being exported. The recent reduction in overall sales of kernels and oil which coincides with the sharp reduction in real producer prices tends to confirm the suspicion that there exists a positive supply response in this sector. Far more striking, however, is the clear relationship between the proportion of palm oil produced which is sold to the Marketing Board and the real producer price.* There seems little doubt that export sales could be increased by raising producer prices.

The production of groundnuts and cotton is similarly potentially price-responsive in that they are annual crops, the acreage of which can easily be altered from year to year. Moreover, there exists the possibility of domestic consumption, particularly in the case of groundnuts, where about 30 per cent of total production is normally not sold for export. But sales to the Marketing Boards are the only data available, and they are greatly affected by weather and other food crops' experiences. Price responses are not therefore observable from existing statistical sources. There exists little reason, however, to doubt that peasant producers of groundnuts react to price changes much as do those of cocoa and palm produce. Supporting evidence is provided by the swift response which has been observed to the introduction of quality differentials in groundnut prices; within three years of the introduction of differentials between special and standard grade, Kano area sales to the Marketing Board of special-grade nuts rose from 2 to 99 per cent of the total.†

---

* A correlation coefficient of $+0.96$ was found between the annual Eastern Nigeria producer price for palm oil deflated by consumer price index, and the annual proportion of Eastern Nigeria palm oil production (implicit in export sales of palm kernels, which are jointly produced with palm oil from the palm fruit and have no domestic use) which was sold to the Eastern Regional Marketing Board between 1949 and 1961.

† Similar experience with quality differentials has been encountered with other Nigerian peasant-produced commodities.

Export taxation therefore clearly may produce current foreign exchange earnings and a domestic product lower than they might be in its absence. This implies an unfavourable distortion of the production structure away from the export production in which the economy is most efficient. At a time when the Regional governments are all anxiously trying to persuade the urban unemployed to return to the land and farmers to stay there, such a distortion away from agricultural production should be viewed seriously. But this in itself is not sufficient objection to the use of export taxes. There remains the crucial question as to what would be done with the extra income which the peasants would enjoy in the absence of the tax.* It is possible that all of it would be spent upon increased imports of consumer-goods—either directly or after a couple of income 'rounds'. If this is the case a higher immediate level of peasant (and perhaps other) living is attained, but there is no gain whatsoever from the higher income from the point of view of capital accumulation and the raising of future incomes. If, on the other hand, the increased income were all saved, the development potential of the country could be greatly increased. This could, of course, occur in a variety of ways. The increased income could be ploughed right back into agriculture either through local investment expenditure such as land clearing or through imports of capital equipment. Alternatively, it could be mobilized in other sectors through direct branching-out of their activities by farmers, direct loans (often to relatives), or deposits with financial intermediaries; or it could, if hoarded, merely free scarce resources (notably foreign exchange) for employment by others in investment activities.

What sort of evidence do we possess on this question? The paucity of research on farm expenditure pattern forces reliance upon three out-of-date studies. An investigation of Yoruba cocoa farmers in 1951–52 showed clearly that, once a family net income of £100 had been reached (below which savings were zero), the percentage of disposable income saved increased with the size of income.† Most of these savings in the year of study went into hoardings of cash, or

---

* This extra income may be greater than the mere amount of the tax collected, particularly if there has been some leisure foregone as a result of the changed terms of trade between leisure and production.

† R. Galletti, K. D. Baldwin and I. O. Dina, *op. cit.*, pp. 462, 473. This study showed remarkable high savings, averaging about 40 per cent of disposable income, but these were attributed to a large and unexpected increase in producer incomes to which final adjustments had not yet been made (p. 461).

what may be regarded as private stabilization and development reserves, rather than productive investment;* but this year may well have been unrepresentative. Very little ever makes its way into the banking system, but considerable sums are lent and borrowed among neighbours and relatives. To the extent that savings are ultimately reinvested the principal outlets for cocoa farmers are into clearing and planting operations (both in cocoa and in food) and houses. More occasionally, investment in transport and business equipment, such as lorries, bicycles, sewing machines and corn-mills, takes place.†

A roughly concurrent study of Ibibio oil-palm farmers in the Eastern Region also showed that savings were occurring even at low incomes. It indicated, moreover, that local (indigenous) credit institutions played a large role in their mobilization. The uses to which they were put were mainly housing, education and such business equipment as bicycles, hand-presses and sewing machines.‡

Similar findings were made in a study undertaken in the Zaria area of Northern Nigeria. Only after a certain (unspecified) level of income is reached do more 'productive' expenditures, such as the hiring of more farm labour, the building of new housing or the purchases of bicycles, corn-mills, sewing-machines, sugar-crushers or lorries, take place. For the majority, it is usual to spend all of the cash income upon consumption goods.§

As far as the increased peasant income which would accrue from reduced export taxes is concerned, two conclusions seem inescapable: (1) the largest proportion would be consumed; (2) of the amounts which were saved, most would be directed to agricultural improvements or extensions at the local level, residential construction, small-scale purchases of equipment, such as sewing-machines and bicycles, and private expenditures on education. Furthermore, it is unlikely that the factors freed by the hoarding of savings, to the extent that this is a significant outlet, would ever be employed at all, given the limited credit availability characteristic in underdeveloped areas and the fact that the size of the government programme is predetermined.

---

* *Ibid.*, pp. 279, 571, 601.
† *Loc. cit.*
‡ Anne Martin, *The Oil Palm Economy of the Ibibio Farmer* (Ibadan University Press, 1956), pp. 18, 21–2.
§ M. G. Smith, *The Economy of Hausa Communities of Zaria, A Report to the Colonial Social Science Research Council* (H.M.S.O., 1955), pp. 165–8.

It remains to be demonstrated that the employment of the taxes collected by the Government from export production was, in some sense, preferable to the consumption and investment expenditures which would have taken place in their absence. This paper will not attempt to demonstrate that this has, in general, been the case. Since the arguments with which it is concerned have to do with Marketing Boards, the discussion here will be confined to the uses which were made of Marketing Board funds. Discussion of the disposal of export duties, so called, cannot, in any event, be separated from a general discussion of the composition of total government expenditures.*

Can it be said that the uses to which the trading surpluses earned by the Nigerian Marketing Boards were put were superior to those to which the peasant farmers would have put them had they been given the opportunity? Since a much larger proportion of the increase in peasant income would have been consumed than that which was actually consumed out of Marketing Board trading surpluses, the rates of return on peasant investments would have had to be much greater than those on Marketing Board ones if peasant uses of the funds in the aggregate were really to have been considered superior. The disposition of Marketing Board surpluses may not have been perfect, but the rates of return from their investments in research, roads, agricultural schemes, universities, modern manufacturing plants and so forth are unlikely to have been any lower than those on housing, sewing-machines, land clearing and the other small-scale outlets for peasant funds discussed above, let alone so much lower as to offset the difference between consumption ratios.† It can therefore unambiguously be stated that Nigerian development has been aided through the device of channelling a portion of its export earnings via the Marketing Boards away from the producer to other (governmental) decision-makers.

---

* It can be argued that Marketing Board trading surpluses should also be considered as part of general government revenues and that discussion of their uses alone is impossible. Such an approach would require that the activities of the Development Corporations and their predecessors, and the research and development responsibilities of the Boards themselves, also be included with those of general government. Since these institutions are, in fact, separate and ostensibly bear responsibilities different from those of the government, narrowly defined, it seems worth while to consider their activities separately.

† It is probable that even if the total economic returns from such items as universities and manufacturing plants were zero, the governments would, in the present climate of opinion, have regarded them as inherently desirable.

Marketing Boards in Nigeria, 1947–61

Table A-1. Cocoa[1]

	Export duties[2]		Marketing Board trading surplus		Produce purchase tax[3]		Total withdrawals, £000s	Producer income,[4] £000s	Potential producer income,[5] £000s	Total withdrawals as % of potential producer income
	£000s	% of potential producer income	£000s	% of potential producer income	£000s	% of potential producer income				
1947–8	307.1[2]	2.2	9,201.8	66.2	—		9,508.9	4,380.4	13,889.3	68.5
1948–9	700.1[2]	5.1	420.6	3.1	—		1,120.7	12,589.3	13,710.0	8.2
1949–50	608.1	3.4	6,479.4	36.2	—		7,087.5	10,792.4	17,879.9	39.6
1950–1	4,461.8	15.2	10,549.6	36.0	—		15,011.4	14,316.6	29,328.0	51.2
1951–2	5,494.2	21.9	1,438.7	5.7	—		6,932.9	18,164.5	25,097.4	27.6
1952–3	4,527.5	19.6	87.3	0.4	—		4,614.8	18,435.1	23,049.9	20.0
1953–4	11,466.0	33.8	5,620.0	16.6	389.7	1.2	17,475.7	16,398.9	33,874.6	51.6
Subtotal 1947–8 to 1953–54	27,564.8	17.6	33,797.4	21.6	389.7	0.2	61,751.9	95,077.2	156,829.1	39.4
1954–5	5,569.8	21.0	5,025.8	19.0	334.3	1.3	10,929.9	15,540.5	26,470.4	41.3
1955–6	3,844.5	19.0	−4,169.0	−20.6	423.9	2.1	99.4	20,101.4	20,200.8	0.5
1956–7	3,223.1	14.8	−1,266.0	−5.8	513.7	2.4	2,470.8	19,231.1	21,701.9	11.4
1957–8	4,153.3	20.8	4,916.3	24.6	294.6	1.5	9,364.2	10,583.8	19,948.0	46.9
1958–9	7,504.5	21.4	7,830.6	22.4	526.1	1.5	15,861.2	19,116.0	34,977.2	45.3
1959–60	5,484.7	18.5	1,098.6	3.7	585.4	2.0	7,168.7	22,471.3	29,640.0	24.2
1960–1[6]	3,938.5	14.1	−3,752.9	−13.5	727.7	2.6	913.3	26,952.3	27,865.6	3.3
1961–2	3,198.1	12.6	3,157.2	12.4	757.5	3.0	7,112.8	18,299.7	25,412.5	28.0
Subtotal 1954–5 to 1961–2	36,916.5	17.9	12,840.6	6.2	4,163.2	2.0	53,920.3	152,296.1	206,216.4	26.1
Total	64,481.3	17.8	46,638.0	12.8	4,552.9	1.3	115,672.2	247,373.3	363,045.5	31.9

[1] Up until 1953–4 inclusive statistics refer to all Nigeria (plus Southern Cameroons); from 1954–5 on they refer only to the Western Region.

[2] Includes a small element of 'inspection fees'.

[3] Obtained by applying tax rate of £4 per ton to tonnages purchased.

[4] Derived directly from Annual Reports of the Marketing Boards. Where necessary, estimates of buying allowances have been made.

[5] Defined as producer income (actual, excluding produce purchase tax) plus export duties plus produce purchase tax plus Marketing Board trading surplus. This equals export proceeds less net Marketing Board trading expenses (trading expenses only) plus increase in stocks.

[6] Results published in the Annual Report for this year were inaccurate. Correct results have been furnished by the Western Region Marketing Board.

Table A-2. Groundnuts[1]

	Export duties[a]		Marketing Board trading surplus		Produce purchase tax[2]		Total withdrawals, £000s	Producer income,[4] £000s	Potential producer income,[5] £000s	Total withdrawals as % of potential producer income
	£000s	% of potential producer income	£000s	% of potential producer income	£000s	% of potential producer income				
1947–8	873·6	8·3	4,267·2	40·5	—		5,140·0	5,376·0	10,516·0	48·8
1948–9	1,065·9	8·0	6,137·0	45·7	—		7,202·9	6,201·6	13,404·5	53·7
1949–50	620·4	8·8	2,440·0	34·6	—		3,064·0	3,985·0	7,049·6	43·4
1950–1	675·9	10·9	3,002·7	48·5	—		3,678·6	2,513·5	6,192·1	59·4
1951–2	2,524·5	14·4	4,851·3	27·6	—		7,375·8	10,185·7	17,561·5	42·0
1952–3	2,638·9	13·5	3,505·8	17·9			6,144·7	13,449·7	19,594·4	31·4
1953–4	2,929·9	12·0	3,588·6	14·7	424·6	1·7	6,943·1	17,515·0	24,458·1	28·4
Subtotal, 1947–8 to 1953–4	11,329·1	11·5	27,796·6	28·1	424·6	0·4	39,549·1	59,227·1	98,776·2	40·0
1954–5	2,633·0	16·6	−133·1	−0·8	372·8	2·4	2,873	12,969	15,842	18·1
1955–6	3,314·0	14·3	1,075·5	4·6	530·2	2·3	4,920	18,303	23,223	21·2
1956–7	2,554·0	13·6	3,075·0	16·3	357·9	1·9	5,987	12,812	18,799	31·8
1957–8	3,059·0	13·6	−4,041·5	−18·0	714·7	3·2	−268	22,686	22,418	−1·2
1958–9	3,195·0	13·6	−1,970·2	−8·4	533·4	2·3	1,758	21,675	23,433	7·5
1959–60	2,686·0	13·2	828·4	4·0	445·4	2·2	3,960	16,464	20,424	19·4
1960–1	3,384·0	13·3	−887·4	−3·5	619·1	2·4	3,116	22,405	25,521	12·2
Subtotal, 1954–5 to 1960–1	20,825·0	14·0	−2,053·3	−1·4	3,573·5	2·4	22,346	127,314	149,660	14·9
Total	32,154	12·9	25,743·3	10·4	3,998·1	1·6	61,895	186,541	248,436	24·9

[1] Up until 1953–4 inclusive figures include all Nigeria: from 1954–5 on they refer only to the Northern Region. Figures for 1947–8, 1948–9 and 1949–50 are calculated from figures in P. T. Bauer, *West African Trade*, p. 401. His figures for later years do not agree with mine, but they are usually not far off; in the absence of any substitutes I therefore employ his annual figures. This produces a slight discrepancy between the relevant total Marketing Board trading surpluses shown in this table and those shown in Table 3 in the text, which was derived directly from Marketing Board Annual Reports.
The 1947–8 and 1948–9 figures refer to Nigerian operations of the West African Produce Control Board (W.A.P.C.B.). The 1949–50 figure is partly W.A.P.C.B. and partly Nigeria Groundnut Marketing Board.
[2] From 1950–1 until and including 1953–4 the export duty figures are taken from the Annual Reports of the Groundnut Marketing Board. For subsequent years there are only calendar-year figures available. I have therefore employed the calendar-year figures for the latter years of the two stated in the crop year; as stated in the Digest of Statistics (revenues due at time of shipment). Figures for these latter years include duties on groundnut oil.
[3] Obtained by applying tax rate of £1 per ton to tonnages purchased.
[4] Same as footnote 4 to Table A-1.   [5] Same as footnote 5 to Table A-1.

Table A-3. *Palm kernels*[1]

	Export duties[2]		Marketing Board trading surplus		Produce purchase tax[3]		Total with-drawals, £000s	Producer income,[4] £000s	Potential producer income,[4] £000s	Total with drawals as % of potential producer income
	£000s	% of potential producer income	£000s	% of potential producer income	£000s	% of potential producer income				
1947	347·6	4·4	2,433·2	30·7	—	—	2,780·8	5,150·8	7,930·9	35·1
1948	784·8	7·9	2,550·6	25·5	—	—	3,335·4	6,638·1	9,973·5	33·4
1949	827·2	5·5	4,512·0	29·8	—	—	5,339·2	9,776·0	15,115·2	35·3
1950	1,080·4	7·9	2,553·7	18·7	—	—	3,634·1	10,000·3	13,634·4	26·7
1951	1,805·1	10·3	4,818·2	27·5	—	—	6,623·3	10,901·1	17,524·4	37·8
1952	2,361·0	11·0	4,044·5	18·9	—	—	6,405·5	14,963·5	21,369·0	30·0
1953	2,280·1	11·4	2,538·4	12·7	—	—	4,818·4	15,096·5	19,915·0	24·2
1954	2,385·7	11·4	1,645·1	7·8	—	—	4,030·8	16,944·3	20,975·1	19·2
Subtotal, 1947–54	11,871·9	9·4	25,095·7	19·9			36,967·6	89,470·6	126,437·5	29·2
1955	1,874·7	12·9	523·1	3·5	593·0	4·1	2,990·8	11,573·4	14,564·2	20·5
1956	2,123·3	13·1	260·6	1·6	657·5	4·1	3,041·4	13,131·5	16,172·9	18·8
1957	1,734·8	11·9	−257·9	−1·7	596·3	4·1	2,073·2	12,393·1	14,466·3	14·3
1958	2,286·5	14·2	−635·0	3·9	647·9	4·0	3,569·4	12,508·9	16,078·3	22·2
1959	2,864·8	13·4	5,780·4	27·1	620·0	2·9	9,265·2	12,050·7	21,315·9	43·5
1960	2,292·7	12·0	4,379·2	23·0	611·5	3·2	7,283·4	11,774·7	19,058·1	38·2
1961	1,948·3	13·1	562·1	3·8	601·2	4·0	3,111·6	11,790·8	14,902·4	20·9
Subtotal, 1955–61	15,125·1	13·1	11,882·5	10·3	4,327·4	3·7	31,335·0	85,223·1	116,588·1	27·1
Total	26,997·0	11·1	36,978·2	15·2	4,327·4	1·8	68,302·6	174,693·7	242,996·3	28·1

[1] Up until 1954 inclusive, statistics refer to all Nigeria (plus Southern Cameroons); from 1955 on, they refer only to Eastern and Western Regions except in the case of export duties. Figures for 1947, 1948 and 1949 were calculated from figures in P. T. Bauer, *West African Trade*, p. 407. 1947 and 1948 refer to Nigerian operations of the W.A.P.C.B. The year 1947 is partly W.A.P.C.B. and partly Nigeria Oil Palm Produce Marketing Board. Other comments in note 1 to Table A-2 apply.

[2] From 1955 on, sum of surpluses earned on palm kernel trading by Eastern Region and Western Region using the latter year of the two included in the Western Region's fiscal year to correspond with the calendar year followed by the Eastern Regional Marketing Board.

[3] Obtained by applying tax rate to tonnage purchased. The 1961 figure, however is my rough estimate.

[4] Same as footnote 4 to Table A-1. [5] Same as footnote 5 to Table A-1.

91

Table A-4. Palm oil[1]

	Export duties[2]		Marketing Board trading surplus		Produce purchase tax[3]		Total withdrawals, £000s	Producer income,[4] £000s	Potential producer income,[4] £000s	Total withdrawals as % of potential producer income
	£000s	% of potential producer income	£000s	% of potential producer income	£000s	% of potential producer income				
1947	75·6	1·8	995·4	23·7	—		1,071·0	3,124·8	4,195·8	25·5
1948	347·5	4·4	3,169·2	40·3	—		3,516·7	4,336·8	7,853·5	44·8
1949	660·1	6·8	2,511·6	26·1	—		3,171·7	6,440·0	9,611·7	32·9
1950	694·4	7·3	1,996·9	21·1	—		2,691·3	6,792·9	9,484·2	28·4
1951	1,167·1	10·5	2,301·3	20·7	—		3,468·4	7,643·7	11,112·1	31·2
1952	1,753·8	10·7	2,508·3	15·3	—		4,262·1	12,081·4	16,343·5	26·1
1953	1,285·1	11·8	-4,647·1	-42·7	—		-3,362·0	14,247·2	10,885·2	-30·9
1954	1,371·9	11·3	-2,292·0	-18·9	—		-920·1	13,041·8	12,121·7	-7·6
Subtotal, 1947–54	7,355·5	9·0	6,543·6	8·0	—		13,899·1	67,708·6	81,607·7	17·0
1955	1,350·0	13·3	377·7	-3·7	658·4	6·5	1,630·7	8,511·9	10,142·6	16·1
1956	1,736·3	14·3	1,669·8	13·7	654·6	5·4	4,060·7	8,094·7	12,155·4	33·4
1957	1,426·8	12·9	1,694·8	15·4	616·9	5·6	3,738·5	7,300·3	11,038·8	33·9
1958	1,343·9	13·3	263·5	2·6	667·9	6·6	2,275·3	7,816·2	10,091·5	22·5
1959	1,416·3	13·6	853·1	8·2	678·9	6·5	2,948·3	7,453·7	10,402·0	28·3
1960	1,270·7	13·6	6·0	0·00064	676·6	7·3	1,953·3	7,377·5	9,330·8	20·9
1961	1,102·4	11·9	195·7	2·1	638·4	6·9	1,936·5	7,323·0	9,259·5	20·9
Subtotal, 1955–61	9,646·4	13·3	4,305·2	5·9	4,591·7	6·3	18,543·3	53,877·3	72,420·6	25·6
Total	17,001·9	11·0	10,848·8	7·0	4,591·7	3·0	32,442·4	121,585·9	154,028·3	21·0

[1] Until 1954 inclusive (1957 inclusive for export duties), statistics refer to all of Nigeria; after, only for the Eastern Region. Figures for 1947, 1948 and 1949 were calculated from figures in P. T. Bauer, *West African Trade*, p. 407. 1947 and 1948 refer to Nigerian operations of the W.A.P.C.B. The year 1947 is partly W.A.P.C.B. and partly Nigeria Oil Palm Produce Marketing Board. Other comments in note to Table A-2 apply.
[2] From 1950 to 1954 inclusive, export duty figures are taken from *Digest of Statistics* (various issues). From 1955 to 1960 inclusive, they are from the *Reports of the Accountant-General of the Federation of Nigeria* (various issues) using the former year of the two calendar years included in its fiscal year to correspond with the calendar year followed by the Eastern Regional Marketing Board. The 1961 figures are taken from the accounts of the Eastern Regional Marketing Board.
[3] Same as note 2 to Table A-1.   [4] Same as note 6 to Table A-1.
[3] Same as note 5 to Table A-1.   [4] Same as note 7 to Table A-3.

Table A-5. *Cotton*[1]

	Export duties[2]		Marketing Board trading surplus		Produce purchase tax[3]		Total withdrawals, £000s	Producer income,[4] £000s	Potential producer income,[5] £000s	Total withdrawals as % of potential producer income
	£000s	% of potential producer income	£000s	% of potential producer income	£000s	% of potential producer income				
1949–50	—		1,185·9	48·4	—		1,185·9	1,266·6	2,452·5	48·4
1950–1	386·0	9·6	2,077·6	51·5	—		2,463·6	1,569·1	4,032·7	61·1
1951–2	713·7	13·6	1,028·5	19·6	—		1,742·2	3,509·5	5,251·7	33·2
1952–3	812·2	16·1	1,440·0	28·5	—		2,252·2	2,795·2	5,047·4	44·6
1953–4	775·1	12·4	1,236·6	19·9	70·3	1·1	2,082·0	4,147·3	6,229·3	33·4
Subtotal, 1949–50 to 1953–4	2,687·0	11·7	6,968·6	30·3	70·3	0·3	9,725·9	13,287·7	23,013·6	42·3
1954–5	813·6	10·3	1,672·1	21·2	92·1	1·2	2,577·8	5,303·1	7,880·9	32·7
1955–6	1,058·2	17·6	500·7	8·3	75·4	1·3	1,634·3	4,378·9	6,013·2	27·2
1956–7	751·1	15·1	230·7	4·6	68·1	1·4	1,049·9	3,934·3	4,984·3	21·1
1957–8	756·3	11·4	−949·5	−14·4	115·6	1·8	−77·6	6,687·6	6,610·0	−1·2
1958–9	918·8	19·4	−983·3	−20·7	81·5	1·7	17·0	4,729·8	4,746·8	0·4
1959–60	693·6	15·4	−990·5	−22·0	80·2	1·8	−217·6	4,726·7	4,510·0	−4·8
1960–1	779·4	9·7	−1,176·5	−14·7	208·7	2·6	−188·4	8,196·5	8,008·1	−2·4
Subtotal, 1945–5 to 1960–1	5,771·0	13·5	−1,696·3	−4·0	721·6	1·7	4,796·3	37,956·9	42,753·2	11·2
Total	8,458·0	12·9	5,272·3	8·0	791·9	1·2	14,522·2	51,244·6	65,766·8	22·1

[1] Until and including 1953–4, statistics refer to all of Nigeria; from then on, they refer only to the Northern Region, except in the case of export duty.
[2] Up until and including 1953–4, from Annual Reports of the Nigeria Cotton Marketing Board. From then on, export duty figures were taken from the *Annual Reports of the Accountant-General of the Federation of Nigeria* (various issues).
[3] Calculated by applying tax rate to purchases data.
[4] Same as note 4 to Table A-1.
[5] Same as note 5 to Table A-1.

24. THE MONETARY EFFECTS OF RECENT BUDGETS IN GHANA

A. J. KILLICK

. . . We have noted that Ghana's economy in the last three or four years has been exhibiting signs of inflationary pressures. This is in contrast to the record of price stability which characterized the economy in most of the nineteen-fifties. The average annual increase in the Accra retail price index in 1952 to 1960 was only 0·7 per cent. The average for 1961–3 was 6·7 per cent and this average was almost certainly exceeded in 1964. We have noted, too, that Government budgetary deficits have frequently been named as a major cause of these pressures. We must now examine this contention in some detail. . . . .

Firstly, there is confusion about the meaning of the term 'budget deficit'. In Ghana the convention appears to be to describe as a deficit an excess of Government spending on current *and capital* account over its *current* receipts. This is the meaning that is given to the term by the *Economic Surveys* and in the publications of the Bank of Ghana.* Defining the term in this way, it is shown that during the fifties almost all the budgets were in surplus and the Government was adding to its reserves, but that from the 1959–60 financial year deficits have appeared and have tended to increase in size.†

An alternative way of viewing this question, however, would be to assign the label of 'surplus' or 'deficit' only to the balance on the current account of the Government, i.e. to the difference between the value of tax and other current receipts and the value of current (non-capital) expenditures. If we do this, we come to the conclusion that Ghana has never yet experienced a budget deficit. This is shown for the years since 1957/8 in the first three columns of Table 1. The Government has always received more on current account than it

* See, for example, *Economic Survey*, 1963, para. 82; and Bank of Ghana *Annual Report*, 1962–3, Table 31.
† See *Economic Survey*, 1963, Table 1.

has spent on current account. It may be the rather free use of the term 'deficit' that has led commentators to assume too automatically that the budgetary balance was having an inflationary effect. In defence of the conventional Ghanaian meaning of budget deficit, on the other hand, it can be replied that it is not just current Government expenditures that constitute claims on resources, but total expenditures. It would also be arbitrary and misleading to isolate only capital expenditures as being potentially inflationary, and in what follows it is not intended to convey that impression.

Table 1. *Current saving and capital expenditure by Government*

Financial year	Revenue on Current A/c £Gm.	Expenditure on Current A/c £Gm.	Current Saving £Gm.	Expenditure on Capital A/c £Gm.	Saving as % of Capital Expenditure
1957–8	60·0	39·2	20·8	23·3	89·3
1958–9	66·8	45·6	21·2	27·7	76·5
1959–60	64·5	50·3	14·2	43·7	32·5
1960–1	71·9	67·0	4·9	31·5	15·6
1961–2[1]	107·6	90·4	17·2	51·9	33·1
1962–3	90·4	79·8	10·6	59·4	17·8
1963–4[1]	126·4	115·2	11·2	58·5	19·1
1965[2]	133·9	100·3	33·6	56·0[3]	60·0

[1] Fifteen months.
[2] Estimates.
[3] Total expenditures on capital account are shown in the 1965 Budget as £G99·7 million. To reduce this figure to one comparable with the earlier years, expenditures of £G26·4 million to be financed by foreign credits have been deducted and subscriptions to the I.M.F., the African Development Bank, etc., amounting to £G17·3 million have also been deducted.

Sources: *Economic Survey*, 1963, tables 3, 4 and 5.
    The Budget, 1965.

The most recent budgetary balances have been complicated by the fact that in 1961/2 and 1962/3 the Cocoa Marketing Board fell into arrears in its payments to the Government of the farmers' voluntary contributions and these arrears were paid off in 1963/4. The sum involved was £G18·6 million and the payment was effected by a 'repayment' by the Government of loans from the Marketing Board to that value, which sum was then accepted again in payment of the arrears. Properly speaking, these arrears should be regarded as relating to the 1961/2 and 1962/3 years. In Table 1, therefore, current revenue and expenditure in 1963/4 have both been reduced by £G18·6 million and this sum has been allocated to the revenues of the previous two years. £G8 million has been added to 1962/3 and £G10·6 million to 1961/2. The public debt figures in Table 2 below have been reduced by the same amounts. The effect of these adjustments is to provide a more realistic picture of fiscal trends in the period concerned.

Table 2. *Size and composition of the public debt, 1957–64*

End of financial year	External debt	Internal debt	Total public debt
1956–7	3·3	21·9	25·3
1957–8	3·2	17·4	20·6
1958–9	7·2	16·8	24·0
1959–60	12·9	38·6	51·5
1960–1	35·7	44·0	79·7
1961–2	49·8	70·1[1]	119·9
1962–3	77·9	114·6[1]	192·5
1963–4[2]	80·6	157·1[1]	237·7

Sources: *Financial Statement*, 1963–4, Table VI. *The Budget*, 1965, Part II, Table VI.
[1] Adjusted for Marketing Board arrears (see text).
[2] Provisional estimates.

The fact remains, of course, that over the period 1957/8 to 1963/4 current expenditures have gone up faster than current receipts and the size of the surpluses on current amount has diminished in relation to expenditures. In the same period, Government expenditures on capital account have increased even faster than current expenditures and, in consequence, the proportion of capital expenditures that could be financed by the current surplus has been falling sharply. This is shown in the final column of Table 1. Thus an increasing share of capital expenditures has had to be financed by using up reserves accumulated in the past and by borrowing.

Reductions in Government reserves have been large in recent years. The following are the total value of reserves in the Consolidated Fund, Development Fund, Contingencies Fund and Special Fund, in millions of pounds:*

1957	63·6	1960	39·0
1958	62·4	1961	31·5
1959	52·7	1962	7·2

Not all of the excess of capital over current surpluses could be finan-

* Taken from *Statistical Year Book*, 1962, Table 148.

ced in this way, however. There was also in this period a large increase in Government borrowing, a process which accelerated as reserves diminished.

At the end of the last financial year the size of the public debt was still small in relation to national income. The total debt of £G237·7 million was equivalent to 40 per cent of the 1963 G.D.P.; it is not unusual for the size of the public debt to exceed the national income in 'mature' economies. What is more relevant, however, is that Ghana's public debt has been growing very fast indeed in recent years. There was a ten-fold increase in the six years 1958-9 to 1963-4. Between these two years the external and internal debts increased at about the same pace, but in absolute terms the enlarged internal debt accounted for 65 per cent of the total increase. It is on the internal debt that we wish to fasten attention in this examination of the effect of the budgets on the price level. Borrowing by the Government from the rest of the world cannot be directly inflationary because the funds obtained in this way give command over an additional volume of real resources, in the form of importables. Domestic borrowing does not necessarily release real resources for use by the Government. It may or it may not, depending on whether the Government is able to tap the real savings of the community. The next step, therefore, is to have a closer look at trends in the composition of the internal debt.

Analysed by type of liability, the increase in the internal debt of the Government between 1958-9 and 1963-4 was made up as follows:

	£Gm.
1. Stocks and bonds	+60·7
2. National Development Bonds (compulsory savings)	+11·9
3. Cocoa Marketing Board Loans	−4·0
4. Treasury bills	+51·7
5. Ways and Means advances	+20·0

What should be stressed here is that the ability of the economy to absorb some of these forms of debt on the scale that it did represents a *once-and-for-all* shift from holdings of foreign debt, mainly United Kingdom securities, to holdings of domestic debt. For example, of the total increase of stocks and bonds, £G37 million was in the form of 'compensatory stocks' issued to public bodies like the Marketing Board in exchange for their foreign assets.* And, as we will see shortly, a further large part of the increase in stocks and bonds and

* See *Economic Survey*, 1963, para. 102.

in Treasury Bills was made possible by a reduction in the external assets of the banking system. In other words, the expansion of the internal public debt and the types of debt which it was possible to issue were intimately connected with the process of running down the country's external reserves. Since the period of large excess reserves could be said to have come to an end by 1961, the ability of the country thereafter to absorb large additions to the public debt in non-inflationary forms has been strictly limited. This constraint was alleviated for a time by the compulsory savings scheme, but that was short-lived and limited in magnitude. It is not surprising, therefore, that the nineteen-sixties have seen rapid growth in Government borrowing from the commercial banks and the Bank of Ghana. The growth of Government indebtedness to the banking system is traced in Table 3.

Table 3. *Net Government indebtness to banking system (£Gm.)*

	Debt to Bank of Ghana	Debt to commercial banks	Total
End of period			
1958	−2·5	−1·8	−4·3
1959	−2·2	−2·1	−4·2
1960	−1·9	1·7	−0·2
1961	3·5	4·6	8·1
1962	9·3	11·9	21·3
1963	5·9	14·6	20·5
1964	21·5	34·0	55·5
Average of period			
1962	5·4	12·5	17·9
1963	10·7	16·8	27·5
1964	10·1	23·7	33·8

Sources: Bank of Ghana, *Annual Report*, 1962–3, Table XLIII.
   Economic Survey, 1963, Table XII.
   Data on 1964 provided by Bank of Ghana.

From this table it can be observed that the Government moved from a small net creditor position at the end of 1960 to a net debtor position of £G55.5 million at the end of 1964. However, the use of year-end figures is not ideal, because of the strong seasonal influences on the monetary situation and also because of the extension of the 1963-4 financial year by three months to the end of the 1964 calendar year. In the lower part of the table, therefore, we have calculated twelve-monthly averages for the three years for which complete data exist. These give a better idea of trends in the period as a whole. Note in particular the very different results obtained for 1964, with the year-end figures much higher than the monthly average figures. Government indebtness to the central and commercial banks was much higher in December 1964 than was typical for the year as a whole. Nevertheless, looking at the lower part of the table there is still apparent in 1962–4 a very considerable increase in indebtness to the banking system; borrowing from both the central bank and the commercial banks approximately doubled in these three years.

The next stage of the analysis is to examine the possible effect on the price level of Government borrowing from the banking system. What will be the effect of this borrowing on the money supply as a whole?

It is well known that borrowing from the *central bank* will have a large expansionary effect on the money supply. By means of this borrowing the fiduciary issue is enlarged. New cash is injected into the economy. Some of this will be absorbed into a permanent increase in the currency circulation, but some of it will find its way into the commercial banks. The commercial banks, finding themselves with enlarged cash reserves, may now extend new credit on a multiple basis. When bank lending is kept at a fixed proportion of bank reserves the size of the credit multiplier will be determined by (be the reciprocal of) the cash reserve ratio. When the banks find it impossible to expand lending as much as they would like to, as is often said to be the case in economies like Ghana's,* the amount of credit is smaller. But, except for the unlikely case of no increase in bank lending at all, Government borrowing from the central bank not only increases the currency but is liable to lead to an expansion of money.

The expansionary effect of Government borrowing from the *commercial banks* will depend upon the kind of debt that is incurred and the way in which the banks absorb these new assets. The following analysis does not pretend to be exhaustive, but rather concentrates on the possibilities most relevant in the Ghanaian context.

Two kinds of Government debt may be identified:

(i) Debt in forms that are liquid assets to the banks. For shorthand, this kind will be called 'Treasury Bills'.

* See Newlyn and Rowan, *Money and Banking in British Colonial Africa* (Oxford, 1954), chapter VIII.

(ii) Debt in forms that do not add to the liquid assets of the bank. This will be called 'Stocks'.

And two ways in which the banks may acquire these assets may be identified:

(*a*) By the utilization of previous existing excess cash reserves or the repatriation of foreign liquid assets. From the viewpoint of the monetary position of the home economy, these may be treated together.*

(*b*) By a reduction in loans and advances to the general public.

Now we combine these in the four possible permutations to trace their overall monetary effects.

The simplest case is the combination (ii)(*b*). The commercial banks reduce the volume of their loans and advances to the general public and instead buy stocks from the Government. This is a change in the structure of the bank's non-liquid assets; a shift of credit from the general public to the Government. The quantity of bank money is unchanged; and assuming that investment is equally productive in both sectors there are no inflationary effects emanating from the monetary system.

A combination of (i) and (*b*) is a good deal more expansionary. The banks have now a more liquid asset structure; they have reduced loans and advances and acquired Treasury bills. Since the bills may be more or less freely converted into cash (in Ghana there is no penal rediscount rate), the cash and liquid reserves ratios of the banks will be increased, permitting a multiple expansion of bank credit. Assuming that there is indeed some expansion of credit, the overall effect of this form of Government borrowing is to increase the quantity of money and the total amount of credit in the economy.

Next the combination (ii)(*a*). Banks lend to the Government by utilizing excess domestic lending power. They acquire stocks by drawing on excess cash reserves or by withdrawing credit from foreigners abroad. The proximate effect is to increase the total amount of credit in the economy. When the Government spends the money it has borrowed in this way total money incomes are increased and a proportion of this amount of credit comes back to the banks in the form of larger demand deposits. This partially replenishes their reserves and leaves them with some excess lending power.

The analysis of the last permutation, (i)(*a*), follows similar lines, except that the initial increase in credit to the Government does not

* The utilization of either type of asset permits a larger volume of domestic credit; they both represent excess domestic lending power.

reduce the excess domestic lending power of the banks. Liquid assets in the form of cash or foreign liquid assets have been exchanged for Treasury bills. The proximate result, as in the previous case, is a net addition to credit, an increase in money incomes and larger demand deposits. At the end of this stage, however, the banks in this case have greater possibilities of credit creation, since the increase in deposits has been achieved without any initial reduction in liquid assets. This is the most expansionary of the four cases considered here.

Table 4. *Asset structure of commercial banks 1959–64 (£Gm. and percentages)*

Asset	(Averages for the year)					
	1959	1960	1961	1962	1963	1964
Cash	6·3 (17)	4·7 (11)	4·5 (8)	7·2 (11)	5·4 (8)	8·7 (10)
Balances with other banks	11·6 (31)	11·6 (28)	10·8 (20)	2·1 (3)	–0·7 (–1)	2·0 (2)
Ghana Treasury bills	—	4·2 (10)	5·8 (11)	17·3 (27)	17·8 (25)	18·8 (21)
Other bills	2·2 (6)	1·6 (4)	3·0 (6)	0·6 (1)	2·2 (3)	4·6 (5)
Total liquid assets	20·1 (54)	22·1 (53)	24·1 (45)	27·2 (42)	24·7 (35)	34·2 (38)
Ghana Govt. securities	0·2 (1)	0·2 (–)	0·6 (1)	1·1 (2)	5·5 (8)	12·6 (14)
Loans and advances	10·6 (28)	13·5 (33)	23·7 (44)	24·5 (38)	30·8 (43)	33·4 (37)
Other assets	6·3 (17)	5·6 (14)	5·8 (11)	10·9 (17)	10·9 (15)	11·5 (13)
Total assets	37·2(100)	41·4(100)	54·2(100)	63·7(100)	71·9(100)	91·2(100)

Figures in brackets are percentages.
Sources: Central Bureau of Statistics *Quarterly Digest of Statistics.*
        Bank of Ghana *Annual Reports.*
        Information for 1964 provided by the Bank of Ghana.

Thus the expansionary effect of Government borrowing from the commercial banks will depend on (1) the type of debt created by the Government; (2) the resulting changes in the asset structure of the commercial banks; (3) the relationship between the volume of bank lending and the reserve position of the banks, i.e. whether reserves will be in a practically constant ratio to lending or whether there are limitations to lending on the side of demand. The figures in Table 3 and Table 4 enable this analysis to be applied to the case of Ghana.

Bank portfolios of Government debt went up from £G0·2 million in 1959 to £G31·4 million in 1964.* Until 1962 almost all of the

* There is a substantial discrepancy between this figure for 1964 and the figure in Table 3. This may perhaps be due to the fact that the figures are still provisional.

CARL A. RUDISILL LIBRARY
LENOIR RHYNE COLLEGE

increase was in the form of liquid assets—Treasury bills. While this component of the asset structure was going up (from zero to 25 per cent), there were reductions in the cash ratio (17 to 8 per cent) and in balances from other banks (31 to *minus* 1 per cent). Balances with other banks are, almost entirely, balances with foreign banks (balances with the London head office in the case of the expatriate banks), so the decline in this item represented a withdrawal of liquid assets from abroad.

The acquisition of Treasury bills rather more than offset the decline in cash holdings and balances with other banks and there was an increase in the total value of liquid assets. Non-liquid assets, however, went up much more with the consequences of a downward trend in the overall liquidity ratio (from 54 per cent in 1959 to 38 per cent in 1964). Nevertheless, at least up to 1962 the liquidity ratio was always higher than was necessary for purely precautionary purposes.

In other words, the pattern of Government borrowing from the banks up to 1962 was akin to the combination of (i) and (*a*) discussed above. This combination we described as the most expansionary of all. The banks were lending to the Government without reducing their total liquidity and hence their ability to lend to the general public. In fact, their loans and advances grew apace—from £G10·6 million in 1959 to £G24·5 million in 1962. On the other hand, loans and advances did not go up by as much as they could have done; the banks were generally under lent in these years and this to some extent mitigated the expansionary effect of the Government borrowing.*

1963 followed a rather different pattern. In the course of that year the Government was able to fund £G10 million worth of Treasury bills into medium-term stocks, i.e. it persuaded the banks to convert Treasury bills into medium-term investments.† This, of course, reduced the overall liquidity of the banks and thus absorbed excess

---

* In other words, bank lending was still generally demand determined in these years as in all previous years. But demand was rising rapidly. For an examination of this increase in demand see my chapter 13 of *The Economic Structure of Ghana*, to be published shortly. Another factor mitigating the expansionary effects of borrowing by Government from the banks is that to some extent the banks act as non-monetary financial intermediaries, re-lending money deposited in savings and time accounts. Between 1959 and 1964 time and savings deposits increased by £G18·2 million.

† See *Economic Survey*, 1963, para. 169. This funding operation, which occurred in the middle of the year, is not fully brought out in the figures of Table 4, which are twelve-monthly averages.

lending power possesed by the banks at that time. As the result of this funding operation the banks' liquidity fell from 52 per cent in July 1963 to 30 per cent in August, and at the end of the year it stood at 27 per cent.* Taking the three commercial banks together, it can be said that they possessed no excess liquidity by the end of 1963. Looking at the banks individually, it seems likely that Ghana Commercial Bank possessed a distinctly low rate of liquidity ratio at that time, while the expatriate banks may still have been under-lent in some degree.

This position changed during 1964. The Government resumed selling Treasury bills to the banks in large quantities, thus re-injecting liquidity in to the system. This is not brought out clearly by the twelve-monthly average figures of Table 4;* it is better for this purpose to work with the year end figures given below:†

	Commercial Bank holdings of Treasury bills (£Gm.)	Liquidity ratio‡ (%)
December 1962	18·0	46·3
December 1963	12·4	26·5
December 1964	26·7	41·0

We see from these the decline in Treasury bill holdings and the liquidity ratio during 1963 and then the large increase in both items during 1964. In other words, 1964 saw a reversion to the pattern established in 1959–62. In March 1964, however, the Bank of Ghana introduced a new element of monetary discipline in the form of statutory minimum asset ratios. The liquidity ratio was to be not less than 40 per cent in March to August and 46 per cent in September to February. The apparently highly restrictive nature of these ratios is rather misleading because for these purposes liquid assets are defined to include approved agricultural and industrial loans.

It is too early to tell whether this measure was effective in introducing a credit restriction. On the face of it, it appears not, for there was a large expansion of credit to the general public by the banking system during 1964 and an even larger expansion in the total money supply. Credit to the public by the banking system during 1964 was an average £G17 million higher than for 1963—an increase of no less than 48 per cent.

---

* See *Economic Survey*, 1963, Table XVIII.
† Sources: *Economic Survey*, 1963, Table XVIII and Bank of Ghana.
‡ Liquid assets are here taken as being cash, balances with Bank of Ghana, balances with other banks, and bills.

Thus taking the period as a whole, the years 1959–64 (*a*) saw a large amount of Government borrowing from the Bank of Ghana and from the commercial banks: (*b*) this borrowing from the commercial banks was in such a form as to keep the banks highly liquid; (*c*) partly as a consequence of this, the banks were able to extend their loans and advances, which went up by more than three-fold. The combined effect of these influences was to speed up the expansion of the total money supply. In the years 1950 to 1959 (a period of rapid economic growth) the average annual rate of increase of the money supply was 6·1 per cent. In 1960 to 1964 (years of relative stagnation) the average was 13·6 per cent.

We come at last to the question—one which we have been very careful not to pre-judge—of whether these monetary trends have been inflationary. So far the analysis has been quite neutral with respect to this question. To show a speeding-up in the expansion of the money supply is not sufficient by itself to identify it as a source of inflation. The crucial issue is whether the money supply has gone up more rapidly that the public's willingness to voluntarily hold money balances, in the form of transactions balances, money hoards, and so on.

The method adopted here is to examine the size of the money supply in relation to the Gross Domestic Product at current prices. In an economy such as Ghana's, where the speculative motive for holding money scarcely arises, we would expect the demand for money balances to be largely a direct function of the total value of current transactions (PT in the equation of exchange). The current price, but not the constant price, estimates of the G.D.P. should be a reasonable index of the trend in the total value of current transactions. So if we expect the money supply:GDP ratio to be constant over time, a decline in the ratio may be taken as *prima facie* evidence of unsatisfied demand for money balances, and an increase in the ratio as evidence of excess money supply.

There are reasons for not expecting the ratio to be constant over time, however. In a low-income country with still quite a large amount of subsistence activity we would expect the money supply to grow relative to the Gross Domestic Product, through the process of monetization. Even in high-income countries there appears to be a secular trend in that direction.* It is of more than ordinary interest to note, therefore, that during the later nineteen-fifties the trend in

* See E. K. Hawkins in *Oxford Economic Papers*, vol. 10, No. 3 (October 1958).

Ghana seems definitely to have been in the opposite direction—a declining money supply in relation to the G.D.P. The money supply as a percentage of the current-price G.D.P. moved in the following way:*

1955	12·5	1960	12·0
1956	13·1	1961	12·8
1957	12·6	1962	12·7
1958	11·8	1963	12·7
1959	11·6		

What is of interest to us here is the trend in the sixties. It will be observed that there was an appreciable increase in 1960 and 1961 and it may be that this expansion did help to pull the price level up again. It was in these years (but also in 1959) that the price level resumed its upward march. Large wage increases were granted in mid-1960 so that the economy was less able to absorb any inflationary forces that may have been emanating from the monetary system. However, the increase in the money supply:G.D.P. ratio in 1960 and 1961 only restored the ratio to approximately its 1956–7 level, so it is difficult to believe that this expansion resulted in any large unwanted money balances. And any unwanted balances were presumably eliminated in 1962 and 1963.†

It is by no means clear, therefore, that the monetary expansion, much of it emanating from the Government budgets, was in excess of the economy's ability to absorb it in voluntary money balances. What expansion did take place in the money supply:Gross Domestic Product ratio only partially offset previous declines in the ratio. 1964, on the other hand, may well reveal a different story. The average money supply in 1964 was 23 per cent up on the 1963 average and it seems highly unlikely that the current-price Gross Domestic Product went up by anything like that extent. Substantial unwanted money balances may well have been created, and since much of the 1964 increase in the money supply was initiated by large Government borrowings from the Bank of Ghana‡ and the commercial banks, it is probable that the extended 1963–4 budget did have a directly inflationary effect.

* See *Economic Structure of Ghana, op. cit.*
† A possibility that should be recognized, however, is that the rising price level was reducing the willingness to hold money, especially in passive hoards. In this case the 1962 and 1963 figures would be compatible with a growing excess supply of money.
‡ £G6 million of the £G10 million deficit for October–December 1964 was financed by Ways and Means advances from the Bank of Ghana. Cf. *The Budget*, 1965, Part II, p. 6.

The conclusion of this analysis that up to 1963 it is doubtful whether Government budgets had a general inflationary effect must, however, be qualified in an important way.

We have already described the inflationary effects of import controls necessitated by balance of payments disequilibria. What must be recognized is that the big increases over the period in total Government spending relative to current revenues led to an enlarged volume of imports and thus contributed in a significant way to Ghana's balance of payments deficits and to the necessity of trade restriction. Hence in this non-monetary way the Government finances even before 1964 were a source of inflationary pressure.

Moreover, while it appears to be the case that the monetary expansion before 1964 was not greater than the public's willingness to hold money, it seems very likely that it at least kept pace with the demand for money. It is difficult to believe that there was any overall monetary tightness in this period. Yet there was a strong case to be made for a restrictive monetary policy in these years. Inflationary pressures were emanating from the foreign trade and local foods sectors and since neither of these sectors could be put right in the short run, fiscal and monetary measures could have been used to neutralize these sources of inflation. A reduction in Government spending with revenue unchanged would both have alleviated the necessity for import restrictions and have slowed down the rate of monetary expansion. The possibility of an anti-inflationary monetary policy would thus have been created.

25. GHANA'S BALANCE OF PAYMENTS SINCE 1950

A. J. KILLICK

The first article surveyed developments in the current account of Ghana's balance of payments and argued that the emergence of Ghana as a deficit country in the second half of the 1950s was to be explained as follows: import values increased more rapidly than export values, with an acceleration of this process in the last two or three years. The increase in imports was due to a rise in the volume of goods imported; their prices were stable. Export earnings were retarded partly by falls in prices and partly by an only slow growth in quantities exported, compared with the growth in import volumes. Export prices and volumes interacted in such a way as to limit Ghana's ability to increase her export earnings, with price changes tending to offset changes in the volume exported.

Current account and overseas assets

The textbooks tell us that a surplus or deficit on current account must necessarily be matched by a converse balance on capital account. That is to say, a current account deficit can be met by obtaining grants or loans from abroad or by running down the country's international reserves, or both. The 1958 Economic Survey put it thus: 'Surpluses in the current accounts find expression in increases in overseas assets or decreases in foreign investments in Ghana. Deficits, on the other hand, imply a reduction in overseas assets or increase in foreign assets in Ghana.'*

In practice, however, this is subject to one important qualification. Whether capital movements of an exactly compensatory nature do in fact take place will depend upon the accuracy of the current account figures. Even countries with most advanced statistical techniques and governmental records cannot hope to eliminate a margin of error altogether. In countries with less substantial bureaucracy the margin of error is likely to be a good deal larger.

Table 1 gives an indication of the relationship between the current

* *Economic Survey*, 1958, para 67.

107

account balance, changes in foreign investments in Ghana, and changes in Ghana's overseas assets.

In all except the last two years the figure for private short-term capital movements is in fact a residual figure, incorporating all errors and omissions, on both current and capital account.* For these years, therefore, it is impossible to say what happened to short-term capital movements themselves. It is thus no paradox to say that the inclusion of an 'errors and omissions' figure in the 1960 Economic Survey represented a major improvement in the balance of payments accounts.

By comparing the first two columns of Table 1 it can be seen that the relationship between the current account balance and what can loosely be called Ghana's reserves is a very imperfect one. The 1959 Survey stated that 'In recent years there has been a tendency for the assets to be reduced more or to increase less than the changes in the

Table 1. *The balance of payments and capital movements*
(net balance: £G millions)

	Balance on current a/c	Official and banking overseas assets	Long-term private capital	Short-term private capital	Errors and omissions
1950	+20·1	−8·8	−1·2	−10·1	
1951	+19·3	−12·8	−10·8	+4·4	
1952	+111·5	−10·2	+0·6	−1·9	
1953	+5·2	−6·7	+6·6	−5·1	
1954	+40·7	−39·8	+8·4	−9·4	
1955	+1·8	−11·6	+4·3	+5·4	
1956	−13·3	+4·3	+2·5	+6·5	
1957	−14·4	+13·3	−3·8	−4·9	
1958	+10·8	−3·4	−3·1	−4·2	
1959	−11·3	+3·4	−1·5	+7·9	+1·4
1960	−33·5	+29·8	+1·9	+1·2	−0·5
1961	−52·7	+56·9	−8·4		+4·2

Notes: A minus sign for the capital account items denotes an increase in reserves or an outflow of private capital, and vice versa for a plus sign.

From 1959, the figures of Official and Banking Overseas Assets include Government capital transactions.

The 1961 figures for private capital movements are not yet available. However, the total movement can be deduced from the remainder of the items.

Sources: Balance of Payment Estimates, 1950–8; *Economic Surveys*, 1960, 1961.

* See *Balance of Payments Estimates, 1950–8; Definitions, Sources and Methods of Estimation*, p. 26.

current balance.'* However, this is to paint the picture too black. While it is true that in surplus years reserves have not been increased to the full extent of the surplus, it is also the case that in deficit years reserves have not shrunk by the full extent of the deficit. Private capital movements (plus 'errors and omissions') have, in other words, behaved in a stabilizing manner. This, however, is not true of 1961.

It should perhaps be added that even now knowledge of private investments is very limited, especially in regard to individual investments and direct investments by foreign firms in Ghana.

The international reserves

There is, to say the least, some imprecision about the concept of Ghana's international reserves. The 1960 Economic Survey speaks of all overseas assets held officially and by banking institutions as 'reserves'. The Bank of Ghana, on the other hand, counts only the overseas assets of the central government, the Bank of Ghana itself, and the Cocoa Marketing Board as 'international reserves'.†

There is something to be said for each of these views. For example, the overseas assets of the commercial banks will, under the sterling exchange system, tend to vary with the balance of payments, increasing when there is a surplus and declining when there is a deficit. In this way they can be said to form part of Ghana's foreign exchange 'cushion' against balance of payments fluctuations and to reduce the need for compensatory financing on the part of the authorities. On the other hand, they will not normally themselves be available for use by the authorities in financing a deficit. In any case, the difference between the two sets of figures is not huge.

A 'second-line' reserve is constituted by Ghana's quota of 35 million dollars (about £G12·5 million) with the International Monetary Fund. In fact, part of these were utilized in August 1962, when the Fund agreed to a £G·5 million drawing in pounds sterling and dollars by Ghana.

One large part of the total official holdings of sterling assets was, during the bulk of the period, not free to be varied according to the need for compensatory financing—the currency backing reserves of the Bank of Ghana. Up to 1960 there was no fiduciary issue of currency, the Bank's currency liabilities being backed 100 per cent

* *Economic Survey 1959*, para. 88.
† *Economic Survey 1960*, Table 85.

by gold and overseas assets. Since it is impossible that 100 per cent of the currency could ever, at any one time, be presented for conversion into sterling or other foreign currencies (especially under a regime of exchange controls), there was a strong case in favour of introducing a fiduciary issue (for which the legal power already existed) and releasing a proportion of the currency reserves to finance balance of payments deficits.* In the second half of 1961 a fiduciary element of over £G6 million was, in fact, introduced, and this is likely to become larger in the future.

It was suggested in the first article that the balance of payments surpluses, and hence the additions to Ghana's sterling assets, of the early fifties were at least partly a by-product of physical difficulties in the way of expanding imports, and of dis-inflationary policies pursued at home, which restricted the level of purchasing power and permitted only a modest rate of capital accumulation.

To this extent, therefore, the accumulation of reserves was not the result of a conscious policy decision. But there was in addition, at least from about 1952 or 1953, a publicly pronounced policy in favour of building up reserves. These two elements, the accidental and the deliberate, were well expressed by Mr. Armitage in his 1953 budget speech:

> These (sterling) balances have accrued over the last four or five years very largely because the raw materials produced in the Gold Coast have brought in large earnings and the Government has controlled expenditure and accumulated reserves. Some of the control on expenditure was of course involuntary and was due to a shortage of materials and skilled supervisory and technical staff. But in addition the Government increased taxation partly in an endeavour to lessen the amount of money which would exert an inflationary pressure on the supply of goods and services in the country, and partly to build up surpluses.†

It might also have been added that the Volta project first became a live possibility in 1952 and it was natural to wish to retain high reserves against the large demands that would certainly be felt if the project got under way.

Whatever the causes, the build-up of reserves gave rise to considerable controversy, especially in pre-independence days, both within the colony and in Britain itself.‡ The build-up of the colony's reserves

* *Bank of Ghana Annual Report* of year ending 30 June 1960.
† On this see article by Hazlewood already cited and Edward Nevin, *Capital Funds in Underdeveloped Countries.*
‡ *Legislative Assembly Debates*, 12 February 1953, p. 151.

was criticized principally on the grounds that it was wrong for the territory in effect to lend capital to Britain when its own capital needs were so great. In reply, the 1954 Economic Survey defended the policy in the following terms:

> If the Gold Coast is to be able to stand on its own feet as an independent country then it is essential that it should be able to demonstrate its ability and will to meet its commitments and so inspire the confidence without which foreign assistance, whether in the form of private investment, managerial ability or financial assistance, will not be forthcoming.*

In the event, there was no radical change after independence; the authorities continued to follow a rather cautious policy. It is true that the first Economic Survey to be published after independence noted the adverse trend in the balance of payments, stating that 'The era of Ghana building up reserves can now be said to have come to an end',† but after discussing the pros and cons at some length, the same Survey came down against a policy of financing the Second Development Plan out of reserves. It preferred a policy of borrowing as much of the foreign exchange cost of the Plan as possible and reducing reserves only by the necessary minimum.‡

This policy of borrowing was, however, slow in bearing fruit. This was tacitly admitted by the 1960 Economic Survey, with the statement that, 'until now Ghana has managed successfully to make large investments out of its own resources only. It is only in the last year that large-scale loans were negotiated successfully'.§ The value of credit agreements with communist countries is now said to exceed £G100 million (West Africa 3.3.62) and, of course, at the beginning of 1962 the American, British and World Bank loans for the Volta River Project were finally agreed.

The policy of keeping reserves as high as possible, especially as defended in the quotation from the 1954 Survey above, is certainly open to criticism. It could be argued that for any underdeveloped country outside Latin America, which is not fortunate enough to be a major oil producer, to hope to attract really large net inflows of private capital is, to put it mildly, unrealistic—whatever the state of reserves.

---

* See, for example, the debate between I. Greaves and A. Hazlewood and others on the implications of the colonial currency system in the *Economic Journal* and elsewhere in the period 1951–4.
† *Economic Survey, 1954*, para. 43.
‡ *Economic Survey, 1957*, para. 19.
§ *Economic Survey, 1957*, paras. 22 and 23.

Moreover, loans from foreign governments are made primarily on political or other non-economic grounds and will thus only marginally be affected by the borrowing country's reserve position. In any case, it by no means follows that high reserves will encourage lending by foreign governments. They may take the reserves as a sign that the country's needs of capital are not so acute and may only be prepared to lend on a large scale when the reserves fall to a crisis level. The recent experiences of India are clearly relevant here.

However, the critics do not get it all their own way. It is for example, difficult to disagree with the 1957 Economic Survey's argument that 'it would be imprudent to spend heavily for three or four years, after which period all development stopped abruptly for lack of funds',* especially since the country was still to a large extent only preparing the way for development and the 'big push' was still to come. It could also be argued that the level of reserves does make a significant impression on the bankers who run the World Bank, and that the decisions of this may often play a crucial part in persuading foreign governments whether or not to make loans. Perhaps the best defence of all is that loans and also large private investments by the aluminium consortium (backed by U.S. government guarantees) are now being received.

Anyway, whatever the merits of the policies in the past, the last deficit eliminated any excess reserves. Ghana needs all the reserves she has got. They fell sharply in the second half of the period under review and quite dramatically during 1961. At the end of 1961 the officially-held reserves represented 40 per cent of the value of imports in that year. The comparable figure for the world as a whole (at the end of 1960) was 53 per cent, and for countries other than the U.S. and Britain was 46 per cent.†

Further details of Ghana's reserves are set out in Table 2.

It is sometimes argued that one of the advantages of membership of the Sterling Area is that the colonies and other members that desire to use London's facilities rather than handle their investments themselves obtain the benefits of the expert management of their reserves in London. It is, however, a long-standing source of grievance that the management of Ghana's reserves was less than expert. More specifically, the complaint is that too high a proportion of the reserves were invested in long-term securities, leaving the

* *Economic Survey, 1960,* para. 364.
† *Economic Survey, 1957,* para. 23.

reserves insufficiently liquid. The dangers of this practice were demonstrated in the later 1950s when long-term rates of interest shifted sharply upwards,* thus depressing the capital values of Ghana's overseas assets. It is true that values would have fallen had the assets been held entirely in short-term paper or if they had been held in some other international money market, such as New York, but they would not have fallen so much.† Official policy is now to increase the proportion of reserves held in short-term securities, but this policy is obviously inhibited by the losses that are liable to be incurred if the longer dated securities are realized before maturity.

Table 2 throws further light on this subject. It can be seen from this that the proportion of short-term holdings to the total increased significantly in 1959 and 1960, due entirely to the dramatic shift in the composition of the Bank of Ghana's assets. This can be explained by the change-over from the old West African currency to the Ghana currency; the Bank of Ghana received short-term sterling securities in exchange for the old currency. Until these years the currency reserve was quite remarkably illiquid, and 1961 showed a return to the previous predominance of long-term assets.

Before concluding, there are two further topics that should be discussed: the regional pattern of Ghana's trade, and the composition of her imports and exports.

Table 2. *Composition of Ghana's reserves (year ends; £G million)*

	1950	'51	'52	'53	'54	'55	'56	'57	'58	'59	'60	'61
Central Govt.												
Short-term	3·0	1·8	—	4·9	12·5	3·4	1·0	2·4	0·5	0·3	2·8	1·5
Long-term	15·6	28·4	34·6	33·9	63·9	78·5	72·6	56·9	57·4	57·8	46·2	10·6
Currency Res.												
Central Bank												
Short-term	—	—	—	—	—	—	—	1·4	3·1	31·4	41·9	5·0
Long-term	32·3	34·5	36·5	35·5	37·1	37·9	40·7	36·7	36·1	41·9	11·9	38·1
G.C.M.B.												
Short-term	25·7	22·0	19·6	24·5	29·5	26·2	14·9	13·0	15·4	6·4	1·5	2·8
Long-term	26·4	41·4	41·4	41·4	36·6	36·4	36·4	36·4	36·4	30·4	28·6	4·0
Others												
Short-term	4·3	3·6	7·3	13·3	10·4	13·8	12·1	12·2	16·6	13·5	10·6	2·5
Long-term	6·0	5·5	5·7	6·6	7·4	12·0	12·1	12·4	12·1	12·0	10·6	10·6
Total:												
Short-term	33·0	27·4	26·9	42·7	52·4	43·4	28·0	29·0	35·6	51·6	51·2	8·9
Per cent of total	29	20	19	27	26	21	15	17	20	31	34	12
Long-term	80·3	109·8	118·2	117·4	145·0	164·8	161·8	142·4	142·0	115·1	97·4	64·8
Per cent of total	71	80	81	73	74	79	85	83	80	69	66	88
Total	113·4	137·2	145·1	160·2	197·3	208·1	189·8	171·5	177·6	166·7	148·6	73·7

* See 1961 Annual Report of the International Monetary Fund. These figures exclude the communist countries.
† See Radcliffe Report, chart on p. 146.

A. J. Killick

Table 3. *Imports by source—selected areas (per cent of total imports)*

	1950	'51	'52	'53	'54	'55	'56	'57	'58	'59	'60	'61
United Kingdom	56	54	56	55	48	47	47	42	43	40	37	36
Rest of Sterling Area	6	6	6	65	6	7	6	6	7	6	5	5
Dollar Area	6	6	8	6	6	6	6	8	8	9	8	11
O.E.E.C. countries	23	25	23	23	27	25	26	27	26	—	—	—
of which												
E.E.C. countries and possessions	—	—	—	—	—	—	—	24	24	22	26	22

Table 4. *Exports by destination—selected areas*
(per cent of total exports)

	1950	'51	'52	'53[1]	'54	'55	'56	'57	'58	'59	'60	'61
United Kingdom	41	41	40	42	40	41	35	37	36	31	31	29
Rest of Sterling Area	4	4	3	4	4	6	6	4	55	4	5	4
Dollar Area	33	33	30	28	17	19	20	17	20	20	16	25
O.E.E.C. countries	19	18	21	22	31	31	37	35	38	—	—	—
of which												
E.E.C. countries and possessions	—	—	—	—	—	—	—	30	34	38	36	32

[1] January–November.
Sources: *Economic Surveys*.

The balance of payments on a regional basis provides the following pattern for the last twelve years*: Ghana consistently has a substantial deficit in her trade with other members of the Sterling Area; she equally consistently has a surplus with the Dollar Area countries, although it is by no means as big as it was in the early 1950s, because of the relative decline in Ghana's exports to these countries; she also has a large surplus with Western Europe, a surplus which has become larger as exports to Europe have increased more rapidly than imports from Europe. As can be judged from this, the balance with the rest of the world† is normally on the deficit side.

Ghana's trading partners are rather more diverse now than they were at the beginning of the period. For example, the regions listed accounted for 91 per cent of imports and 97 per cent of exports in 1950, whereas in 1961 the proportions were 74 per cent and 90 per cent respectively. One important source of imports into Ghana which

* See Peter Ady on 'Ghana and the Sterling Area', *Bulletin of the Oxford University Institute of Statistics*, November 1959.
† Excluding Sterling Area countries.

is not shown is Japan, which accounts for up to one-tenth of total imports. A recent development is the growth of trade with what the United Nations coyly describes as the 'Centrally Planned Economies'. In 1961 they accounted for 5 per cent of imports and 3 per cent* of exports, and although in relation to total trade they are still of very limited importance, their share in the total has grown considerably in the last three years and is likely to continue to do so in the future. Trade with other African countries is growing too, although only rather slowly in relation to the total. Excluding South Africa, African countries (including African members of the Sterling Area) accounted for 7 per cent of imports and 3 per cent of exports in 1961. These figures, however, understate the true position; there is certainly a good deal of unrecorded commerce with neighbouring territories.

Britain's share in total trade, on the other hand, has declined sharply since the mid-fifties. One explanation that has been suggested is that there was bound to be some shift from sterling countries to dollar countries following the relaxation of restrictions on trade with the latter. In fact, trade with the dollar area has been pretty stable in recent years and the relaxation of controls does not seem to have made a great deal of difference. Probably the decline in Britain's trade with Ghana has occurred for the reasons that have caused Britain's share in total world trade to decline. Finally, note should be taken of the importance of trade with the Common Market countries. Over the last decade the West European market for Ghana's exports has been by far the most rapidly expanding one, notwithstanding the decline in the last two years. The share that it has taken of Ghana's exports has probably doubled in these years.

It seems likely that the controls imposed in December 1961 will be used to effect some change in the pattern of Ghana's trade and, more specifically, to increase trade with communist countries. One suggestion that has been made recently is that a third of Ghana's trade should be done with communist countries 'because the Socialist world now constitutes one-third of humanity'.† This is a novel principle on which to base a country's trade. Its more general application would lead to surprising results. Some 55 per cent of trade would then be carried on with Asian countries, only 8 per cent with other African countries, Britain's population would qualify her

---

* See *Economic Survey, 1961*, Table 104.
† See *West Africa*, 9 December 1961, p. 1350, which appears to give support to this proposal.

for about 2 per cent of trade and the whole of Europe for less than 25 per cent. It should be emphasized that the objection is not against more trade with communist countries; on the contrary, it will be argued later that Ghana needs to expand her trade in this direction. The resulting volume may turn out to be greater or smaller than a third of the total. But the general principle on which any country's trade should be based is not some demographic one, but that it should buy in the cheapest markets and sell in the most profitable ones.

Composition of exports

It has for many years now been official policy to try to diversify Ghana's exports and to lessen the heavy reliance on cocoa. Thus the 1953 Economic Survey commented in its opening paragraph that the 'reliance on the world price of cocoa and the volume of cocoa exports is outstanding and it is apparent that if the Gold Coast is to develop a prosperous and balanced economy a much broader basis of production has to be realized'.* It is useful here to distinguish three aspects of a policy of diversification: (a) reducing the proportion of primary product exports to the total; (b) reducing the proportion of cocoa exports to the total; (c) reducing reliance on imports by the domestic production of substitutes, a matter which will be touched on in the next section.

Regarding (a)—the desire to reduce dependence on exports of primary products (foodstuffs, agricultural and mineral raw materials) —virtually no progress has been made in recent years, as is acknowledged in the 1960 Economic Survey.† In 1951 the five commodities listed in Table 5 accounted for 96 per cent of all domestic goods exported: by 1961 the figure was 95 per cent. The re-export of goods from abroad accounted for rather over 2 per cent of total exports at both the beginning and the end of the period.

The record on the second aspect of diversification—reducing reliance on exports of cocoa—depends on the time perspective chosen. Mr. Green has shown that dependence on cocoa in the post-war period has been greater than pre-war. Thus, the percentage of annual domestic exports contributed by cocoa in the period 1935–9 was 52 per cent, in 1950–4 was 69 per cent, and in 1955–9 was 62 per cent.‡ So if we concentrate attention on the fifties there was some

---

* *Economic Survey, 1953*, para 1.
† Para. 338.
‡ R. H. Green, 'The Ghana Cocoa Industry', *Economic Bulletin*, vol. 5, 1, 1961.

reduction in the reliance on cocoa, albeit an involuntary one arising from the declining cocoa price.

Table 5. *Shares in the value of exports of domestic goods (Selected goods—per cent of total)*

	1951	'52[1]	'53[1]	'54	'55	'56	'57	'58	'59	'60	'61
Cocoa beans	68	62	63	75	68	59	56	60	61	59	61
Timber (logs and sawn)	5	5	7	6	8	11	11	11	12	14	13
Manganese	8	10	10	5	5	8	10	8	6	6	5
Diamonds	6	6	4	4	6	9	10	8	8	9	6
Gold	9	11	11	9	9	9	11	10	10	10	10

[1] January–November.
Sources: *Economic Surveys.*

Composition of imports

Probably the most illuminating break-down of imports is a classification according to the use that is made of them. Such a break-down is given in Table 6.

Table 6. *Imports by end-use (per cent of total value)*

	1952[1]	'53	'54	'55	'56	'57	'58	'59	'60	'61
Non-durable consumer goods	47	50	49	47	44	47	45	42	41	41
Durable consumer goods	5	9	7	10	10	9	10	8	9	8
Raw and semi-finished materials	27	22	24	24	26	24	25	26	24	28
Capital equipment	12	13	15	13	15	13	14	19	22	19
Fuels and lubricants	9	5	6	5	5	6	7	5	5	4

[1] January–November.
Sources: *Economic Surveys.*

The 1955 Economic Survey, it will be recalled, stated that a 'definite limit has to be set to the increase in total expenditure on consumer goods'. In fact, expenditure on imported consumer goods continued to rise, although it is true that the share of consumer goods imports in the total has never since been as high as the 57 per cent of 1955. However, only in the last three years of the period has the share dropped at all significantly.

In fact, the proportion of consumer-goods imports has throughout been very high by comparison with other countries. Yates has examined the relative shares of consumer goods and producer goods in the imports of a large number of countries for the year 1953. The Gold Coast had the second highest proportion of consumer imports

117

of all the countries listed, with a proportion nearly half as high again as the average.*

The U.N. Economic Commission for Africa provides a more recent comparison with other African countries. They show that in 1959 Ghana's imports of food, beverages, tobacco and textiles were, proportionately, the third highest of all the countries listed, with only Senegal and Sudan importing higher proportions. Ghana's 43 per cent can be compared with the unweighted average of all the countries listed of 32 per cent.†

As Yates notes, a high proportion of consumer goods imports seems to be a characteristic of under-developed countries and especially of colonies or countries that have only been independent for a short time. This is presumably because colonial governments give lower priority to economic development (necessitating large capital goods imports) than nationalist governments, and are in a weaker position to hold down consumption. The position in Ghana would seem to conform to this pattern, with some recent movement away from the pattern of imports established before independence.

It is hardly necessary to point out that consumer-goods imports are not necessarily useful. They are not synonymous with 'unnecessary luxuries'. Indeed, most of them are essential to the Ghanaian economy. Nevertheless, there remained the suspicion that some of these imports could be cut without any loss of efficiency or any great hardship being felt. Faced with the difficulty we have seen in expanding export earnings, consumer goods imports had to suffer a relative reduction if the capital goods necessary for development were to be obtained. This is merely an application of the general economic principle that increased investment necessitates the postponement of consumption.

Without detailed research it is impossible to be sure whether the third aspect of diversification—the consumption of domestically-produced substitutes for imported goods—has made much progress. There certainly has been some saving on imports, for example, of beer, tobacco and rice, but the overall impact has probably been no more than marginal so far. There is a long way to go before local production will effect really large reductions in consumer-goods imports.

* Yates, *Forty Years of Foreign Trade*, pp. 196–7.
† U.N.E.C.A., *Economic Bulletin for Africa*, June 1961, annexe of African Statistics.

Future prospects for Ghana's balance of payments

It is certainly much easier to be pessimistic about the future balance than it is to be optimistic. As Mr. Nypan has shown,* Ghana's marginal propensity to import is almost certainly substantially above the marginal propensities of her trading partners to import goods from Ghana. This means that only if real incomes grow more slowly in Ghana than in the industrial countries will there be no serious additional pressure on her international payments. If Ghana maintains an average or (and this is what is hoped for) an above-average rate of growth, the pressure for ever-increasing deficits will become intense.

To spell out this gloomy conclusion in more concrete terms, there are obvious reasons for thinking that the demand for imports is likely to continue to rise, but few substantial grounds for expecting exports to rise at all at the same pace. Imports, it was suggested in an earlier article, are sensitive to both current expenditure and capital formation by the Government and other public bodies, to private capital formation, and to changes in personal incomes, of which cocoa farmers' incomes are a particular important element. Whatever happens to private investment and personal incomes—and it must be hoped that these at least will not fall—it is quite obvious that government expenditure will continue to rise. Clearly, the greater emphasis now being placed on economic development will create additional demand for imported goods.

In this respect, it is worth having a closer look at the Volta project. Firstly, it is by no means certain that the foreign loans that Ghana will receive for the dam, power station and transmission grid will cover the direct foreign exchange requirements of this part of the project. The Ghana Government is to meet half of the £G70 million needed and expects the other half to be covered by loans. But in 1956 the Preparatory Commission estimated that nearly three-quarters of the capital expenditure on this phase of the work would need to be on imported goods.† To be sure, the actual sums estimated by the Commission to be necessary for the project have since been substantially reduced, but there is no reason to think that the *proportions* of internal and external expenditures have changed very

* See E. Nypan, 'Demand for Imports in Ghana and Demand for Ghana Products in other countries', *Economic Bulletin*, January 1960.
† *Report of Preparatory Commission on Volta River Project*, Vol. II, Appendix XIII, Annexe L, p. 406.

much. If they are right on this, then, something of the order of £G15 million, out of Ghana's total contribution of £G35 million, will have to be provided in the form of foreign currencies, which is no small thing.

Quite apart from the immediate direct foreign exchange cost to Ghana of the project and the costs of servicing the foreign loans, the secondary effects are also likely to be important, for the project will generate, besides electricity, new incomes on a large scale. Something like £G130 million is going to be invested in the project in the next few years (including £G60 million by Valco), and even though much of this will be spent on imported capital goods, Ghana's economy can be expected to experience substantial 'income effects'. Hence the demand for imported consumer goods will also rise.

Considering this, then, and the large development expenditures that are likely in other sectors of the economy, it is obvious that the pressure for greatly increased imports will be very large.* Small wonder, therefore, that President Nkrumah recently cited an estimate that food imports would have to be increased four-fold by 1970.†

On the side of exports, there are great difficulties in the way of increasing Ghana's foreign earnings to match her increasing require-ments of imports. It was shown in an earlier article‡ that the price Ghana receives for her exports tends to vary inversely with the volume of her sales and therefore that it was very difficult for her to greatly increase her export earnings. For example, the volume of Ghana's exports increased by nearly a quarter, but her export earnings remained stationary.

Of course, this situation could change, especially if the world market for cocoa became more buoyant. But if demand in the traditional cocoa-consuming countries continues to grow only slowly increased revenue from cocoa exports will depend crucially on the ability to find potential customers who are not at present partici-pating on any scale in the market—a point emphasized by the 1960 Economic Survey. The obvious candidates here are the European communist countries, which have *per capita* income sufficiently high that they might consume large quantities of chocolate, could their

---

* The continued urbanization of the population, with its resultant changes in consumer-preferences away from domestic products and towards imported goods, will also add to this pressure.
† *Daily Graphic*, 27 March, 1962.
‡ *Economic Bulletin*, vol. 6, No. 2, 1962.

governments be persuaded that this was desirable. It is also possible that some Asian countries and others would provide another substantial market, if the terms were suitable.* Any reduction in export production costs through greater efficiency could also be a valuable stimulus to greater sales.

The other main hope on the side of exports is that Ghana will be able to reduce her reliance on primary products (and cocoa in particular) and develop important new exports. There are very few signs of this happening at the moment. Eventually, of course, the Volta Project will provide important aluminium exports, but that is to look some way ahead.

He would be an optimistic man, however, who would pin his faith on these possibilities. In fact, if the taxes imposed in the 1961 Budget make goods imported from the industrial countries more expensive than in neighbouring countries, Ghana's re-export of manufactured goods to these countries will decline and those neighbouring countries may instead start re-exporting to Ghana.†

The conclusion to be drawn from all this prognostication is that unless fairly drastic action is taken, further large deficits will only be avoided by an increasingly tight regime of direct controls. As the IMF men would say, Ghana is faced with a 'fundamental disequilibrium' calling for equally fundamental solutions. The final question to be examined, therefore, is what effective lines of action are open to Ghana?

There may be some temptation here to slip into determinism and to argue that Ghana's trade balances will be fixed by world forces and that there is not much Ghana can do about it. In support of this thesis can be brought the evidence that it is a long-term and world-wide phenomenon that the primary producing countries are experiencing difficulties in their balance of payments, due mainly in recent years to a deterioration in their terms of trade—a deterioration which is liable to continue in the future.‡ Since the terms of trade are not under Ghana's control, it might be argued, there is very little she can do about her balance of payments.

However, this will not stand up to examination. Strictly speaking, it is not the case that there is nothing that Ghana can do about her

* See Green, *op. cit.*, p. 28.
† Recorded re-exports in 1961 were about £G2 million; the true figure was probably larger.
‡ See G.A.T.T., 'Trends in World Trade', *Economic Bulletin for Africa*, January 1962, notes a continuation of this trend.

terms of trade. As we have seen, she has had a great deal of influence on the terms through variations in the quantity of cocoa exports.* More important, we have also seen that the recent deficits cannot wholly be explained in terms of movements of import and export prices. At worst, the terms of trade have merely aggravated what would in any case have been a deteriorating situation, with import volumes increasing faster than export volumes.

As short-term measures the deficits could be met by borrowing from abroad and by running down Ghana's international reserves. Further borrowing will certainly be attempted, although Ghana's indebtedness is now large and the interest and repayment costs of the existing loans and credits will themselves impose an additional strain on the balance of payments in the future. In any case, past experience does not altogether encourage reliance on foreign capital: it is hard to come by and is so discontinuous that there is no prospect of being able to look to an assured inflow of capital over a period of years.

There obviously can and will be some running down of reserves, but equally obviously there is a limit to this: another deficit on the scale of that of 1961 would eliminate the reserves altogether.

Thinking of longer-term solutions, there are three major possibilities to discuss: (1) internal deflation; (2) devaluation of the Ghana pound; (3) strict limitation of imports by the continued use of direct controls.

Whatever was the case in the 1950s, it would probably be generally agreed that at the present time Ghana is suffering from both internal and external disequilibrium, with trade deficits combined with inflationary pressure (partially suppressed) at home. With such a combination of circumstances the text-book solution would be for the Government to embark upon deflationary policies that would both kill off the danger of inflation and, by reducing incomes and, possibly, costs and prices, reduce the demand for imports and encourage exports.

The trouble with the text-books is that they largely confine themselves to equilibrium within a static framework. As yet, economic theory provides no clear guidance when internal and external disequilibria are combined with the need for a high and sustained rate of economic growth. Given the high priority accorded to

* Of course, this influence would have been less if import prices had not been so constant.

122

economic development in Ghana, it is inconceivable that deflationary policies could be pursued to such an extent that the balance of payments problems would be solved.

But to say that a *general* policy of deflation is not a possible solution to the problem is not to say that nothing could be done along these lines. There is a strong case for imposing a damper on sectors of the economy where this will not have a seriously adverse effect on development: the 1961 Budget and the policy of 'wage restraint' can be best understood in this light. But the room for manoeuvre is not great; a selective use of the damper will not produce a solution by itself.

One obvious area where there is scope for more positive action is the marketing board's payments to the cocoa farmers. The need here is for a far more conscious policy to be adopted towards the *incomes* of the cocoa farmers as distinct from the price they are paid. It was suggested in the first article that changes in cocoa incomes have had an important impact on imports. Frequent fluctuations in these incomes can only have a destabilizing effect not only on Ghana's international trade but on her whole economy, yet virtually no attempt seems to have been made to use the marketing board to smooth out these fluctuations.

While it is true of recent years that the prices received by the farmers have been more stable than the prices received by Ghana on the world market, it is also the case that the incomes received by the farmers year by year have been *less* stable than the revenue earned for Ghana by cocoa sales.*

It is not suggested, of course, that a policy of income stabilization would be without complications. But it is suggested that the adoption of a conscious policy in the sphere of cocoa incomes would be an important step in the direction of both internal and external stability.

The second possibility is a devaluation of the Ghana pound. The possible use of devaluation is not something that the authorities should shy away from. It is something that merits close and detailed investigation. At the moment only guesswork is possible. The issue revolves round the elasticities of the demand for and supply of Ghana's exports, and the elasticities of the supply of and Ghana's demand for her imports, and the 'income' effects of such a move.

---

* In the period 1954–5 to 1959–60 the average year-to-year fluctuation in Ghana's earnings from cocoa exports was 13 per cent p.a., while the fluctuation in marketing board payments to farmers was 15 per cent p.a.

The following are the writer's own guesses as to the nature of these factors.

On the side of exports and on the crucial assumption that other competing exporters like Nigeria would not follow suit and devalue their currencies, it seems quite possible that the demand for Ghana's exports would be fairly elastic—her cocoa, timber and so on would become more attractive in relation to other suppliers. Ghana would thus be in a good position to increase her export earnings provided that she could meet the extra demand for her goods. But this may well prove very difficult, at least for a time. Supply would probably be inelastic, for a considerable period—the output of agricultural products and minerals can only be much increased after a lengthy gestation period. The immediate impact of devaluation on Ghana's foreign exchange export earnings would therefore be limited.

Turning to imports, there is every reason to expect Ghana's elasticity of demand to be very low—this is a widely noted phenomenon of underdeveloped countries and stems, of course, from the absence in most fields of home-produced substitute commodities. So the fact that domestic prices of imported goods would be increased may lead to a relatively slight reduction of imports. Foreign elasticities of supply, on the other hand, can be taken as very elastic because Ghana only represents a very small part of the total demand for the products she imports. There is therefore no question of the reduction in Ghana's demand forcing down the world prices of her imports. Overall, then, expenditures on imports may not be greatly reduced by devaluation.

The general conclusion suggested by the guess-work is that devaluation may bring a smallish improvement in the balance of payments in the short run and a more substantial improvement over a long period, when export supply elasticities have improved and more import substitutes are being produced at home—all this on the assumption that competing export countries do not retaliate.*

One other point to bear in mind is that the devaluation tends to have an inflationary effect—which may be serious where trade is a very important element in the economy as a whole and where that economy is already subject to inflationary pressures.

It is not the intention here to advocate devaluation; still less to

---

* The conclusion that devaluation is more likely to be effective in the long run than in the short is a familiar one. However, the gestation period is likely to be longer in primary production than in manufacturing.

suggest that this is at present an active possibility. The point to be made is that devaluation is a measure which is worth detailed investigation.

This leaves the third possibility—the one that has been adopted—of the physical limitation of imports by a system of licensing, quotas, exchange controls and the like. By itself, this is no solution at all, for the deficits will reappear the moment the controls are removed. It also distorts the international price mechanism and reduces 'the gains from trade' in a way that is not true of the other policy measures already discussed. But it possesses the advantage of having a dependable and more or less immediate effect (as the 1962 import figures show) and has more to be said for it than economists are sometimes inclined to admit, if it is combined with other measures that will go to the root causes of the trouble and in time render the direct controls unnecessary.

The general rather pessimistic conclusions reached above about the speed, reliability and effectiveness of the alternative lines of action suggest that the regime of restrictive trade controls now in operation in Ghana is necessary and likely to remain for some years to come. But it should be considered as a stop-gap pending a more fundamental solution, and not as a self-contained policy requiring no further action.

26. THE FISCAL SYSTEM AND THE GROWTH IN NATIONAL INCOME

P. OKIGBO

In this chapter we propose to focus on the interrelationship of the fiscal system and the national economy by analysing the burden of the taxation on the private sector of the economy and the role of government as a prime mover in capital formation. The level of government receipts and expenditures influences the level of the national income; even more, it affects the way in which the private sector disposes of its income. The government's fiscal operations, by direct and indirect taxation, can induce an expansion or contraction of private business activity. Through its investment policy the government can influence the pattern, the volume, and the direction of aggregate investment. For these reasons our proposal to focus on these questions will underscore the role that the government plays in the growth of the Nigerian economy and in the finance of development.

Our starting-point is the impact of government taxation on the gross product of the private sector. Tax receipts take away from households and companies some of the income that they may wish to spend on consumption or on investment goods or that they may wish to have lie idle. Government disbursements on the purchase of goods and services, on the other hand, place resources in the hands of households and companies. But the government, through its disbursements, does not put into the same pockets the identical amounts that it takes from them through taxation. Consequently the government's budgetary operations lead to a redistribution of income. In addition, through its deficits or surpluses in its fiscal operations, the government influences the expansion or contraction of economic activity.

Table 1 sets forth the government's tax receipts as a proportion of the gross product of the private sector. The latter figure is obtained by deducting from the gross domestic product the net output of all

126

public authorities represented by the following components: coal mining, public utilities, rail and air transport, government, and the marketing boards. On the side of tax receipts we have taken direct taxes on persons and companies, all indirect taxes levied by all tiers of public authorities—local, regional, and federal.

The entries in column 3 of Table 1 (government tax receipts) exclude the surpluses of the marketing boards, representing the difference between the total external receipts for those export crops controlled by the boards and the disbursements by the boards to the producers. The addition of this element (column 5) significantly alters the picture: gross receipts by the public authorities increased from £29·4 million to £64·9 million in 1950 and from £103·9 million to £116·0 million in 1960. In Table 2 government tax receipts are further divided between direct taxes (on companies and persons), indirect taxes, and marketing boards' surpluses for the years 1954, 1957, 1960, and 1962.

Table 1. *Burden of government tax receipts on the private sector, 1950–60*[1]

Year	Gross product of private sector	Government tax receipts (excluding marketing boards)	Tax receipts as percentage of product of private sector	Government tax receipts (including marketing boards)	Government tax receipts (including marketing boards)
	£ million	£ million	%	£ million	%
(1)	(2)	(3)	(4)	(5)	(6)
1950	459·4	29·4	6·4	64·9	14·2
1951	533·9	40·5	7·6	60·0	11·2
1952	553·6	51·4	9·3	87·9	15·9
1953	601·8	58·5	9·7	94·7	15·7
1954	694·3	67·5	9·7	118·7	17·1
1955	777·4	83·4	10·7	99·7	12·8
1956	786·7	77·5	9·8	118·5	15·1
1957	853·4	81·1	9·5	92·8	10·9
1960	966·2	103·9	10·8	116·0	12·0

[1] Source: Reports of the Accountant General; Annual Reports of the Marketing Boards; The Nigerian National Plan 1962–8; P. N. C. Okigbo, *Nigerian National Accounts, 1950–7*.

Table 1 shows that the proportion of the gross product of the private sector taken by government through direct and indirect taxation (excluding taxation by marketing boards) was relatively low. In 1950 the proportion stood at only 6·4 per cent, rising to 10·7 per cent in 1955. It declined to 9·5 per cent in 1957, but rose subsequently to 10·8 per cent in 1960. In the ten years between 1950 and 1960 the proportion remained at just under 10 per cent.

When we introduce marketing boards' surpluses (Table 1, column 6) we see that the proportion reached its highest level in 1954, when it was 17·1 per cent. After 1956 it was well under 15 per cent. This level is clearly low relative to the budgetary needs of most developing countries. Table 2 shows that receipts from personal income taxes represented an abnormally low proportion of government tax receipts from all sources. It suggests that there is still considerable room for manoeuvre and ... that there is a great deal more to be done by the regions to increase the yield from existing revenue sources.

Table 2. *Government tax receipts, 1954–62* (£ million)

	1954	1957	1960	1962
Direct taxes				
Personal income taxes	19·8	25·0	27·5	23·4
Taxes on company incomes	5·6	5·3	4·8	5·8
Indirect taxes				
Customs and excise	42·1	50·8	71·6	74·1
Marketing boards' surpluses	51·2	11·7	12·1	15·0 (estimated)
Total	118·7	92·8	116·0	108·3

The future of the governments of the Federation lies, therefore, in the fullest possible exploitation of the existing revenue sources. The inelasticity of the receipts from direct taxes with respect to the national income is due primarily to difficulties encountered in extending the tax base beyond the wage and salary earners who are the main contributors. The ease with which self-employed persons (who form the bulk of the taxable population) escape the tax net shows that a more vigorous and efficient fiscal administration should bring in a substantial increase in direct tax receipts. Receipts from company taxes can be increased not necessarily by raising the rate, which is high enough at 40 per cent (relative to other parts of the world), but by re-examining the system of reliefs and allowances from gross profit. It should be noted that a good many of the existing companies already benefit from tax holidays and other forms

128

of relief. The system whereby only 55 per cent of gross profit is liable to tax would appear to be relatively generous. However, whatever the change that may be contemplated, there is the danger of an erosion of public confidence in the business and financial community, especially among potential overseas investors. In any case, the magnitude of the receipts suggests that additional revenues from this source cannot significantly alter the structure of government revenues.

Indirect taxes—customs and excise—which constitute the bulk of the tax receipts of the governments, seem to us to offer the greatest opportunities. The increases in customs duties in April 1962 led to a sharp drop in customs revenue, from £61·7 million* in the calendar year 1961 to £55·6 million in 1962. The danger here is that if adequate care is not taken, the increases in duty will lead to immiseration of the poor, because of the regressiveness of these taxes, and to inflation of the cost of development. Certain luxury goods, however, can be taxed still more heavily—large-capacity passenger cars, certain categories of textiles, radios and television sets, etc.

Marketing board margins are now a vanishing source of revenues. The surpluses of marketing boards have been declining since 1954 (except for an unusual rise in 1956), as shown by these figures for 1950–62:

	1950	1951	1952	1953	1954	1955	1956	1957	1960	1962
Marketing boards' surpluses (£ million)	35·5	19·5	36·5	36·2	51·2	16·3	41·0	11·7	12·1	15·0 (estimated)

These surpluses represent gross margins out of which the marketing boards have to meet their trading and sales expenses. It is clear, therefore, that the extent to which the government can draw on marketing boards for the finance of development is now severely limited. The boards cannot push producer prices down to a point where investment in new plantings is endangered. The decline in external receipts for exports since the late 1950s has forced the boards to dip into their reserves for the stabilization of producer prices. In the decade 1950–60 the finance of development in Nigeria has been carried to a large extent on the back of the peasant farmer. It is the farmer who has borne the brunt of the taxation through indirect taxes and direct imposts by the marketing boards.

One of the objectives of the government s tax policy is to reduce the fluctuations in the level of economic activity through the impact

* Excluding export duties and excise taxes.

of the government's revenue and expenditure policy on the level of total demand for goods and services. Downward swings in the level of economic activity leave resources idle, while inflationary pressures make it more difficult to maintain the rate of economic growth. In the Nigerian experience the dependence of the public authorities on indirect taxation for the bulk of public revenues hampers the use of fiscal instruments for reducing fluctuations in activity. Consequently the authorities have to rely more on automatic, built-in stabilizers than on deliberate policy instruments.

Such built-in stabilizers are to be found in those elements of the revenue structure that are very sensitive to changes in the level of economic activity. For example, personal income taxes and company taxes show greater sensitivity to fluctuations in the national income than do customs and excise taxes, which are more sluggish. If the government wishes to use direct taxes as instruments to combat fluctuations it has to strengthen the flexibility of those taxes with a view to making their response more automatic. Unfortunately the yields of these taxes constitute only a very small fraction of government revenues.

By their nature, indirect taxes tend to be more regressive in their incidence than direct taxes. With the expansion of the needs of the regions and the local authorities, the role of indirect and inherently more regressive taxes will tend to increase. As dependence on this source of revenues increases, the overall fiscal system will be less responsive to changes in national income unless the built-in flexibility of the revenue structure is improved. For this reason there is a strong need to look at the tax base with a view to broadening the yield from direct taxation.

The relevant considerations are the size of the tax base relative to the actual income of the individual and corporate taxpayers, the items of income in the tax base that are responsive to changes in the level of activity, and the effectiveness of the progression in the tax rates at the base. Although practice varies from region to region, nearly all of what is described as employment income enters the tax base. Of this category of items that enter into the base, salaries and wages form the largest single element.

Any flexibility sought in the system must be achieved not through changes in the rates themselves, but through the broadening of the concepts of income for purposes of taxation. Policy can profitably be directed to a widening of the concept to cover those items of income that respond relatively quickly to changes in activity and those items whose deduction would tend to offset fluctuations.* Over 90 per cent of all taxable individual returns are subject to tax in the first income bracket (this group, however, pays only 48 per cent of the total tax). Consequently graduation in the tax schedules is of interest mainly to the remaining 10 per cent. It is therefore possible to strengthen the flexibility of the system by improving the exemption system and by additional marginal graduation at the bottom of the scale. The argument for this type of improvement has not been compelling in Nigeria because of the upward trend in business activity since the end of World War II. Further, the administrative cost of further graduation at the bottom of the income scale has often appeared enormous. However, this is a possibility that can be borne in mind for application, should the need arise.

At Nigeria's stage of development it would be difficult to apply the concept of a neutral tax policy—that is, a policy whose impact on the growth of consumption and investment leaves the balance to be maintained by the interplay of market forces. In the first place, if market forces were to determine the pattern of development, many existing monopolistic and oligopolistic elements in the economy would become entrenched. These are to be found in most of the branches of activity except perhaps in agriculture and in retail trade. In the second place, the public authorities have taken the view that there is a need for deliberately accelerating the pace of development. One of the main objectives of public policy may therefore be to correct the inadequacies of the market forces.

Differences may exist in the actual economic circumstances of some groups that may require differential tax treatment in order to assess the tax base correctly and apply the correct tax rates to each category of income. In a federal fiscal system, equity may demand variations among geographic or economic areas to offset differences in fiscal capacities. The application of this criterion may prove much more satisfactory than the adjustment of fiscal receipts through grants or transfers passing through the Central Authorities. It would remove one of the sources of contention in the administration of federal grants by eliminating the necessity for the donor authority

---

* Income excludes gifts and allowances, which can be substantial for the upper income bracket. See my *Distribution of National Income in African Countries*, International Economic Association, Conference on the Distribution of National Income, 1964.

to direct the recipient states or fiscal units in the allocation of their expenditure.* Alternatively, differential rates may be applied to different groups of income recipients within the same income category. For example, in Britain from 1947 to 1961 the tax rate on company profits was differentiated between dividends and undistributed profits, with a view (although the effectiveness is disputed) to influencing the apportionment of profits between reserves and dividends.†

Preferential treatment, on the other hand, involves a smaller tax burden for a taxpaying unit than the economic circumstances warrant. The public authorities can attempt to reduce the area of preferential treatment. Whereas there are economic justifications for differential tax treatment of particular income groups, the overall effect of preferential treatment is to distort the use of resources. By making the tax burden lighter for particular activities or particular units than the economic circumstances warrant, the public authorities would be encouraging idle capacity in other activities.

In Nigeria the government has decided to regard some types of activity as more essential to the progress of the economy than others. This judgment is reflected in the types of initial allowances for plant and equipment relative to those for buildings and in the tax reliefs granted to pioneer industries. To minimize the distorting effects of preferential treatment, the tax laws must leave some room for correcting a bad judgment in particular cases. This is especially important in a country like Nigeria, where each concession evokes other claims with a snowball effect, leading to a constriction of the tax base.

In principle, tax concessions should be as general as possible. Since customs and excise taxes constitute the major source of revenue in Nigeria, it is in this field that corrective action needs to be taken to reduce the distortion of the growth of the economy due to preferential treatment of selected industries. For the health of the economy encouragement should be given to new entrants to prevent existing favoured beneficiaries from entrenching themselves and perpetuating the inefficiencies that the preferential treatment may engender.

* See J. M. Buchanan, 'Federalism and Fiscal Equity', reprinted in American Economic Association, *Readings in the Economics of Taxation* (London, Allen and Unwin, 1959), pp. 93–109; see also the references cited therein.
† See A. Rubner, 'The Irrelevancy of the British Differential Profits Tax', *Economic J.*, vol. 74, June 1964, pp. 346–59.

It is possible to use tax policy to encourage the growth of small businesses and to make them more competitive with the larger established concerns. It is common knowledge that the larger firms have access to a line of credit and finance denied to smaller firms that have to rely on internal finance for the growth of their business. The government can, therefore, use a differential tax policy to encourage small businesses by making it possible for them, through fiscal methods, to finance the expansion of their business out of internal funds more easily than can the larger concerns with access to other sources of funds.

The role of government in the finance of development

The United Kingdom Colonial Office, which until 1960 had responsibility for the administration of Nigeria, promulgated in 1945 a Colonial Development and Welfare Act authorizing the expenditure of special funds for the economic and social development of colonial territories. These funds were available not only for capital construction but also for recurrent expenses on personnel engaged in approved schemes and projects. The colonial governments were accordingly requested to submit plans and programmes spread over ten years to serve as a guide in allocating the funds between territories and, within territories, between schemes. In response to this request the government of Nigeria formulated a ten-year plan (1946–55) setting forth a number of schemes in respect to which an application would be made for Colonial Development and Welfare funds.

The Nigerian authorities had no guiding set of principles or priorities in framing this ten-year plan; the major consideration was to formulate schemes that would attract the funds set aside by the United Kingdom government. There was apparently £50 million available in the ten-year period for capital installations and for personnel. Very little thought, however, was given to the problem of carrying the schemes forward after the Colonial Development and Welfare funds ran out.

In 1950 it was realized that ten years was too long a period for planning the development of a country that was rapidly changing in structure. A decision was therefore taken to break the interval into two five-year periods and to formulate a new plan for the five years 1951–6. Much of this new plan was a revision and updating of the original plan in the light of performance difficulties—shortages of men and materials.

133

The most significant step was taken in 1953 when the International Bank for Reconstruction and Development, at the request of the government of the Federation of Nigeria, sent a mission to survey the economy and to prepare a development programme. Its report,* published in 1954 on the eve of the establishment of the regional governments, served as the basis for the 1955–60 programme. The economic programme of the federal government alone amounted to £91·3 million, with an estimated recurrent burden of £4·2 million per annum.†

Meanwhile constitutional changes had been introduced that made it necessary to prepare the 1955–60 plan on a regional basis. The federal government saw its own responsibilities as consisting in the provision of a country-wide system of communications in the widest sense of the term, provision for higher education and fundamental research, provision for security and prisons, provision of loan finance for the statutory corporations, and provision of services in the federal territory of Lagos.‡

The approach of independence in 1960 led the Nigerian authorities to extend the span of the planning period to 1962. The 1955–60 programme was accordingly revised and extended to enable works undertaken within the period to be completed. In the meantime the energies of the governments were directed toward preparing the first national plan, which was launched in 1962 and with the finance of which we are now concerned. It is a matter of interest that between 1955 and 1962 the Nigerian public authorities budgeted for a capital expenditure of nearly £300 million.

The role of government in the economic development of the country can be seen from the data in Tables 3, 4, and 5, showing the government's share in the gross domestic fixed investment for the period 1951–61.

Government investment rose from £11·5 million in 1951 to £70·5 million in 1961, while gross fixed investment from all sources rose from £37·8 million to £172·1 million in the same period. The government's proportionate share remained remarkably stable, in the range of 30 to 35 per cent, between 1951 and 1957 but rose steadily to 41 per cent in 1961. Investment by households has been

* International Bank for Reconstruction and Development, *The Economic Development of Nigeria* (Lagos, Government Printer, 1954).
† *The Economic Programme of the Government of the Federation of Nigeria 1955–60*, Sessional Paper No. 2 of 1956.
‡ *Ibid.*, p. 4.

Table 3. *Gross fixed investment by type of sponsor, 1951–61 (£ million)*

Sponsor	1951	1952	1953	1954	1955	1956	1957	1960	1961
Government and public corporations	11·5	18·2	19·9	25·8	29·9	33·5	37·4	60·1	70·5
Major companies (including voluntary agencies, such as missions)	11·2	15·6	18·5	18·7	24·3	28·9	31·3	20·8	18·1
Households	15·1	20·2	20·4	27·0	31·5	38·8	44·2	73·6	83·5
Total	37·8	54·0	58·8	71·5	85·7	101·2	113·0	154·5	172·1

Table 4. *Distribution of gross fixed investment by type of sponsor, 1951–61 (percentages)*

Sponsor	1951	1952	1953	1954	1955	1956	1957	1960	1961
Government and public corporations	30·4	33·7	33·9	36·1	34·9	33·1	33·1	38·8	40·9
Major companies	29·6	28·9	31·5	26·2	28·4	28·6	27·8	13·8	10·6
Households	40·0	37·4	34·6	37·7	36·7	38·3	39·1	47·4	48·5
Total	100·0	100·0	100·0	100·0	100·0	100·0	100·0	100·0	100·0

consistently higher than investment by government. It should be noted, however, that this takes the form mostly of dwellings. What is significant is the rate of increase in the investment by the government between 1951 and 1961, relative to the investment by major companies over the same period.

Further, the overall distribution of investment by type of asset is dominated by the pattern of distribution of government investment. In Table 5 we see that civil engineering works (roads, buildings, railways, harbours and rivers, waterworks and wells), including maintenance of roads and bridges, have constituted the largest single group of government investment expenditure. Next in importance were buildings—offices and dwellings. By 1961 investment expenditure on plant, machinery, and equipment by the government stood at about one-fifth of the expenditure on civil engineering works. By contrast, the major private companies spent most of their investment funds on plant, machinery, and equipment.

135

Table 5. *Government fixed investment by type of asset, 1951–61*
(£ million)

Type of asset	1951	1952	1953	1954	1955	1956	1957	1961
Buildings	3·2	5·1	7·1	8·1	7·4	9·0	12·8	26·7
Civil engineering	5·1	7·1	7·0	10·3	13·6	14·9	13·0	31·5
Vehicles	0·7	1·7	1·2	2·2	3·7	2·3	3·8	4·1
Plant and machinery	2·0	3·8	4·1	4·5	3·9	6·6	6·7	5·6
Plantations and mineral explorations	0·5	0·5	0·5	0·7	1·3	0·7	1·1	1·6
Total	11·5	18·2	19·9	25·8	29·9	33·5	37·4	70·5

That public authorities accounted for no less than one-third of the gross fixed investment underlines the importance of public capital programmes for the future growth of the Nigerian economy. It emphasizes the role that the plans for the public sector are bound to play in the future and the problems that the finance of these plans raises for the country. The part played by the government as an engine of development and economic change becomes magnified when we recall that the government's share in the gross fixed investment is expected to rise from 33 to 35 per cent in the decade 1951–61 to nearly 67 per cent in the decade 1962–72. This is bound to have important consequences for the future structure of the private sector as the public agencies acquire a pervasive influence in the ordering of economic activity. The national plan is, however, optimistic about the future role of the private sector. The large role assigned to the public sector in the 1962–8 planning period arises from the 'intention of the Governments to provide the basic services needed for a more vigorous growth of the private sector in future Plan periods'.*

The national development plan for 1962–8 was formulated (see Table 6) in the expectation that the gross domestic product would grow at 4 per cent per annum, that investment would maintain a proportion of 15 per cent of the gross domestic product, and that the composition of this investment would be biased in favour of the more directly productive forms. It was estimated that by 1967–8 the level of government consumption would stand at 204 per cent of the 1960–1 level and that it would amount to £841·3 million in the plan period. Private consumption allowed for was estimated to grow by only 2·8 per cent per annum, just a notch above the then estimated

* *National Development Plan 1962–8*, p. 36.

136

rate of growth of population. This last objective is a severe one; the success of the authorities in implementing the plan will doubtless depend very much on the extent to which the growth of private consumption can be held down by fiscal and other measures.

Table 6. *Planned expenditures in the framework of national accounts, 1962–8 (in constant 1960 prices) (£ million)*

	1960	1961	1963	1964	1965	1966	1967	Totals
Private consumption	922·0	986·5	1013·8	1036·8	1062·3	1094·6	2235·1	6319·1
Government consumption	85·0	110·2	118·9	132·9	154·4	162·4	173·3	843·1
Gross fixed investment	158·0	179·7	186·8	193·6	200·6	207·2	215·4	1183·3
Increase in stocks	10·0	5·7	3·6	3·4	3·5	3·3	4·1	23·6
Import surplus	62·5	83·9	77·6	76·1	74·7	86·4	81·8	480·5
External debt service	—	5·1	5·9	10·9	16·4	26·6	27·9	92·8
G.D.P.	1112·5	1203·3	1251·4	1301·5	1353·5	1407·7	1464·0	7981·5

The plan envisaged a total capital programme of £676·8 million in the public sector and a total recurrent expenditure of £996·5 million (including the existing commitments). The problem for the fiscal authorities is, therefore, twofold: First, how can the public authorities carry the recurrent burden without breaking the back of the taxpayers? Second, how can the capital programme be financed? It was estimated that the finance of the capital programme of the public sector would come partly from new internal resources (£262 million) and partly from external aid (£327 million), with the balance of £87 million explained in part by an assumed under-spending (£23 million) and in part by a gap not covered by foreign aid (£64 million).

In practice, of course, it is the search for additional recurrent revenues required to meet the burdens generated by the capital programme that raises the most serious difficulties. Even if the funds can be found for building a school or a hospital, the search for funds to run it after construction is often a much more serious problem.

The financial plan proposed for the public sector can be represented as in Table 7. From this table it is evident that the recurrent revenues of the public authorities are expected to increase by one-

third in the plan period. Just over half of this increase is expected
to come from new taxes and fees, mainly from direct taxes on
personal and company incomes and from indirect taxes. Our discussion in the first part of this chapter indicates that the scope for
substantial increases from this source, through increases in rates, is
limited. In the first two years of the plan only £11·0 million out of
the projected £146·5 million was realized. Nor was the government's
experience with changes in customs tariffs in 1962 very rewarding.
Further increases in customs duties were introduced in August 1964,
but it is still too early to assess the full impact of these changes on
the public revenues.* There may still be some room for increasing
the yield from company taxes by raising the effective tax paid from
the current level of 22 per cent of gross profit to about 30 per cent.
This should bring in an additional £3 million per annum. Similarly
there may be some room for tightening up the administration of

Table 7. *Sources of funds for the public sector plan, 1962–8 (£ million)*

1. Revenues from existing sources		834·4
2. Revenues from new sources		262·0
Taxes and fees	146·5	
Profits of statutory corporations	89·0	
Profits of marketing boards	26·5	
	262·0	
3. Total recurrent revenues		1096·4
4. Receipts from other sources		123·2
Cash balances	57·5	
Central Bank borrowing	33·7	
Nonbank borrowing	32·0	
5. Total	123·2	1219·6

taxes and fees. However, the only guess that can be made for the
future is that the target of £146·5 million by 1967–8 appears too
optimistic.

Between 1954 and 1962 the governments of the Federation
endeavoured with great success to realize substantial savings in their
recurrent budgets. This procedure assured them that funds would be
available for development purposes through transfers from the
recurrent budget to the capital development fund. By 1962 the level
of recurrent budget surpluses had fallen sharply, and by 1964 the
surpluses of the federal government had practically disappeared.

* These changes may yield up to £15–20 million per annum, but they are bound
to raise the cost of development through their impact on the price of imports.

Growth in National Income

The following figures, showing the government's budgetary surpluses from 1957 to 1964, illustrate the plight of the federal government. (The figures represent millions of pounds.)

Table 8. *Budgetary surpluses of the federal government, 1957–64* (*£ million*)

	1957	1958	1959	1960	1961	1962	1963[1]	1964[1]
Revenue retained by federal government	41·92	46·22	50·36	70·29	67·57	68·85	69·96	79·40
Budgetary surplus	10·40	17·53	10·63	17·25	14·54	8·70	2·99	1·39
of which contribution to development fund	4·00	6·34	3·00	7·14	8·43	4·24	2·80	1·35
Other	6·40	11·19	7·63	10·11	6·14	4·46	0·19	0·04
Surplus as percentage of revenue	24·8	37·9	21·1	18·1	21·5	12·6	4·3	1·8

[1] Data are derived from Approved Estimates of the Federal Government for 1963–4 and 1964–5; for the period 1957–62, the data are taken from the audited accounts.

With the prospect of these surpluses disappearing, the governments of the Federation have to undertake a more serious control of expenditures and simultaneously a thorough search for ways to improve the yields from existing revenue sources, if they are to maintain the normal level of services.

The statutory corporations that were expected to realize a profit of £89·0 million from their current operations were by 1964 turning to their governments for financial support, not only for the continuation of their capital programmes but also for their recurrent obligations. Consequently the continued support of the operations of the corporations by the governments would make it even less likely that any significant saving could be made in the ordinary budgets of the governments.

The regional governments raided their marketing boards so much in the 1954–62 period that these boards have very little reserve left for use, should the need arise to stabilize producer prices. Their gross margins, out of which they meet their sales and marketing expenses, have fallen to a level far below that of 1950–4. Even if they are able to save the £26·5 million assigned to them in the plan, the marketing boards will find that the need to build up their reserves for stabilization purposes will considerably reduce their capacity to contribute this amount in full. The picture could, of course, change if the world market prices for exports should rise well above the current level.

The financial plan in Table 7 also envisages the raising of another £123 million through drawing down cash balances and reserves and through borrowing from the Central Bank and from the non-bank public. All these avenues were tried in the first two years of the plan. The reserves available to the Central Bank and the governments have already been drawn down heavily, partly as a result of government fiscal operations and partly as a result of pressures on the balance of payments.

Borrowing from the non-bank public has been less than successful. The Central Bank has had to come to the rescue of the governments by taking up nearly £20 million of the development stock in the first two years of the plan. In other words, borrowing both from the Central Bank and from the non-bank public has been undertaken at a faster rate than was envisaged. Consequently the Nigerian public authorities are finding that the finance of the national plan will impose a severe strain on their fiscal resources and capacities. Although the tax burden may appear light, it should be recalled that it falls heavily on a relatively small segment of the population. What is therefore indicated is an immediate and vigorous method of extending the tax net, coupled with the possibility of changing the rates. On the success with which the fiscal authorities meet this challenge will the fulfilment of the objectives of the national plan depend.

27. THE COST AND FINANCE OF EDUCATION

P. WILLIAMS

[. . .] Cost and finance

... For a developing country as poor as Uganda, and with a heavy dependence on the world market prices of a few commodities, the financing of education imposes unusual strains. Because of sharp and often rapid movements in the price of coffee and cotton, it is extremely difficult to plan public expenditure ahead satisfactorily. It is all too easy at times of economic boom to use windfall surpluses to increase too much the rate of capital investment in schools and colleges. It is true that it may be possible to turn off the capital expenditure 'tap' when recession next hits the economy, but it will not be feasible to avoid the wake of recurrent costs that inevitably follows a spell of capital spending. On the other hand, against the dangers—political as much as economic—of taking on excessive liabilities in respect of teachers' salaries and maintenance costs of buildings must be set the risks of going too slowly. Uganda is a country in a very great hurry and the present mood is to take a few chances on the continuation of the prosperity of the last two or three years. It is hard to blame Uganda for this approach. With economic conditions being as uncertain as they are, she can't avoid taking some chances. She must risk either going too far too fast, or keeping resources unnecessarily idle.

Education is very expensive in Uganda. At the primary stage equipment needs are not great and the simple buildings required are normally provided 'free' by voluntary agencies or as a result of community effort. Nevertheless education at this level costs about £9 per pupil p.a. in government schools. This may not seem a high figure, but it has to be compared with the average income per head of about £25, and it means that the aggregate cost for primary education of £4–5m. accounts for a sizeable proportion of both national income and public expenditure. That education is expensive is even more true at secondary level, where the total recurrent cost per pupil of a completed six years up to Higher School Certificate

141

has been working out at over £1,000 in boarding schools and £560 in day schools if one includes capital charges. At Makerere University College, the average annual cost per student (excluding capital charges) is about £800–900 p.a., plus £125 p.a. boarding charges: or about £2,800 for a complete degree course of three years.

Why should education be expensive in a country where the annual *per capita* income averages only about £25? There are several reasons. First, teachers' salaries. These are not perhaps excessive by comparison with earnings in other professions, and indeed it could be argued that teachers' salaries need substantial improvement, especially at the secondary level where many potential teachers have been tempted into other jobs. But in relation to the national income, and more particularly that part of it which becomes available through taxation for public spending, the level of teachers' salaries constitutes a serious obstacle to rapid expansion. Thus, in primary schools the untrained teacher starts at £126 p.a.; the trained vernacular teacher at £132 p.a.; and the person with eight years' primary schooling and four years' training starts at £189 p.a. and is on a scale rising to £354 p.a. £189 is seven to eight times the national income per head in Uganda: in Britain, a trained primary teacher starts at about £730 p.a., or under one and a half times the British national income per head. Richard Jolly, in his *Planning Education in Developing Countries*, gives a most interesting comparison (see Table 1) between Uganda and Ghana showing how the actual levels of teachers' pay have been very similar in the two countries, despite the wide difference in income per head in Uganda and Ghana. The very high rate of remuneration of the better qualified teachers in Uganda in relation to *per capita* Gross Domestic Product is also clearly revealed.

In Ugandan primary schools, where the standard enrolment per class is forty pupils and teacher-class ration is 1:1, the average teacher cost per pupil works out at about £6–£7 per head. But in senior secondary schools at S1–6 level, the teacher cost per pupil is eight times as much at over £50 per head (£75 if various expatriate allowances are also added), partly because of higher salaries—the average teacher salary (cost to the Uganda Government: not including any overseas aid element) is £1,000–£1,200 at this level—but also because the teacher-pupil ratio is higher. At Makerere University, staff are on more or less international scales rising from £1,000 for a local assistant lecturer (£1,300 plus education allowances for expatriates). These salary levels in the upper branches of the education system are certainly no less than those required if teaching is to have an attraction comparable with other professions. The scales have in fact been fixed with the general level of civil service and other salaries in mind. But such salaries are too high in relation to Uganda's present resources and are a formidable obstacle to further expansion. Their inappropriateness will become more and more obvious over the course of the next decade or so as the supply of CSC—and HSC —holders for the teaching profession becomes more plentiful.

The teachers' salaries' element in educational costs has risen very

Table 1. *Starting salaries of teachers in Uganda and Ghana as a multiple of per capita GDP 1955–61 (selected years)*

	1955	1957	1959	1961
Uganda				
Per capita GDP (£)	23·8	23·7	22·9	23·0
Teachers' salaries as a multiple of *per capita* GDP				
Vernacular	2·8	3·3	5·0	5·8
Primary	4·6	5·0	5·1	8·2
Junior Secondary	8·6	9·9	10·3	13·0
Senior Secondary	21·0	24·3	25·2	26·6
Graduate—pass	27·2	28·6	29·6	33·4
hons	29·1	30·6	31·7	36·0
Ghana				
Per capita GDP (£)	56·5	59·0	66·6	72·0
Teachers' salaries as a multiple of *per capita* GDP				
Unqualified Primary	1·5	1·7	1·5	2·0
Cert. B Primary	2·0	2·5	2·3	2·8
Middle School (Cert. A)	2·7	3·2	2·9	3·5
Senior Secondary	7·6	7·8	6·9	7·0
Graduate	10·6	10·5	10·2	9·5

Source: Richard Jolly, *Planning Education in Developing Countries*.

quickly despite Uganda's poverty. To some extent, this has been the result of teachers ageing and so earning increments on their scale. Another contributory factor is the constant up-grading of entrants to the teaching force, causing a progressive shift in the teacher force towards higher qualifications and higher pay.* This is likely to become

* Richard Jolly points out that the typical teacher today in Uganda is the primary teacher starting on £189 p.a., whereas in the 1930s the typical teacher would have been a vernacular teacher earning £15 p.a. Of course, the value of money has declined and the quality of education now being given by the 'typical teacher' is much improved. Even so, the cost implications of the change are certainly startling.

a major issue in future because, although more well-qualified Ugandans should become available for teaching in the next decade, it may be too expensive to replace poorly qualified teachers with well-qualified ones on much higher salary rates. But the main reason for increased cost is that teachers' pay scales themselves have risen enormously. Taking 1947 as 100, the index of starting salaries of teachers in 1964 stood at 554 for vernacular teachers, 416 for primary, 400 for junior secondary, and 678 for senior secondary: the corresponding actual rates of starting pay are £132 p.a., £189 p.a., £312 p.a., and £612–£828 p.a. (depending on qualifications of the teachers).

Second, the cost of buildings has been too high. This has partly been a matter of excessive standards, partly that the buildings that have been erected have involved high maintenance charges. It has been calculated that the average replacement cost of a Cambridge School Certificate place is about £500 (it has been considerably higher than this in the past—over £800 in many cases), and that annual interest and amortisation charges on this sum may represent a figure as great as annual teaching costs per pupil! The new girls' secondary school at Tororo, built from U.S. aid funds, has involved capital costs of as much as £1,250 per pupil. At Makerere, the cost of halls of residence has been working out at over £1,000 per student —largely because prestige buildings have been erected with a good-sized room to each student, and all the furnishings which one might find in a well-equipped university in Britain. Many European and American students at Makerere have found the provision of amenities considerably better than at their home universities. The European and American tradition of penurious students starving in garrets is one of those that East Africa has not adopted.

The high cost of buildings is closely connected with the pattern of boarding education in Uganda at secondary and tertiary levels. While the need for boarding education is regrettable from an economic point of view, there are of course compensating benefits—in particular the social and political contribution to nation-building and the educational value resulting from the mingling of students from different areas and backgrounds. To a great extent boarding education has been an inevitable result of the distribution of population in the country and of the low levels of income which have made it necessary to confine educational opportunities to the minority. Uganda has few towns of any size and over most of the country the people live in scattered farms rather than villages. In order to create schools of economic size, pupils have had to be drawn from an area much wider than could be reached by the vast majority of pupils on a day attendance basis. If one includes interest and amortisation charges on capital, then secondary boarding places in Uganda are nearly twice as expensive as day places to maintain, and it has been calculated that in boarding schools the buildings and equipment connected with boarding work out at about 75 per cent of total capital costs. Of course, the lower cost of day schooling is not all saving, for the parents of day children have to make provision for their food and board. At the University the remedy, traditional in advanced countries, of cutting down on the capital costs of student accommodation by putting students into lodgings could only be used on a modest scale in Kampala. The number of houses where students could be found suitable lodgings is rather limited, though one would have thought that some accommodation would be available if an intensive effort were made to find it. From an economic point of view, this would certainly be preferable to extending halls of residence at present lavish standards, and might be cheaper than the doubling up in rooms and introduction of the cafeteria system which Makerere is now beginning to introduce. But if fresh residential building on the campus itself is to take place, it might be worth thinking of far more radical changes such as the provision of dormitory-type accommodation supplemented by liberal quiet-room space. Those who throw up their hands in horror at such ideas should reflect that it is not post-Robbins expansion in Britain that is under discussion, but facilities for very poor countries with an average national income of £25 a head.

Another aspect of the situation where many of Uganda's secondary schools are boarding schools located in remote areas is the need to provide staff housing. This is generally provided to European standards, since most of the staff tend to be expatriate, and three-bedroomed houses cost at least £3,500, often more (the Ministry of Education hopes to reduce this to £2,800). In spite of the relatively low level of wages in Uganda, building is expensive because of the high cost of imported building materials by the time they have been brought up from the coast and because building is often inefficient in the absence of experienced foremen and clerks of works. Since many secondary schools are aiming at three streams, S1–4, their twelve classes will need about 18 to 20 teachers on present staffing ratios. Non-teaching staff also require accommodation, so that it is not surprising that housing requirements account for a high proportion of the costs of building a secondary school. It is not only European staff, however, who are entitled to receive housing—the same applies to Ugandans. In many areas, government assistance with the provision of housing is justified because there may be no houses that teachers could buy or rent on the open market. But in other places there seems to be little reason—apart from non-discrimination between the races—for this privilege inherited from the colonial regime. Unless care is taken, Uganda will find herself continuing to provide at great expense the benefit of free or subsidized housing to her indigenous civil servants long after the majority of expatriates have departed.

Fourthly, high teacher-pupil ratios have undoubtedly been a cause of undue expense in the past, even though the position has steadily improved. Many primary schools and secondary schools have not in the past attained the standard enrolment per class (at present forty in primary schools, thirty-five in classes S1–4, and twenty in S5 and 6) expected of them. This has been partly due, particularly at primary level, to duplication of schools on a sectarian basis in some areas and it may be partly accounted for by the dispersed pattern of population, making it difficult to maintain a standard size school in some places. It is also the result of pupils dropping out, for economic or other reasons, leaving smaller enrolments in the upper forms of primary and secondary schools—something that teachers (as opposed to the education authorities) are not unwilling to see. In the higher reaches of secondary technical education and at university level, the higher teacher-pupil ratio reflects the distorted structure of the educational pyramid in Uganda, with its shortage of facilities at secondary level and the consequent shortage of candidates for higher courses. The teacher-pupil ratio for the University of East Africa as a whole is about 1:6·5 and is about 1:8 at Makerere. This is a far cry from the ratio of 1:15 envisaged at Tananarive in September 1962 at the Conference on the Development of Higher Education in Africa. And it is difficult to see how the figures can be much improved upon so long as the University authorities set their sights on a target of under nine contact-hours a week between a member of staff and his students. A final reason for the excessive number of staff in relation to the pupils they are teaching is the heavy reliance above primary level on expatriate staff and the practice of giving them their overseas leave in blocks of three months or more at a time. This means that staff may frequently be away on holiday during term time and the overall staff-pupil ratio has to be higher to make this possible. It has been calculated that in senior secondary schools the teacher-class ratio could be reduced from 1·5:1 to 1·25:1 if this difficulty could be overcome; and, as indigenous staff take over, the ratio will, of course, fall.

When it comes to meeting these high costs, the resources of Uganda are limited. As compared with an advanced country, Uganda is in any case handicapped, like many developing countries, by the age-structure of her population. With at least 42 per cent of her population under 14, Uganda has proportionately far more children to educate and, even allowing for her smaller proportion of retired people, comparatively fewer people of working age to provide the resources to support the education system. Britain, by contrast, has only about one-quarter of its population under 15. Partly as a result of the differences of age structure and partly because of the high unit costs of education in Uganda, it has been estimated that it would cost seven to eight times as much in relation to GDP in Uganda as in Britain to attain a given level of primary school enrolment.*

With education already accounting for over one-quarter of the Central Government budget (if one includes the local authority grant element), it is almost inconceivable that a higher proportion of Uganda's government revenue could be devoted to it. Yet the present proposals of the Uganda Government for expanding education would require additional recurrent and capital expenditure by 1970—on a scale involving doubling educational outlays in six years at present costings. This in turn presupposes a Government budget twice as big as at present. For an economy so dependent on the level of world coffee and cotton prices, it is indeed a tall order to guarantee such an increase. There could hardly be a gloomier omen than the Budget Speech by the Minister of Finance in June 1965 which gave the following comparison for the years 1964–5 and 1965–6:

	£m. Recurrent Revenue	£m. Recurrent Expenditure	£m. Surplus/ Deficit
1964–5 revised estimates	32·9	28·2	+4·7
1965–6 estimates	28·8	33·3	−4·5

* See Ursula Hicks in *The Economics of Educational Expansion in Low-Income Countries*, Three Banks Review, March 1965, who actually gave (p. 15) a figure of ten times.

Will the plans prove feasible from a financial point of view? Almost everything depends on the strength of Uganda's economy over the period ahead. If things go badly, what alternatives are there? First, taxes might be adjusted so as to yield greater revenue for the Central Government. This is politically difficult to put into effect and would have far-reaching repercussions on the rest of the economy, but ways of increasing sources of public finance must nevertheless be found urgently. A second possibility, that a greater part of the responsibility for financing education might be devolved on to local authorities or parents, seems hardly possible so long as the structure of local government is so weak or when parents have been encouraged to hope that *free* education may not be too far away. Thirdly, it may also be considered justifiable to finance students in higher education by means of individual loans, repayable either in money or in service at below market-rate salaries. A degree course costs perhaps £2,500 of public money and yields the individual beneficiary additional income to the same amount over not more than five or six years. Student loans were mentioned as a possibility by the Castle Report and merit serious investigation. The final possibility is increased external aid, and this is discussed in Chapters 4–7. None of these suggested alternatives precludes the necessity of introducing cost-reducing measures.

PART VI

ECONOMIC DEVELOPMENT

---

28. IMPORT SUBSTITUTION AND EXPORT PROMOTION AS AIDS TO INDUSTRIALIZATION IN EAST AFRICA

B. VAN ARKADIE

1. General considerations

During the coming years the East African countries will be seeking to encourage the growth of local industries. This paper sets out the relative merits of export promotion and import substitution as alternative strategies for industrial development in East Africa. It also attempts to measure the rate of industrial growth which would be attainable with a strategy of import substitution.

Import substitution creates domestic industries to produce for local use goods which were previously imported. Export promotion involves the creation and expansion of domestic industries for the production of goods for the export market. The two strategies are not mutually exclusive. An industry could expand to supply both domestic and foreign markets. . . .

2. The East African case

It has been the conclusion of all the commentators consulted in preparing this paper that the correct strategy in the East African situation is import substitution.* The only exception to this proposition is the possibility suggested by many of these writers that trade between differing African countries be developed; the argument is usually presented as a case for import substitution in a wider market area. Most of the suggested expansion in manufactured exports

---

* See the World Bank Reports, *The Economic Development of Uganda*, p. 270; *The Economic Development of Tanganyika*, p. 232; *The Economic Development of Kenya*, p. 162. (All page references are to the Johns Hopkins University Press editions.) Also, Arthur D. Little Inc., *Tanganyika Industrial Development*, p. 18; B. F. Massell, 'Industrialization and Economic Union in Greater East Africa', *The East African Economic Review*, December 1962, p. 111–16.

outside the greater East Africa area consists of projects for extending the local processing of primary products (e.g. food packing and processing). Greater East Africa refers to East Africa plus some or all of the following countries: Burundi, Congo (Leopoldville), Ethiopia, Mauritius, Rhodesia, Zambia, Malawi, Rwanda, Somalia, Sudan.

The first step in evaluating this support for the import substitution case is to ask whether likely possibilities exist and to compare them with the possibilities of export promotion. The rest of this section takes up this question, attempting to identify the likely industries which will provide major scope for import substitution. The issue is only partly treated, as this discussion is mainly from the demand side and does not involve any very rigorous treatment of the cost side. The final section of the paper provides a rough measure of the total impact of an import substitution programme on the rate of industrial growth during the coming decade.

Perhaps the strongest evidence for the import substitution case is the current extremely high degree of import dependence of the East African economy. The extent of this dependence is indicated by Table 1, in which East African imports and monetary gross domestic product are compared. Imported goods have amounted to more than one-third of gross domestic product during the past decade. The decline in the relative importance of imports since 1955 is to be explained more by the decline in fixed capital formation, than by success in import substitution. There was a peak in capital formation in 1955, the same year as the peak in imports, while there was a sharp decline after 1957, matched by a decline in imports. Investment spending, particularly on machinery and equipment, has a much higher import content than other forms of spending.

Evidence on the import content of different types of spending is shown in Table 2. This table is based on the EACSO analysis of imports classified according to end use, modified so as to allocate producers' materials and spares and accessories according to their end use. Table 2 presents such a reallocation of 1961 data.* Thus an attempt has been made to allocate imports among consumption activities, investment, agricultural inputs, and general industrial inputs. For East Africa as a whole consumption imports are about half the total, investment imports about a third. The fourth group is a class of materials which it is not possible to classify according to

* 1961 is chosen because allocation of imports by end use is available for Uganda, Kenya and Tanganyika as well as East Africa as a whole for that year.

end use—packaging materials, metals not used in the building industry, industrial chemicals.

A rough test of import dependence is to compare the imports in Table 2 with final expenditures in the national income and product accounts. Official estimates of final expenditures do not exist for East Africa. However, certain crude yet interesting comparisons have been made in Table 3. These figures indicate the high degree of import dependence particularly in so far as capital goods expenditure is concerned. For East Africa as a whole something like one half of capital formation in 1961 consisted of imported goods, while for consumption the import content was about one-quarter. This degree

Table 1. *East Africa: total imports and domestic product, 1954–62* (£ *million*)

Year	Total imports	Monetary gross domestic product
1954	117·5	286·2
1955	149·0	320·2
1956	133·8	337·3
1957	140·1	356·6
1958	121·4	359·8
1959	121·5	375·7
1960	133·9	400·3
1961	135·2	404·3
1962	135·5	409·7

Total net imports by country, 1954–62 (£ *million*)

Year	Uganda	Kenya	Tanganyika
1954	25·2	60·3	32·0
1955	34·0	71·5	43·5
1956	28·1	69·8	35·9
1957	28·9	72·0	39·3
1958	27·0	60·9	33·6
1959	25·5	61·5	34·5
1960	26·0	70·1	37·8
1961	26·5	68·9	39·7
1962	26·2	69·5	39·8

Sources: East African Statistical Department, *Economic and Statistical Review*, various issues, and East African Common Services Organization, *Annual Trade Reports*, various years.

of import dependence is very high, particularly when it is considered that a quarter of gross domestic product in East Africa derives from services, rents, and government employment, which can have only a negligible import content.

Table 2. *Allocation of imports according to end use: East Africa, 1961*
(£ *million*)

1. Consumption activities	
a. Food, Drink and Tobacco	12·2
b. Finished Durable Goods	8·0
c. Finished Non-Durable Goods	27·1
d. Manufactured materials used in domestic production of consumers' goods	6·2
e. Spares and Accessories	1·5
f. Crude materials used in domestic production	2·3
g. Miscellaneous	5·4
	62.7
2. Agriculture inputs	
a. Agriculture Inputs	2·3
3. Investment activities	
a. Producers' Capital Goods	27·6
b. Spares and Accessories	4·7
c. Building Materials	8·4
	40·7
4. Industrial inputs (not elsewhere classified)	
a. Explosives and Chemicals	2·6
b. Crude materials N.E.C.	0·3
c. Manufactured Goods N.E.C.	9·4
d. Mineral Fuels and Lubricants (not classified as consumers' goods)	7·5
e. Metalliferous Ores and Metal Scrap	0·9
	19·9
Total Imports Retained for Domestic Uses	124·7
5. Re-exports	10·4
Total imports*	135·2

* Figures do not add to total because of rounding.

Sources: East African Statistical Department, *Economic and Statistical Review*; *East African Retained Imports: Stage of Production and End Use Analysis, 1960–1961*; East African Common Services Organization, *Annual Trade Report.* 1961.

Table 3. *Approximate relation of retained imports and final expenditure, 1961*

A. East Africa

	Final expenditures (£ million)	Retained imports ((£ million)	%
	(1)	(2)	(3)
Gross domestic expenditure (net of indirect taxes)	404	125	31
Of which:			
Capital formation plus capital goods, spares and accessories	79	41	52
Central Government current spending and net foreign investment	64	*	*
Consumption plus local government spending	261	63	24
Unallocated imports		21	

* Not readily estimable.
Sources: same as for Tables 1 and 2.

The feasibility of import substitution cannot be tested solely through such evidence on the level of overall import dependence. It is also necessary to investigate the viability of individual industries.

The characteristics of a potential import substitution industry are the existence of a domestic market large enough to consume more than the minimum output necessary for the viability of at least one plant, the possession of simple enough technical characteristics, and either a high transport cost content (e.g. cement) or the acceptability of protection for that type of product (e.g. cotton textiles and other consumer goods). Thus the production of machinery is limited at the early stages of development for a number of good reasons—the complicated and changing techniques, the low transport cost content as a percentage of final value, the small size of the domestic market, and the importance of established reputations for competence and service (as compared, for example, with a standardized building material susceptible to straightforward specification and quality analysis).

As development proceeds the possibilities for import substitution will change with the growth and evolution of the structure of domestic demand on the one hand and the increasing sophistication of local skills and adequacy of the industrial infrastructure on the other.

Properly, any exercise assessing the feasibility of a particular

153

industry should therefore involve both a projection of demand and of the likely cost structure after the initial learning period. Short of such a series of detailed project analyses, however, the broad outlines of existing import substitution possibilities can be identified from an examination of existing import patterns. Using the 1961 import bill, an assessment of the possibilities for the coming decade can be attempted.

The experience of countries which have previously pursued the import substitution path suggests that textiles and clothing provide an early candidate for major industrial development. This is borne out by the East African evidence, which suggests that for the immediate future this provides the most serious posssibility. In 1961 total imports of textiles, yarns and fibres (including jute), clothing, leather consumer goods, footwear and parts of footwear were £24 million for East Africa as a whole. In a number of lines firms are already in successful operation and the market is large enough, with enough room for specialization, for there to be development in each of the East African countries.

There are certain disadvantages, however, to concentration on the textile industry. From the point of view of underdeveloped countries as a group it has already been noted that other low income countries are major exporters of textiles to East Africa (particularly India and Hong Kong). Also, textiles and clothing share with most primary products an income elasticity of demand generally less than unity, i.e. spending on these items grows less fast than income.* Thus world textile production has grown much more slowly than manufactured production as a whole during the past sixty years.† This, plus the fact that the textile industry is an early candidate for import substitution in most industrialization programmes, suggests that export possibilities for this industry are poor.

Therefore, although the development of a textile industry will be the major feature of East African industrial development during the coming decade, this will be almost entirely for the home market.‡

The second major possibility, iron and steel, is more speculative, because of the large scale of installation needed for successful operation. At present, East Africa imports considerable quantities

---

* For a survey of evidence on this subject see A. Maizels, *Industrial Growth and World Trade*, pp. 336–9.
† Total manufacturing output grew over three times as fast as textile production, 1899–1959. Maizels, *op. cit.*, p. 335.
‡ And adjacent countries in the event of preferential trading arrangements.

of basic iron and steel products (133,000 tons in 1961; 125,000 tons in 1962).

The value of these imports in 1961 was £8·7 million.* Steel demand is volatile, being closely dependent upon building and construction activity; in 1955, at the peak of the mid-50s boom, 174,000 tons of basic steel products were imported. Although such figures contribute heavily to the East African import bill, they still represent a small steel market by the standards of modern steel industries.† On the other hand, steel industries do operate elsewhere with outputs within the East African consumption range (e.g. in Rhodesia and Egypt) and, at the early stages of development, steel consumption tends to grow faster than growth in gross domestic product.‡

If a domestic steel industry were able to supply a substantial proportion of local steel needs, construction activity would be that much less of a strain on the balance of payments, making substantial increases in construction possible at the government initiative. As a rough estimate, with ambitious development programmes, East Africa could well be consuming as much as 300,000 tons of basic steel products by the end of the decade. There is therefore a serious possibility of development in this industry, although the diversity of steel forms is such that it is not likely that one plant could supply all needs.§

Paper and paper products, rubber products (mainly tyres and tubes), soap and cleansing preparations, accounted together for imports into East Africa of £7·8 million in 1961. Soap is already substantially supplied domestically. By the end of a decade the same should be true of paper and rubber products.

East African imports of chemicals (basic products, not including pharmaceuticals, cosmetics, soap, etc.), fertilizers, disinfectants and insecticides, and paints and varnishes were £4·4 million in 1961.

---

* This includes primary forms, sheets, plates, hoops and strips, railway track material, and tubes, pipes, fittings, castings and forgings. In addition, £1¾ million of simple manufactures of iron and steel were imported in 1961— this includes nails, wire, metal doors and frames, netting, etc., but does not include tools or more complicated manufactured products.

† See Duncan Burn, *The Steel Industry 1939–1959*, pp. 270.

‡ Maizels, *op. cit.*, p. 239; and United Nations Economic Commission for Europe, *Long Term Trends and Problems of the European Steel Industry*, Geneva 1959, pp. 119–22.

§ For a more cautious view of the wisdom of establishing steel mills in developing economies see Walter P. Blass, 'Steel Mills for Developing Economies', *Social and Economic Studies*, vol. 2, 2 June, 1962.

Although demand for chemical products is likely to grow faster than overall economic growth,* particularly as a result of development policies in agriculture, it must be admitted that this 'industry' covers a heterogeneous group of products. Moreover, as they are mainly agricultural or industrial inputs, heavy protection would be undesirable. This industry is therefore likely to develop only insofar as it is able to compete with imports, as is the case with some insecticides and fertilizers.

In addition to these fairly substantial industries there are numerous fairly small industries which could provide a role for small-scale enterprise in the industrial sector. The following list is of commodities each accounting for imports ranging from £150,000 to £750,000 in 1961 which might well be produced domestically: building materials (other than steel, paper and wood), glass (plate glass, etc.), glassware, chinaware and plastic householdware, household sanitary fixtures, furniture and fixtures, matches, wood products and plastics (not included elsewhere), brooms and brushes, toys and games, pens, pencils and office supplies (not included elsewhere).

A number of manufactured imports have not been considered in this analysis: electrical equipment, tools, all kinds of machinery, pharmaceuticals, metals other than iron and steel, miscellaneous chemical products. The presumption is that import substitution is unlikely in these areas in any major fashion, though it may be feasible for selected products. It might also be possible to begin assembly of transport equipment in East Africa, but for the immediate future this is unlikely to result in a high proportion of the total value being transferred to domestic value added, and heavy protection to encourage such a transfer is probably premature.†

Also, the considerable food imports into East Africa (£11·5 million in 1961; £12·3 million in 1962) provide some opportunity of manufacturing expansion through the growth of food processing industries which have already been established in East Africa. With urbanization and the expansion of income, the domestic market for processed foods will grow. Food processing should develop throughout East Africa and make its contribution to manufacturing value added both for the domestic and the export market.

There are two important pieces of *prima facie* evidence that East

* Maizels, *op. cit.*, pp. 287–8.
† Although higher taxes to discourage consumption of such items as these which enter the consumer budget may well be in order.

Africa will have little opportunity to expand manufactured exports in the near future. Kenya, which has the most developed manufacturing sector in East Africa and possesses a distinct locational advantage over Uganda and much of Tanganyika for purposes of international trade, is hardly less dependent on primary goods for export earnings.* Although 'manufactured goods' exports under the S.I.T.C. classification accounted for as much as 13 per cent of the Kenya total in 1961, this percentage was largely illusory as two-thirds of this total was essentially primary production.†

The second piece of negative evidence is the level of protection existing industries require in the domestic market from competitors who would have to be met on equal terms, or even at a transport cost disadvantage, if competing in some third country. Thus of the fifteen principal manufactured products exchanged in inter-territorial trade in 1962, four had tariff protection of 33⅓ per cent, five at 25 per cent, three at 12½ per cent, two had specific rates amounting to at least 25 per cent *ad valorem*, and only one (insecticides) was free of protection.‡

Kenya has succeeded in exporting substantial quantities of cement, mainly to countries in which she possesses a transport cost advantage (Mauritius, Aden, Réunion in particular). Kenya has also established a small export market in canned foods, notably meat and pineapples (1961, gross value of £1·8 million). Tanganyika has a meat packing industry which accounted for exports of £1·8 million in 1961. A canning industry may be viewed as being at least in part in the industries sector.

For the immediate future, the further processing of foodstuffs and other primary products would seem to be the main source of manufacturing value added in the exports sector. The other major possibility is the development of the tourist trade. This invisible export has the desirable property that it decreases dependence on primary products for foreign exchange earnings, although it does not contribute to industrialization as such.

Despite the existence of these export possibilities, the examination

* Exports are a much less important source of domestic income, however, because of the much greater progress already achieved in import substitution in Kenya. Also Kenya's primary exports are much more diversified.
† Soda ash, wattle bark extract, and copper.
‡ See Dharam Ghai, *Territorial Distribution of Benefits and Costs of the East African Customs Union*, paper prepared for the University of East Africa Conference on Federation, Nairobi, 26–30 November 1963.

of the range of industrial possibilities does suggest that for the coming decade import substitution is the more feasible strategy for industrial development.

3. Estimating the impact of import substitution

Although the survey of possibilities briefly attempted in the previous section confirms the existence of import substitution possibilities, it is still necessary to assess the total impact of an import substitution programme, to see if it is likely to provide sufficient industrial expansion. Excluding any possibilities in food processing or machine assembly, the disaggregated analysis of the previous section included commodities resulting in imports worth £51 million in 1961.

Approaching the problem at the aggregate level, it is possible to define broad categories of import spending which would provide the market for import substitutes. The advantage of the more aggregative approach is that it allows for the effect of the considerable restriction of the range of consumer goods which is likely to accompany an aggressive import substitution programme. As protection increases the consumer will substitute in his budget the limited range of domestic products for the much more diverse range of products previously imported. The size of the market for domestically produced goods therefore depends partly on the degree to which consumers are willing to substitute one good for another in the consumer budget in response to relative price changes. In the extreme, if consumer goods imports are virtually eliminated through prohibitive tariffs and quotas the consumer will be forced to purchase whatever goods are available on the domestic market—night clubs might become substitutes for imported cars. Short of such a stringent view of the process, however, it is possible to identify broad categories of commodities for which demand can be substantially shifted from imports to the use of potential domestic products.

Finished manufactured products as a group (excluding agricultural and industrial inputs, food, drink and tobacco, building materials and miscellaneous imports—i.e. postal packages) accounted for imports of £68·9 million in 1961.* By comparison, value added within East Africa in the manufacturing sector was only £36·3 million.† However, from the discussion in the previous section it is clear that

---

* That is, items 1b, 1c, 1e, 3a, and 3b in Table 2.
† Cotton ginning, coffee curing, and sugar manufacturing are not counted as manufacturing for this purpose.

even at the aggregate level a more specific estimate of substitution possibilities must be made. For reasons suggested above it seems likely that during the coming decade such opportunities are likely to be found in non-durable consumers' goods, building materials, and to a lesser extent agricultural and industrial inputs (excluding fuels and crude materials—the latter because of the concern with manufactured products in this analysis). These items amounted to a £56 million import bill for East Africa in 1961.* This compares with the total import bill for the categories covered in the detailed analysis of the previous section amounting to £51 million.

These estimates of the likely limits on import substitution possibilities are in gross terms. To translate them into effects on domestic value added it is necessary to allow for the fact that even if they are produced domestically, some of the inputs will be imported. Further, in evaluating the effect of import substitution on the growth of value added in manufacturing, it is necessary to recognize that some of the material inputs will originate in the primary sector.

Some estimate of the adjustments necessary to allow for these effects can be made from data available on the structure of the Kenya economy. The Kenya Survey of Manufacturing, 1961, indicated that, for industry as a whole, value added was 38 per cent of gross output.† From the same source it may be estimated that about 33 per cent of the materials used by Kenya industry were imports. These figures are aggregate ratios, the figures for particular industries varying considerably. If these average figures can be taken as a rough guide for the future, however, it could be expected that net import substitution, i.e. additional domestic value added in the manufacturing sector, would be of the order of 65 per cent of the gross value of the substituted imports.‡ This percentage would be far less if the

* That is, items 1c, 1d, 2a, 3c, 4a, and 4c in Table 2.
† Value added is derived for the Survey in a somewhat different fashion than for the domestic product estimates; for our purposes the census concept, gross output net of materials and fuel purchases, is quite appropriate.
‡ This percentage is estimated as follows: if the proportion of material inputs to gross output is m (where $1-m$ is the proportion of value added to gross output) and the proportion of material inputs domestically produced is d (where $1-d$ is the proportion imported), then the domestic value added resulting from a given import substitution (where S equals the gross amount of imports substituted for) is:

$$(1-m)S+m.d. \ (1-m)S+(m.d.)^2 \ (1-m)S+.. = \frac{(1-m)S}{1-m.d.}$$

All these effects would not be in the manufacturing sector as some material inputs would be primary products.

159

substitution simply took the form of final stage assembly. On the other hand, Kenya industry is a considerable mixture, ranging from processing of locally produced goods to assembly of imported parts, so that the current structure provides at least a reasonable illustration of the net effect of future substitution.

Viewed in these crude terms, a hazardous estimate of the upper limit on net import substitution with existing levels of domestic spending is about £36 million of additional manufacturing value added.* Alternatively the disaggregated analysis of substitution possibilities with its somewhat lower total of £51 million gross, or £33 million in terms of estimated manufacturing value added, may be used. Both these figures may be conservative to the extent that import substitution of food and drink leads to manufacturing (i.e. processing) value added and the assembly and finishing of machinery and transport equipment proves feasible in East Africa.

This suggests that the total consumption of imported goods which might be displaced by domestic production during the coming decade is such as to result in additional value added roughly similar to the size of the existing manufacturing sector. However, in a growing economy both the market currently supplied by imports and that supplied by existing domestic industries will be growing. Therefore import substitution involves not only the capture of markets currently supplied by imports but also involves the satisfaction of additional demand which, in the absence of substitution, would have been supplied by a growing level of imports. Thus a growing economy provides an opportunity for import substitution even without any absolute decline in the imports of those lines in which domestic industries have been created.

Under the simplest assumptions, with demand for manufactured goods growing at the same rate as overall growth, this point may be illustrated with a simple arithmetical example. The strength of the point is increased, if it is realized that demand for manufactured goods is likely to grow faster than overall demand. Assume 'substitution possibilities', in the net sense defined above, are roughly equal to the size of the existing manufacturing sector. With a growth rate for the economy as a whole of 5–6 per cent per annum over a ten-year period, under the assumption of constant structure of demand, the market for the import substitution possibilities would rise to a level 1·6 to 1·8 times current manufacturing value added. Thus as the

* That is 65 per cent of the £56 million import bill.

Table 4. *Rates of growth in domestic manufacturing: value added resulting from alternative demand and substitution projections*

(Figures represent percentage rates of growth compounded annually over a decade)

Rates of growth of demand for manufactures[1]	Case A: Import substitution bill = manufacturing sector of beginning of period			Case B: Import substitution bill = three-quarters manufacturing sector of beginning of period[2]		
	(i) No net reduction of imports of substituted goods by end of decade	(ii) 50% net reduction of imports of substituted goods by end of decade	(iii) 100% net reduction of imports of substituted goods by end of decade	(i) No net reduction of imports of substituted goods by end of decade	(ii) 50% net reduction of imports of substituted goods by end of decade	(iii) 100% net reduction of imports of substituted goods by end of decade
	Rates of growth of domestic manufacturing value added					
5	8·5	10·7	12·6	7·6	9·5	11·0
6	10·0	11·9	13·6	9·1	10·7	12·0
7	11·4	13·2	14·7	10·4	11·9	13·2

[1] In the text it is assumed that the rate of growth of demand for manufactured products is the same as the overall rate of growth of the economy. This is not a necessary assumption; if the income elasticity for manufactured products is 1·2, for example, then a 6 per cent growth in demand for this sector will be achieved with a 5 per cent overall rate of growth, and the relevant rates of growth of domestic manufacturing value added with substitution will apply.

[2] The import substitution bill and the manufacturing sector are defined in values added terms. Case B is included to illustrate the effect of a more conservative assumption regarding substitution possibilities. Three alternative assumptions are made regarding the degree of net substitution (i.e. actual reduction in imports of substituted goods).

economy grows at 5–6 per cent, the manufacturing sector could achieve a growth rate of $8\frac{1}{2}$–10 per cent without any absolute reduction in the volume of substituted imports. With any net reduction the growth rate could be even higher. By the end of the decade a new set of substitution possibilities will appear.

A comparison of hypothetical possibilities is shown in Table 4, which shows the annual rates of growth which can be achieved over the decade under differing assumptions regarding the size of substitution possibilities and the success with which they are implemented. In practice it must be expected that somewhat higher rates of growth in manufacturing could be sustained because of the tendency for the demand for manufactured products to rise faster than the overall rate of growth. This table suggests that rates of industrial growth of the order of 10 per cent per annum could be achieved with an import substitution strategy and with an overall rate of growth of the order of 6 per cent per annum, without achieving self-sufficiency in those lines for which import substitution seems to be currently appropriate.

Whether this is a satisfactory rate of industrialization depends on the assessment of a number of issues not considered here relating to the broad development strategy. If it were considered desirable, for example, to pursue an industrialization strategy requiring a rate of growth of industry as high as 15 per cent per annum it seems likely that the range of items would have to be extended and the speed of expansion accelerated to the point where costs would rise markedly. In such a case export promotion might become a relatively more attractive proposition, with export subsidization in those industries already established. If, on the other hand, a rate of industrial growth of 10 per cent per annum is considered satisfactory, then it seems much more likely of attainment within a strategy predominantly directed towards import substitution. In the writer's judgment, a rate of growth of 10 per cent per annum in the manufacturing sector in the immediate future would be a highly successful performance, particularly in the light of overall constraints on expansion not explicitly considered in this paper.

29. COMMODITY EXPORT EARNINGS AND ECONOMIC GROWTH

G. BLAU

The high degree of economic dependence of the less developed countries* on their traditional exports of a limited range of primary products should be lessened *eventually* by the progressive development and diversification of their economies. Meanwhile, however, the very process of economic growth and diversification of these countries will inevitably continue to depend in large measure, in any case within the course of this decade, on the possibilities of expanding earnings of foreign exchange from these very same traditional exports for which, in many cases, the outlook in major markets, namely those of the high-income developed countries, is indifferent or poor.

This is the crucial problem facing the governments of the underdeveloped countries in their economic relations with the rest of the world and in the shaping of their own national development programmes. It is also the subject of this paper which comments on some of the main issues involved, in three parts. The first part considers the probable extent of continuing dependence, by 1970, of the economies of most of the less developed countries, and of their growth prospects, on the levels of their primary export earnings. The second part is mainly concerned with some key problems of the primary export sector as such, and the third with some possible forms of international action.

Part One: Commodity export earnings and economic growth— quantitative framework of reference

The traditional exports of primary products, predominantly of agricultural origin, account at present for no less than 90 per cent

* Throughout this paper, the group of *less developed countries* is meant to comprise the countries of Africa, Latin America, Asia and the Far East (excluding Japan and the Asian centrally planned economies). The terms 'less developed', 'developing', 'underdeveloped', and 'low-income' are used interchangeably throughout the text.

Table 1. *Exports from less developed countries to the rest of the world:
main categories only, 1959–61 averages*

	All exports		Primary commodities per cent of total	
	$ billion	Per cent of total	Incl. petrol	Excl. petrol
Agricultural commodities (food and raw materials)	10·9	54	60	83
Non-agricultural raw materials	2·3	11	13	17
Petroleum	5·0	25	27	–
All primary commodities	18·2	90	100	100
Manufactures	2·1	10	–	–
All exports from less developed countries to the rest of the world	20·3	100	–	–
Of which: To developed market-economy countries	19·2	95	94	92
To centrally planned economies	1·1[1]	5	6	8

[1] Almost entirely primary products.
Source: Summarized from Table 5 [not reprinted here – Editors], and from United Nations and FAO basic data.

of the combined foreign exchange earnings, from their total exports to the rest of the world, of the countries of Africa, Asia excluding Japan, and Latin America.*

Moreover, primary export earnings account for about 70 per cent of all foreign exchange inflows, including aid and other net long-term capital transfers, from the rest of the world to the group of less developed countries, as a whole.

The role of the primary export sector

In the light of these figures, it does not take much arithmetic to

* This is shown in Table 1, which also illustrates the predominant importance of the share taken by the developed market-economy countries (North America, Western Europe, Oceania and Japan). Of the total exports of $20·3 billion from the group of less developed countries to the rest of the world in 1959–61, $19·2 billion, or 95 per cent, went to the Western developed countries (including Japan). The *centrally planned economies* (U.S.S.R., Eastern Europe excluding Yugoslavia, and Mainland China) accounted for 5 per cent ($1·1 billion, consisting predominantly of primary products), though their imports in recent years have been growing at much faster *rates* than those of the Western developed countries.

164

see that even on very optimistic assumptions for large *percentage* expansions of earnings, or savings, of foreign exchange under any items other than primary export earnings, the main burden as a provider of foreign exchange will inevitably continue to fall on the primary export sector, in any case within the course of this decade.

At the same time, in contrast to the controlling influence of the primary export sector on the typical underdeveloped country's rate of economic growth, there is relatively little that such a country itself, or by itself, can do in turn to control the rate of growth of the earnings of its primary export sector. This adds to the importance of looking for possible forms of international action which can contribute to a solution of the problem.

The assurance of adequate levels of foreign exchange inflows from the rest of the world, while it is an essential condition for the economic progress of the less developed countries, is not, of course, a sufficient one. There is a great deal that the underdeveloped countries themselves must do to promote their chances of economic growth. The *main* effort will have to be their own. Similarly, because of the precariousness of the outlook, it is essential that underdeveloped countries do all they can individually and jointly to work for the optimal utilization of their resources by means of improved programming and, where possible, closer integration and resulting improvements in the division of labour and planned sharing of resources for the group as a whole, or for any of its main regions. Special care will have to be taken to strike the right kind of balance in the delicate process of weighing the relative advantages of export promotion and import substitution. This last-mentioned aspect forms part of the wider case for strengthened international programming which will be referred to below.

At the same time, for reasons well known, the problems of the less developed countries cannot be solved solely by taking the line that in view of the generally unpromising outlook for a major expansion of their export earnings beyond the levels calculated on assumptions of unchanged trends and policies in the rest of the world, they should rely, instead, on more rapid internal development or on expanding trade among their own number. Such advice, taken by itself, would not be much better than the kind of attitude which Marie Antoinette might have taken by asking why these countries cannot simply solve their own problems by having more cake, baking and saving more cake, or selling more cake to each other.

165

G. Blau

Quantitative framework of reference

While the importance of the prospective foreign-exchange problems of the underdeveloped countries has come to be increasingly recognized, their practical consideration in international discussions was handicapped until fairly recently by the lack of a sufficiently comprehensive framework of reference in quantitative terms. It is an astonishing fact, for instance, that the growth targets set by the United Nations Development Decade had to be framed and adopted in the absence of any adequate quantitative indications of the cumulative effect of commensurate rates of expansion of import requirements for the underdeveloped countries, taken as a whole, and of the prospective widening of foreign exchange gaps on current account which would result, for most of these countries, under assumptions of a continuation of current trends and policies for their export earnings.

This is now changing. Much more is still needed, but some beginnings have been made toward presenting such a wider framework. Of the four sets of general calculations available, two important ones were published in June–July 1963.* There are also more detailed projections available for particular commodities and groups of commodities.†

The four sets of general projections are each based on somewhat different assumptions, coverage, and techniques, but they are, none the less, broadly parallel in their results, showing the same gloomy story of the large 'hypothetical gap on both current and long-term capital account' which would result from accelerating growth, in the absence of major new changes of policies and trends.‡ I shall here

---

* The two most recent studies are: United Nations, *World Economic Survey*, 1962; Part I: *The Developing Countries in World Trade* (United Nations, 1963); and Alfred Maizels, National Institute of Economic and Social Research, *Industrial Growth and World Trade* (Cambridge University Press, 1963). The two earlier sets of projections were published by the United Nations Economic Commission for Europe: *Economic Survey of Europe in 1960* (United Nations, Geneva, 1961); and in the GATT annual report on *International Trade, 1961* (Geneva, 1962).

† See in particular, *Agricultural Commodities—Projections for 1970*; Special Supplement to the *FAO Commodity Review, 1962* (FAO, Rome, 1962); and also *Prospective Demand for Non-Agricultural Commodities* (United Nations, New York, 1962).

‡ In contrast to a prospective gap on current account, a 'hypothetical gap on both current and long-term capital account' is, of course, one that cannot happen, since to the extent that it cannot be closed or narrowed by means of further expansions of net foreign exchange inflows (or savings), due to the

take, as my starting-point, the calculations shown in the recent United Nations study.

Assuming a hypothetical growth rate of 5 per cent by 1970 for the total gross domestic product of the less developed countries, taken as a whole, the United Nations study calculates that the group's combined imports from the rest of the world would have to rise to a total of $41 billion (at 1959 prices), or about twice the 1959 volume.* At the same time, the earnings from all their exports to the rest of the world, which in 1959 had amounted to $20 billion, i.e. a total sufficient to pay for the bulk of their import bill in that year of $21 billion, could not be expected (on assumptions of continuing current trends and policies) to rise to more than $29 billion, an expansion of less than one-half over the 1959 level (all figures at 1959 prices).

On these assumptions, allowing also for the doubling of debt service charges and the other net service cost from $4 billion in 1958 to $8 billion in 1970, the deficit on current account would be quadrupled, rising to $20 billion by 1970. Thus, while it had been possible, in 1959, to meet the deficit on current account for the group as a whole by inflows of aid and other net capital transfers of a total of $5 billion, the near-doubling of all such net capital inflows to $9 billion in 1970 (a figure based on extrapolating past trends) would not be sufficient to meet more than 40 per cent of the prospective deficit on current account in that year. The remaining 'hypothetical gap' on both current and long-term capital account would amount to no less than $11 billion in 1970, unless new means could be found for reducing it.†

Nor is this the whole of the story. It must also be remembered that any such calculations based on an average growth rate for the gross national product of the group of less developed countries taken

---

possible effects of changes of trends and policies, the only alternative left, by definition, is to assume slower rates of growth in the underdeveloped countries than those which had been stipulated to start with in arriving at the size of the 'hypothetical gap'.

* 1 billion equals 1,000 millions.
† These projections are being re-calculated by the United Nations Secretariat and may undergo some revisions, in the light of modifications of assumptions. In any case, it is clear that any such calculations cannot be taken at their face value and must be treated with caution. Nevertheless, the approximate indications which they do provide are better than none. It is in this sense that they are here being used for purposes of general reference.

as a whole inevitably tend to understate the growth problems of the poorer members of the group. Their progress, starting from lower-than-average rates, would need to be faster than average, while their prospects for expanding export earnings, depending in typical cases on one or two agricultural products, with indifferent or poor market outlook, may be worse than average.*

The need for caution in interpreting any figures relating to a large group of countries is also illustrated, in this particular case, by the relative weight in the group's total exports of the value of oil exports which represents the earnings of just a few out of about a hundred countries, but accounts for more than one-quarter of the group's total earnings from primary exports to the rest of the world. The better-than-average prospects for oil exports are thus bound to have a disproportionate effect on the calculations of export prospects for the group as a whole.† If the oil-exporting countries are excluded, more than 80 per cent of the remaining group's total primary export earnings are found to be accounted for by agricultural products (as compared with merely 60 per cent for the larger group, including exporters of oil). The significance of the large agricultural component in the export earnings of the vast majority of underdeveloped countries results from the fact that agricultural exports have expanded at slower rates in volume, and suffered from sharper declines in prices, than nearly all other products (see Table 2). The high degree of dependence of individual under-developed countries on agricultural exports (and high degree of concentration, in most cases, on one or few agricultural products) is illustrated in Table 3.

Moreover, with population increasing in the underdeveloped parts of the world at an average rate of $2\frac{1}{2}$ per cent a year, a 5 per cent average rate for overall growth would merely allow for a growth rate of $2\frac{1}{2}$ per cent of GNP per head of population. It is evident that continuing high rates of population growth in most underdeveloped countries are not merely bound to retard rates of growth of real incomes per head, but they are also bound to contribute to the

* The 5 per cent growth target set by the General Assembly for the United Nations Development Decade was meant to represent a target rate for each of the less developed countries which had not yet reached that rate, not an average rate for the group as a whole.
† The inclusion of oil-exporting countries may also be one of the reasons why the United Nations study arrives at an actual (calculated) average growth rate of as much as 4·65 per cent a year for the gross national product of the group of underdeveloped countries taken as a whole in the 1950s.

prospective size of the 'gap' for any *given* growth rate of real incomes per head.

All figures presented so far were based on constant price relationships. If, instead, it were assumed that the average unit value of the assortment of imports required by the underdeveloped group in 1970 were 10 per cent higher (relative to the average unit value of exports which is assumed constant) than in 1959, the resulting assumed deficit on current account, in 1970, would be widened by a good part of the $4 billion, which would have to be added to the $41 billion import bill, as a result of the higher import unit values.

Table 2. *Indices of export prices (1950 = 100)*

	Exports from under-developed areas				From developed areas	
Year	Non-ferrous metals	Raw materials mineral	agricul-tural	Food	Food	Manu-factures
1954	126	106	83	124	107	115
1959	118	105	82	89	104	121
1960	122	102	85	85	103	123
1961	115	101	78	83	103	124
1962	117	102	74	83	105	126
1963 i	116	102	76	91	108	126
1963 ii	117	102	74	104	112	124
1963 iii	118	103	74	98	113	125

Source: *United Nations Monthly Bulletin of Statistics.*

While more recently the decline in the terms of trade of a number of primary exporting countries has been arrested or in some cases reversed, the underlying causes for assuming continuing problems of a structural character for primary export earnings remain unchanged.* If the adverse trends for primary products, which until recently had

---

* Moreover, even for the period of rising composite price indices for primary products, an assessment of individual price movements and of their causes, commodity by commodity, gives a diverse picture from the exporter's point of view. For some commodities, prices continued to fall, while the rising movements for others reflected in a number of cases the operation of short-term factors, aggravated in some cases by the effects of speculative activity for a small share of total market transactions, the so-called 'free market'. The influence of such short-lived peaks of 'free-market' quotations may well prove to be against the best long-term interests of primary exporters, by causing further disequilibrating forces to be set in train (and in particular by weakening the defences against protectionist longer term policies for competing high-cost industries in importing countries).

Table 3. *Agricultural exports as per cent of total exports: selected countries (based on 1958–59 averages)*

Exporting countries (illustrative)	All agricultural exports as per cent of country's total exports	Exports of major agricultural products (see list) as per cent of country's total exports	
Latin America			
Brazil	90	64	coffee, cocoa
Colombia	79	78	coffee, bananas
Costa Rica	91	80	coffee, bananas
Ecuador	95	92	bananas, coffee, cocoa
Honduras	86	67	bananas, coffee, cocoa
Mexico	59	34	cotton, coffee
Panama	94	71	bananas
Near East			
U.A.R.	80	75	cotton, rice
Syria	72	47	cotton
Sudan	94	70	cotton, gum arabic
Turkey	77	60	cotton, tobacco, fruit and nuts
Far East			
Burma	94	69	rice
Ceylon	98	82	tea, rubber
India	41	27	tea, cotton, tobacco
Indonesia	62	47	rubber, copra
Malaya	72	64	rubber
Pakistan	76	63	jute, cotton
Philippines	79	48	sugar, copra
Thailand	80	66	rice, rubber
Africa			
Ghana	80	66	cocoa
Nigeria	88	66	cocoa, groundnuts and oil, palm kernels and oil
Senegal	89	86	groundnuts and oil, palm kernels and oil
Ivory Coast	85	79	coffee, cocoa
Mauritius	95	94	sugar

Source: FAO Commodity Policy Section and Trade and Price Analysis Branch.

been operating without interruption since 1954 (particularly for agricultural exports), were assumed to continue, the results would show an even more gloomy story, particularly for the large number of countries which depend primarily on agricultural exports.

Commodity Export Earnings

How to close the 'gap'?

In considering possible effects of changes in trends and policies (at constant prices), it is logical to start off by taking account of the limited prospects of expansion of the largest and stodgiest item, namely that of primary export earnings, and then to go on to review the possibilities of policy changes in other directions where prospects of rapid expansion of earnings or savings on current account appear more promising, ending up with a 'residual gap' for which a further expansion of aid and other net long-term capital inflows, beyond the levels of expansion assumed on trend, is the only remaining way out, short of slower growth. The prospective size of net inflows of aid is a natural 'residual' which is bound to be influenced, in some measure, by the limits of expansions open to underdeveloped countries under all other sectors, whether earnings from exports or savings from imports.

My order of proceeding here will be slightly different, however, since my main purpose, at this stage, is to provide a framework for the further discussion of the future role of the primary export sector which is, therefore, taken as the 'residual', after allowing for expansions (or savings), due to possible policy changes under all items *other than* primary export earnings, while holding primary export earnings on trend. This is done in Table 4,† which shows the following three alternatives:

Alternative I: Assuming unchanged trends and policies; constant prices.

Alternative II: Allowing, on a purely illustrative basis, for possible effects of changes in trends and policies under all items *other than* primary exports; holding expansion of primary products on trend.

Alternative II/1: At constant prices.

Alternative II/2: Assumptions as under II/1, except for assuming a 10 per cent increase in the average unit value of 1970 imports, relative to the average unit value of exports (which is held constant).

The figures shown in Alternative I are those of the United Nations calculations. The additional expansions of earnings, and savings, as assumed on a purely illustrative basis under Alternative II, are also based, in part, on some illustrative data shown in the United Nations study, to which are added for good measure some further favourable

* (Not reprinted here—*Editors.*)

171

assumptions, for all items *other than* primary exports on as generous a scale as seems feasible rather than on what might be regarded as the 'most probable'. For one thing, no one really knows what the 'most probable' is, since we are dealing here with the effects of possible *policy* changes. By taking some 'probable upper limits' of expansions rather than 'probable expansions' as such, the resulting purely illustrative figures are not meant to stand up as such, but are merely intended to provide some broad framework of reference by showing a magnitude of what might be regarded as the 'probable hypothetical minimum residual gap' rather than as the 'probable gap' as such. The details of the assumptions made are given in the explanatory notes to Table 4.

The resulting figures show that in the absence of much more drastic favourable changes than those assumed on a generous scale for exports of manufactures, import savings, and expanded aid, including food aid, there would remain under Alternatives II/1 and II/2 a 'hypothetical probable residual minimum gap' of $3 billion and $7 billion respectively which, by definition, could be closed only by one or the other of the two remaining alternatives, or a combination of them: larger primary export earnings or slower rates of growth. The total earnings from primary exports which on these assumptions would be required to close the gap, under each of the three alternatives, are shown below.

	Alternatives			Alternatives		
	I	II/1	II/2	I	II/1	II/2
		($ billion at 1959 prices)			(per cent increase over 1959)	
1. Exports (assumed) of primary products from underdeveloped countries in 1970, assuming unchanged trends and policies		←——25——→			←——39——→	
2. 'Hypothetical gap' on both current and long-term capital account	11	3	7	('gap' nil in 1959)		
3. Total primary export earnings that would be required to close the 'gap' by 1970	36	28	32	100	53	77

For detailed data and explanatory notes, see Table 4.[1]

[1] (Not reprinted here—*Editors.*)

Under the most favourable of these three assumptions (Alternative II/1), primary export earnings would still have to provide 85 per cent of all earnings from exports and 60 per cent of total foreign exchange requirements in 1970, for the group of less developed countries taken as a whole.

Part Two: The typical commodity problems of the less developed countries

Structural problems

The typical commodity problems of the underdeveloped countries are easier to understand than to remedy.

On the side of *supply*, the root of the trouble is, of course, the very fact of the poverty of these countries which is not only the result, but also the main cause, of the obstacles that stand in the way of becoming less poor. In particular, it is a main cause of their lopsided production structure, of the high degree of dependence on a limited range of primary products, and of the lack of other remunerative outlets, capital, and skills, which makes the primary export sector into the one-eyed king of opportunities. Similarly, it is poverty which causes the high degree of dependence of these countries on markets outside their own group, the vulnerability to adverse market trends, the low degree of mobility in responding to such trends, and the low levels of reserves required to cushion sudden shocks. In such circumstances, technological advance, which has been manifest in the sharply rising yields for a number of tropical export products (resulting largely from the greater care and research applied to export crops than to domestic subsistence crops), cannot, in itself, provide a solution, but may merely aggravate the problem by leading to structural overproduction.*

* The problems which may result from leaving levels of agricultural output to be determined entirely by the free play of market forces were no doubt in the mind of Mr. Pisani, the French Minister of Agriculture, when he argued, in a statement to FAO in 1961, that the biblical phrase 'In the sweat of thy face shalt thou gain thy bread' was in need of amendment; it should now be made to read: 'In the sweat of thy face shalt thou lose thy life, for the more thou bringest forth out of the earth, the less shalt thou gain' (Statement before the seventh session of the FAO Conference, ninth plenary meeting, 9 November 1961; cf. C61/PV/9). At the same time, the phenomenon of structural over-production of agricultural industries in the developed countries differs sharply in character from that in the underdeveloped countries. In the case of the former, the main difficulties in commercial world markets arise from the combined effects of rapid technological advance and unco-ordinated national

173

Added to this are the technical problems resulting from long gestation periods, and even much longer life cycles for some of these products, notably for tropical tree crops and rubber. This leads, on the side of entry, to the delayed-action effect of successive layers of excess capacity resulting from earlier boom periods. It also adds to the difficulties of exit, which is even slower and costlier than entry and altogether not likely to happen unaided, in sufficient volume, in response to adverse market trends, due to the problems facing producers in poor economies in their search for alternative opportunities of at least equal interest to those of export cash crops. Much the same is true with respect to established capacity for extraction industries.

Similarly, on the side of *demand*, the main factors influencing market trends in the high-income countries (which absorb, as was noted earlier, 95 per cent of all primary exports from the underdeveloped countries to the rest of the world) are not accidental, but inherent in the structure of high-income communities. The main factors can be broadly grouped under the following two headings: (1) factors influencing total consumption in major markets, and (2) factors influencing the probable degree of control, on the part of the underdeveloped countries, over total market supplies, including identical products from other sources and close substitutes (originating outside the underdeveloped exporters' group).

The extent to which *factors influencing levels of total consumption* in major markets are inherent in the characteristic structure of high-income communities will be clear, without explanation, merely by looking at the following list of the main influences at work:

1. Low rates of population growth (generally much lower in high-income countries than in the underdeveloped parts of the world).
2. Near-saturated markets for foods, including tropical beverages, and low responsiveness of demand to income changes.
3. Low responsiveness of demand to price changes, *at the retail level.*

policies of agricultural support in both exporting and importing countries. The cost of such support is borne out of taxation or by means of higher prices to consumers. In the case of the underdeveloped countries, on the other hand, the primary export sector is in typical cases not merely the main provider of foreign exchange, but also a major source of fiscal revenue for financing programmes of assistance to the even poorer agricultural subsistence sectors and for general purposes of development and diversification.

4. Very low responsiveness of *retail demand* to changes in import unit values for basic imported products, due to large shares of retail cost being accounted for by processing charges and trading margins (shares which are being increased by the growing sophistication of products and services and other factors characteristic of high-income countries), and in some cases revenue duties and other fiscal charges.

5. Rapid technological advance, leading to higher output of finished product per unit of input (e.g. electrolytic process of tinplating).*

6. Shifts in industrial patterns away from industries with large requirements of imported raw materials per unit of output.

Of these six main factors influencing total consumption levels, all are irreversible and none (except for the fourth, in part) are easily amenable to change by means of governmental policies in the importing countries. The second, third, and fourth provide the main arguments, from the viewpoint of constellation of markets, in favour of restriction agreements.

Differing degrees of control over market supplies

The situation is different, in some respects, for the other main set of factors, namely those influencing the probable *degree of control over market supplies*, which the underdeveloped exporting countries, acting as a group, can hope to attain in their major high-income markets. On the one hand, this second set of factors, just like the first set, reflects intrinsic features of high-income economies and, in my view, is largely irreversible. On the other hand, one major factor among them, namely that of agricultural support measures in both exporting and importing countries, is amenable to change, at least in principle, by means of changes in governmental policies. The other main difference from the first set is that the second set includes some of the main arguments against the chances of effectiveness of any 'do-it-yourself' versions of producers' restriction schemes for other than a very few commodities. These factors are the following:

* The reference here is to new technological processes which lead to savings (in volume) of raw materials, whether natural or synthetic, per unit of output, as distinct from the reference below which relates to technological advances influencing competition, or degrees of interchangeability, among different kinds of raw materials.

1. Agricultural support policies, which add to the problems facing underdeveloped countries, due to:
   (a) competition from high-income exporting countries;
   (b) protected agriculture in importing countries.
2. Technological advance and dynamic industrial structure, which lead not merely to:
   (a) the expanding use of synthetics, but also, more generally, to
   (b) greatly extended openings for 'interchangeability' of materials, due to new techniques, in ways which strengthen the bargaining powers of the users *vis-à-vis* the sellers, while at the same time yielding a responsiveness of substitution at the manufacturing level, with respect to *upward* price changes for the older *established* materials (seeing that upward price changes stimulate new processes of interchangeability), but not to the same extent with respect to *downward* price changes (since the process is not symmetrical). Moreover, new processes, which may have been started originally in response to higher prices of the established materials, often take on a momentum of their own and develop into irreversible trends. . . .

Attitudes of high-income importing countries

The high-income importing countries, their governments and public opinion, have become increasingly aware of the seriousness of the trade problems of the low-income countries, and they do want to help. They are also becoming increasingly aware of the 'indivisibility' of problems of trade, aid, and economic growth. There is ample evidence to show that it would not be quite just to maintain (as has, at times, been maintained) that Government Jekyll, coming from a Special Fund meeting, becomes Government Hyde at the trade conference table. But it would be nearer the truth perhaps to say that the government of a typical high-income importing country (and this seems to apply more or less equally to any of them) comes to the trade conference table full of good intentions and weighed down by the responsibilities of which it has become conscious, but, nonetheless, with a personality which for understandable reasons is split in more ways than one.

The first inherent conflict concerns the basic decision as to the *total* net long-term capital transfer, whether by means of special arrangements for trade or aid, which such a country agrees to entertain from its own resources. Closely linked again is the question as to how much of the total should take the form of aid (and what kind of aid) and how much might have to be allowed by means of any built-in element of international assistance in arrangements ostensibly designed for trade, not aid.

Next, to the extent that the concept of such a built-in element of assistance in arrangements ostensibly designed for trade is accepted, a decision has to be taken as to how much of *that* total might take the form of measures which would mainly constitute a financial burden, through higher prices, for the consumers in importing countries; how much should be allowed to show up as net transfer in the Treasury accounts, to be financed by the taxpayers; and how much should take the form of measures which would involve adjustments of policies affecting producers (who, in turn, might be compensated by means of domestic programmes of adjustment-assistance) in the high-income countries. . . .

A programme of international adjustment assistance

Some of the elements of such a programme of international adjustment assistance might be as follows:

The case for improved international programming. As a very minimum, strengthened efforts are required to assist underdeveloped countries in the joint planning and direction of their national programmes, so as to provide each of them with full knowledge and understanding of the plans of others and of the market problems in the rest of the world. Such indicative planning should be supplemented, wherever possible, by long-term contracts or other forms of market assurance which would give to each of these countries a sufficiently firm basis for the elaboration of their development programmes geared to a definite knowledge of the external conditions with which they will be individually confronted. The development of such a quantitative framework is an essential pre-condition (though not, of course, a substitute) for attaining a more rapid rate of economic development as such.

Absorptive capacity and capacity to repay. A set of new principles is needed (reinforced by better knowledge to be obtained by means of improved international programming and projections) to relate current efforts and plans with respect to all forms of trade, and 'aided trade', as parts of one comprehensive programme of international adjustment assistance.

G. Blau

In the case of an international programme, or policy, for aid, the main elements of definitions which can help to provide a logical framework, are these: first, the *definition* of what constitutes 'aid', namely 'those parts of net capital inflows, which normal market forces do not provide';* second, the *purpose* of an international aid policy which is 'to maximize the traditional effort of, and catalytic effect in, the economy of the recipient country'; third, the recipient country's *absorptive capacity*, which is defined as a measurable auxiliary concept for indicating the size of total aid required; fourth, the *capacity to repay*, which is supposed to influence merely the *forms* of aid, not the total amount (since the total amount is to be influenced by absorptive capacity and not by the ceiling of capacity to repay, which may be considerably below that of absorptive capacity).

The formulation of such a framework of reference for an international policy of aid has been an important step forward, but by now it is no longer enough in itself. It needs to be supplemented, or broadened, by definitions relating to the wider concept of international adjustment assistance, which would apply to all transfers, by whatever means, and which would have to come to be recognized as a determinant of positive action (in the same way as the concept of absorptive capacity is a determinant for positive action re aid), not merely as the basis for a set of policing rules of the kind which until hitherto had been foremost on matters of trade.

A new set of principles might take as its basis the key concept of an underdeveloped country's 'absorptive capacity' for the effective utilization of net capital inflows for purposes of development. To the extent that the country's 'capacity to repay' has a lower ceiling than the one set by the measurable concept of 'absorptive capacity', the country concerned would be regarded as having a *prima facie* case for some form or other of international assistance.

Compensatory financing as a special case of international adjustment assistance. The consideration of possible arrangements for partial compensation for the effects of adverse market trends would become a special case within the wider framework of international adjust-

* I am here using the concepts and terminology which have been developed by the economic school of the Massachusetts Institute of Technology and explained in a number of their publications, of which I am here making use for reference of the report by P. N. Rosenstein-Rodan, *International Aid for Underdeveloped Countries* (Massachusetts Institute of Technology, Center for International Studies, Cambridge, Mass., January 1961).

ment assistance. The latter, even though it would not be fully automatic, would, nonetheless, be measurable on the basis of objective criteria.

The role of commodity agreements. The basic role of commodity agreements would be to provide an instrument for improved international programming. Beyond that, commodity agreements could also be used, in certain conditions, for raising earnings or, at a less ambitious level, as means for safeguarding market shares which are being threatened by the inroads of protectionist national policies or other market-limiting factors. Importing countries might be expected to co-operate actively, once they were committed to the wider programme of international adjustment assistance, and would regard such instruments as merely a part of the wider plan and of its obligations which in any case would have to be met in one way or another. As far as possible, commodity agreements should also provide for co-ordinated measures influencing consumption, internal price and production levels, and related national commercial and fiscal policies, not merely for measures relating directly to the regulation of exports and imports. Where formal agreements cannot be obtained, the best possible use should be made of other forms of consultative machinery.

Some unco-ordinated elements of adjustment assistance can be found in three instances of existing international commodity arrangements, even though in one of these three (the new International Coffee Agreement) these elements are merely indirect and not perhaps very clear, while in the other two cases (the Commonwealth Sugar Agreement and the near-historical case of the French *caisses de stabilization*) they are less than world-wide and partly based on preferences.

At the same time, the coffee agreement appears to reflect a more positive opinion on these matters on the part of the high-income importing countries which are beginning to recognize that the 'commodity problem' cannot be regarded as something apart from the 'development problem'.* A negotiating United Nations Cocoa Conference, on the other hand, held in 1963 just after the coming

---

* ... The new Coffee Agreement since its coming into force in 1963 has had a series of difficult problems to contend with, first as a result of a large number of requests for revisions of basic quotas and more recently through the need for adjustment of quotas due to a sharp rise in coffee prices which was caused by a combination of factors. The period of operations of the new agreement has been too short for an appraisal of the record to be made at this stage.

into force of the Coffee Agreement, had to adjourn without reaching agreement.

Possible use of import levies as tools of international adjustment. Among possible forms of international adjustment assistance, consideration might be given by governments to the possibility of a programme of import levies (or of restitution rather than abolition of revenue duties and other fiscal charges) for commodities with inelastic markets. Such import levies might be restituted, in whole or in part, tied or untied, directly or by means of contributions to an international fund, to assist the governments of the less-developed countries.

As compared with a programme solely run by the exporters, such a programme based on exporter/importer co-operation might have some advantages. For one thing, the imposition of levies at the point of entry would give a better assurance of effective control and equal treatment of exports from all sources. At the same time, low-income importing countries could be left free to pay the price without tax (provided that problems of transfer shipments could be solved). Moreover, even though the exporters themselves may prefer an alternative which leaves them in full control of the proceeds, there may be something to be said for the other version of creating an international fund. In addition, if the funds were earmarked in part for purchases of, say, machinery equipment in the countries imposing the levy, the proposition would become more acceptable to the high-income importing countries.

One main difficulty in my view, however, concerns the question of determining a price level, in cases where there is no internal reference price for a protected domestic product. Wherever there *is* such an internal reference price, the chances are that returns to exporters, under the levy-restitution system, will reflect some additional proceeds over what they would have been in the absence of the system, because prices minus levy in the import market will not be allowed to fall below the reference point. There is no such guarantee for non-competing commodities from low-income exporting countries. Here again, however, the situation might be different if such a system, like any other forms of special measures, were anchored as part of a wider framework of reference of international adjustment assistance, geared to the attainment of stipulated growth targets in the less developed countries.

At the same time, the present review appears to me to underline further the need for a *concerted attack*, proceeding simultaneously on various fronts, since there is no one line of action which is likely to be anywhere near sufficient for a solution of the problems with which we are faced.

30. PROJECTED CHANGES IN URBAN AND RURAL POPULATION IN KENYA AND THE IMPLICATIONS FOR DEVELOPMENT POLICY*

D. M. ETHERINGTON

'No estimates of future population or depopulation formed upon any existing rate of increase or decrease can be depended upon.'— T. R. MALTHUS, Essay on the Principles of Population (1803).

Introduction

The population of Kenya is growing very rapidly. While it is notoriously hazardous to engage in prediction, it is nevertheless important to examine the general order of magnitude of the population problem facing Kenya. Some writers are beginning to assess the implications, but few people appear to appreciate that most of the increase in population will have to be absorbed in the agricultural sector. The present proportion of the population in agriculture, and the coefficient of differential growth,† preclude their absorption by the non-agricultural sector unless major discoveries of new recourses, acting as prime movers, are forthcoming.

The purpose of this paper is, in the first instance, to indicate briefly the significance of different rates of growth of urban and total population, and then to make provincial projections up to 1990 for the rural African population‡ for all provinces, except the North-East. This latter province is of little significance in terms of population numbers, and is unique in its problems and way of life. The second aim is to examine the extent of the land resources and hence

---

* This paper was presented at the East African Institute of Social Research Conference held at Makerere University College, December 1964.

† F. Dovring, 'The Share of Agriculture in a Growing Population', *FAO Monthly Bulletin of Agricultural Economics and Statistics*, vol. 8, 8/9, 1959. See also Bruce F. Johnston and Soren T. Nielsen, 'Agriculture and Structural Transformation in a Developing Economy' in *Economic Development and Cultural Change*, April 1966.

‡ Throughout this paper, unless explicitly stated to the contrary, all the references to population refer to African population only.

the implications to agriculture of the very large increases in numbers of people that will have to be supported in the rural areas, within the next two or three decades, if the population increases are as large as the calculations below suggest.

It is a common feature of low income countries that large proportions of their population are engaged in agricultural pursuits. The relatively low elasticities of demand for foodstuffs and other agricultural products and the greatly increased average output per man available from specialization and mechanization in non-agricultural pursuits are often used to suggest that the development of secondary and tertiary sectors of the economy are necessary conditions for economic progress. Assuming this to be true, the proportion of the population in each sector is of considerable interest. The rate at which the urban and rural sectors of the economy can change in relative importance depends on the present proportions and the differential rates of growth of the urban and total populations. The expansion of the urban population does not necessarily mean, as is sometimes implied, that there will be any reduction in the rural population, either relatively or absolutely. An absolute decline in Kenya's agricultural population is only a distant theoretical possibility. A relative decline in the numbers engaged in agriculture is more feasible but, as will be seen, is also of rather academic interest in Kenya's circumstances.

The Rate of Population Growth

The population censuses which have taken place in East Africa over the last five years have indicated rapid, and possibly increasing, rates of population growth. The 1962 census in Kenya has been particularly alarming, suggesting, as it does, a rate of growth of 3 per cent per annum. This is the estimate of the Statistics Division of the Directorate of Planning,* but it must be realized that this is based on census data only since, for the African population, the statistics on vital registration and migration are inadequate. Thus this estimate of Kenya's rate of population growth is formed mainly upon a comparison of the 1948 and 1962 census data. Because of the difficulties raised by boundary changes and possible variation in coverage in the different censuses, it was inappropriate to take the total

---

* The author is particularly indebted to the generous help of Dr. J. G. C. Blacker, the Kenya Government Demographer, in providing him with access to census data and some of his, as yet, unpublished analysis.

increase in the intercensal period (equal to a 3·3 per cent mean rate of growth). The distribution of districts by percentage increase was fairly heavily skewed, hence it was considered that the median or mode would possibly act as a better measure than the mean rate. The median rate was 2·94 and the modal rate 2·64 per cent per annum.* These conclusions have been supported by data on fertility and mortality obtained from the 10 per cent post-enumeration survey which followed the 1962 census which indicated crude birth and death rates of 50 and 20 per thousand respectively. The official population projections assume that the crude birth rate will remain constant but that the rate of population growth will increase because of a decline in the death rate consequent on an increase in life expectancy at birth of half a year per annum.

In the past there has been considerable debate when growth rates in the order of 2·0 per cent per annum were suggested for East Africa.† It is significant, however, that the Kenya Government accepted the 3 per cent per annum rate of population growth when drawing up its Six Year Development Plan (1964–1970). This is a realistic approach since it would require a startling decline in the birth rate (or a series of natural catastrophes) to alter the trend materially. While recent developments in birth control techniques (inter-uterine devices) now make rapid declines in birth rates a real possibility, these techniques have yet to be tried on a large scale in Africa. It is therefore sensible for economic planners to work on the assumption that the present high rate will continue for a considerable time. It would be foolhardy for any government to underestimate the effects that a rapidly growing population may have, and as Indian planners have come to realize, it may be equally foolhardy to consider the rate of population growth as an exogenous factor in planning.‡

Nevertheless, this paper in using the official projections of population which are based on an increasing rate of growth from about 3·1 per cent in the 1960s to about 3·5 per cent in the 1980s does make the assumption that population growth is not capable of manipulation. The rapid decline in birth rates in Japan since 1949

* *Kenya Statistical Digest*, vol. 1, 1, September 1963, pp. 3–4.
† *East African Royal Commission 1953–1955 Report*, Cmnd 9475, H.M.S.O. 1955, p. 31.
‡ This point is adequately discussed by Aaron Segal in an article entitled 'Unemployment, Population and the Plan' in the *Kenya Weekly News*, No. 2017, 9 October 1964, p. 27.

following legislation legalizing induced abortions merely demonstrates the hazards of prediction.

Table 1 shows comparative population growth figures for Kenya and selected countries.

Table 1. *Total population estimates and estimated annual rates of population growth in selected countries*

Country	Year of last census	Total population mid-year 1962 (000,000)	Rates of growth % p.a.
Kenya	1962	8·6	2·9
Tanzania[1]	1957	9·9	1·9
Uganda	1959	7·0	2·5
Ghana	1960	7·1	n.a.
Congo (Leopoldville)	1955–7	14·8	2·4
South Africa	1960	16·6	2·6
U.A.R. (Egypt)	1960	27·3	2·6
Mexico	1960	37·2	3·1
Brazil	1960	75·3	3·4
Malaya	1957	7·4	3·2
India	1961	449·4	2·3
U.S.S.R.	1959	221·5	1·7
U.S.A.	1960	186·7	1·6
U.K.	1961	53·4	0·8

Source: *United Nations' Demographic Yearbook 1963*, Table 1, pp. 123–42.
[1] Zanzibar and Tanganyika.

Provincial rates of population growth

The census data in Kenya show beyond doubt that the provincial rates of population growth differ markedly. The projection of provincial population is, however, rather hazardous since both the former censuses were based on the pre-1963 'provinces' and the present provinces have few common boundaries with them. Whereas there were six provinces, there are now seven. The censuses bureau has, however, reanalysed its data on the new provincial basis and has made annual projections up to 1970.

The provincial populations were reconstructed for 1948 and 1962, making allowance for boundary changes and under-enumeration in some districts in 1948. The percentage which each province formed of the national total was then calculated for the two census years, and the change in the percentage was extrapolated linearly.*

In the absence of logical alternative hypotheses, projections for 1980 and 1990 were made on the same basis and are shown in Table 3.

Urbanization

The size of the urban population has been taken as an indication of those engaged in non-agricultural pursuits. In conformity with United Nations definitions, all towns with populations of 2,000 and more have been classified as 'urban'.† This may give an optimistic assessment of the non-agricultural population, particularly as the whole of the Nairobi extra-provincial district has been included.‡

In the 1948 census there were seventeen and in the 1962 census thirty-four towns with populations of over 2,000 people. This meant that in 1962 6·3 per cent of the African or 7·8 per cent of the total population was urbanized, about two-thirds of whom were in Nairobi and Mombasa. The degree of urbanization is compared with other countries in Table 2.

The data for the seventeen towns with populations of more than 2,000 in 1948 provide a reasonable basis for the calculation of the rates at which urbanization had taken place in the period 1948–1962. For the projections of future growth of the urban population the thirty-four towns (with populations of more than 2,000 in 1962) were assigned to their provinces and the growth rates which had been calculated for the seventeen towns (by provinces) were applied to them (see Table 3).

Urbanization in Africa is undergoing rapid change not only in terms of numbers but also in composition. The system of migratory

---

* For example in 1962, 16·1768 per cent of the total population was in the Central Province, but as a proportion of total population its share is decreasing by 0·1009 per cent p.a., hence its share in 1970 should be 15·3696.

† With the exception of Bungoma in Western Province which had a population of less than 2,000. An additional observation could be added: since we are primarily concerned with the *African* rural areas, commercial (i.e. large-scale) farm and plantation labour, which shows many of the characteristics of the urban labour force, could be considered as urban labour. However, in Kenya, a major resettlement scheme is being undertaken whereby the large-scale mixed farms are being subdivided for African farmers. As a consequence, only urban population as defined by towns of over 2,000 is used.

‡ This adds about 60,000 persons, which is probably not an unreasonable figure to assign to the population supported by the bicycle commuters of the city.

labour, so common over most of Africa, appears to be breaking down so rapidly that the publications on the subject run the risk of becoming out of date before the printer's ink is dry.* No longer can the typical urban worker be regarded as merely temporary. As the urban labour force becomes more permanent, so the workers look to the towns to provide them with improved facilities in terms of housing, roads, sanitation, schools and hospitals, so that families may be brought up suitably in these towns. The composition of the population in Nairobi in the two censuses indicate the nature of this change. In 1948 71 per cent of African population in Nairobi were adult males. This percentage had fallen to 47 per cent in 1962. The ratio of women and children to adult males had increased from 0·42:1 to 1·06:1† between censuses and it can be expected that over time this ratio will tend towards the national average of 3·57:1. Thus the assumption that the very rapid rate of growth of the urban population of 6 per cent per annum which took place between 1948 and 1962 will continue may not be unreasonable, at least up until 1980. This rate of increase would be attributed to both increased employment opportunities and the increasing size and permanence of the urban family. It must be noted, though, that projections for individual towns at rates of 7 per cent and more must naturally be subject to severe criticism when carried over too long a time period, since, as the base increases, this would imply incredibly large migratory moves. Such rates of growth would, of course, call for fairly sophisticated planning by town and city councils if large slums are to be avoided.

While it is not the subject matter of this paper, it is pertinent to note that the investment in the necessary urban infrastructure required to allow even a 6 per cent annual increase in urban population would be very high, for this is a sphere in which the capital-output ratio is likely to be particularly high. This feature substantially affects the shape of the transformation curve from 'agriculture' to 'industry' and prevents simple comparisons of opportunity costs between the sectors.‡

With projections for the urban and total African population, by subtraction, the difference indicates the size of the rural populations in the provinces. The projections are given in Table 3. The figures in

---

* Cf. 'Migrants and Proletarians': A Review by E. Rado, *East African Economic Review*, New Series, vol. 1, 1, p. 81.
† Dr. J. G. C. Blacker, private communication.
‡ S. Enke, *Economics for Development* (Prentice-Hall 1963), pp. 136–8.

D. M. Etherington

Table 2. *Urbanization in Kenya and selected countries*

Country	Year	Percentage of Total population	
		Urban	Rural
Kenya	1962	7·8	92·2
Tanzania[1]	1957	4·1	95·9
Uganda	1959	2·4	97·6
Ghana	1960	23·1	76·9
Congo (Leopoldville)	1955-7	22·3	77·7
South Africa	1960	45·0	55·0
U.A.R. (Egypt)	1960	37·7	62·3
Mexico	1960	50·7	49·3
Brazil	1960	45·1	54·9
Malaya	1957	42·7	57·3
India	1961	18·0	82·0
U.S.S.R.	1959	47·9	52·1
U.S.A.	1960	69·9	30·1
U.K.	1961	78·3	21·7

Source: *UN Demographic Yearbook 1963*, Table 5.
[1] Zanzibar and Tanganyika.

Table 3. *Rural and urban African population projections for Kenya by provinces; mid-year estimates 1962-90*

Province	1962		1970		1980		1990	
	Urban '000	Rural '000	Urban '000	Rural '000	Urban '000	Rural '000	Urban '000	Rural '000
Coast	120	535	201	624	388	762	755	826
Eastern	25	1,528	44	1,937	93	2,663	197	3,724
Central	24	1,287	58	1,529	175	1,884	524	2,193
Rift	95	1,651	124	2,074	173	2,819	242	3,927
Western	5	1,003	9	1,292	19	1,818	41	2,609
Nairobi E.P.D.	220	—	333	—	555	—	918	—
Total Kenya[1]	507	7,599	799	9,530	1,459	12,897	2,781	17,563

Source: Calculated from Kenya Census Statistics. See text for the bases of the projections.
[1] Excluding the North-East Province.

this table were used to draw up the semi-log diagrams (1-7).* These diagrams show in a rather dramatic fashion the insignificant effect that urbanization is likely to have on the urban/rural distribution of population of Kenya during the next few decades. What is true of

* Only Diagram 1 is here reproduced (*Editors*).

188

Changes in Urban and Rural Population

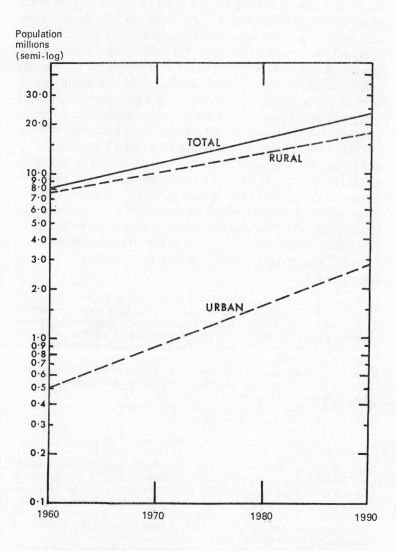

Projected sector changes in the Kenya population of 1960-90

the country as a whole (diagram 1) is true to a greater or lesser extent of each province except the Coast (cf. diagrams 2-7). Kenya's 6 per cent per annum rate of urban growth compares very favourably with many other countries,* but few of the industrialized countries had to contend with rates of growth in the total population approaching 3 per cent per annum. Kenya's coefficient of differential growth between her urban and total population will increase by about 3 per cent per annum.† That is to say, on these assumptions, that the urban population will increase from 6·3 per cent of the total African population in 1962 to about 6·5 per cent in 1963 and 6·9 per cent in 1965 and so on. The very small proportion of population in the urban areas, and the rate at which the total population is growing, precludes the absorption of the increase in the total population by the urban sector. A country with 8 per cent of her population in the urban areas and a 3 per cent per annum increase in her total population would initially require increases in the urban population of the order of 38 per cent per annum if the rural population were to remain static.‡

* E.g. Egypt's rate has increased in the last ten years to 3·1 per cent p.a.; the Republic of South Africa to 3·2 per cent p.a., and the Congo (Leopoldville) 5·9 per cent up to 1960. The present developed countries experienced rates of urban growth of between 0·7 per cent (France) and 4·2 per cent p.a. (U.S.A. 1850–80). Dovring, *op. cit.*, Table 2. See also *Economic Bulletin for Africa*, vol. 5, January 1965.
† This is calculated by subtracting the rate of growth of the rural population (about 3 per cent p.a.) from the rate of growth of the urban population (about 6 per cent p.a.) over the period.
‡ The identity which explains the relationship between urban, rural and total rates of population growth is as follows:

$$P'_A \equiv \frac{P_T}{P_A} P'_T - \frac{P_N}{P_A} P'_N$$

where P'_T, P'_A and P'_N refer to the *rates of growth* of the total (T), agricultural (A) and non-agricultural (N) populations respectively; and P_T, P_A and P_N refer to the size of the total, agricultural (i.e. rural), and non-agricultural (i.e. urban) populations. An example will help illustrate the relationships: say that the country has a total population of 10 million of whom 8 per cent are in the urban sector, and the total population is growing at 3 per cent p.a. What rate of urban population growth would be required to prevent the rural population from expanding? By substituting our information into the identity we have the following:

$$O \equiv \frac{10}{9·2} \, 0·03 - \frac{0·8}{9·2} \, P'_N$$

$$P'_N = \frac{0·3}{9·2} \cdot \frac{9·2}{0·8} \equiv 37·5\% \text{ per annum.}$$

These facts justify an attempt to examine the implications for agriculture of the very large increase in the rural population during the next two or three decades. They also justify policies making the agricultural sector in Kenya the residual holder of population rather than the alternative of planning agriculture for a specific population and assigning the residual to urban development. It is also made clear that such questions as whether there are low elasticities of demand for agricultural products and whether the average *per capita* output from secondary and tertiary sectors is higher than in the agricultural sector, are of secondary importance. Where the proportions are so heavily weighted towards agriculture, it can be only through agricultural development that significant changes can be made in average *per capita* income levels.

Implications

While the 'Kenya population problem' has usually been used in the context of political issues in relation to land, this has not always been the case and there is fairly extensive documentation of early fears of population growth. Thus the evidence of one of the District Commissioners before the Carter Commission in 1933* could well have been made today and is a warning to all prophets.

> The future of the next thirty years or so may be imagined as a race between the tendency of a growing population to congest the land and a growing skill to make the same land support a larger population. During the earlier years of the period skill will be in the lead and will result in greater individual prosperity, but the rate of betterment will decline and it seems likely that in about twenty years from now (unless remedial measures are taken), approaching congestion will decrease the standard of life, as much as growth in skill will raise it. After that a long flat top to the graph is the best we can expect.†

On the other hand, the Royal Commission (1953–5) wrote in 1955:

> There is no evidence to suggest that up to the present the general rate of growth of the African population has exceeded the overall ability of the economy of the three territories to support it. Indeed, we believe that the recently accelerated growth of population is in part both a cause and a consequence of the greater economic opportunities which are open to the indigenous population. Thus the growth of the population should in itself present no serious overall problem of

---

* *The Kenya Land Commission Report*, Cmnd 4556, H.M.S.O. 1934.
† This is actually quoted from *Land and Population in East Africa*, Colonial 290, H.M.S.O. 1952, p. 2.

population pressure provided the many obstacles to the economic mobility of the factors of production necessary for the development of the modern exchange economy can be overcome.*

While the Commission was not too worried with the overall problem of population growth it was more than a little concerned when it faced the problem, as the D.C. had to, on a local level. Thus the members of the Commission stated that:

> Throughout our enquiry we were impressed by the recurring evidence that particular areas were now carrying so large a population that agricultural production in them was being retarded, that the natural resources themselves were being destroyed, that families were unable to find access to new land and that land which should have been lying fallow was being encroached upon. Such a situation clearly implies that with the existing state of agricultural technique and economic organization and in the absence of other types of economic activity, the population is unable to support a growth in its numbers without a deterioration in its average standard of life. It implies that there either must be a change in the use of land or reduction in the number of people whom the land has to sustain.†

The Commission was particularly concerned with the 'dual economy' and how to bring peasant agriculture into the modern exchange economy. A great deal has been learnt and done since the report was published and there are many striking examples in Kenya of small-scale commercial farmers. The serious problem for the future is that small-scale farming must become commercial and at the same time smaller-scale. The problem is how continually to shift the production function upwards so that the full effects of diminishing returns so feared by the District Commissioner may not be felt.

Attempts at assessing population pressures and the maximum populations that certain districts in Kenya could hold have also been made by officers of the Department of Agriculture. Not surprisingly they started with the individual family farm. Assuming a farm was to support eight persons, or six adult equivalents, they made estimates of the full subsistence needs, and the excess income needed to purchase the other necessities, for such a family. Then, on the basis of contemporary technical knowledge and taking into account the ecology of an area, adequate farming systems were planned to achieve the desired income levels. In order to obtain the total population

* Royal Commission, *op. cit.*, p. 34.
† *Ibid.*, p. 37.

that could be supported in an area, each ecological zone was divided by the average size of the planned farm and the answer multiplied by eight, allowance being made for the use of a small proportion for public purposes (roads, villages, etc.).

The most detailed of such plans were those worked out by L. H. Brown for Central Province in 1952 and Nyanza Province in 1954 while he was Provincial Agricultural Officer in each of these provinces.* The 'Swynnerton Plan'† incorporated the findings of these and other studies in drawing up a national agricultural policy for African farming. The ultimate aim of this plan was to establish '600,000 African economic farming units and raise the productivity of each unit from present sales (i.e. gross income) valued at a mere £5 to £20 per family to £100 a year or more after providing for the needs of the family'.‡

Owing to boundary changes Brown's calculations cover districts in five of the six provinces for which population projections have been made. Sufficient details however are only given for the districts now in the Central and Eastern Provinces. These are shown in Table 4. For those areas of Nyanza Province now in Western, Nyanza and Rift Provinces Brown gave gross estimates by ecological zones, but did not show sub-totals by district. His estimates were significantly above those given by previous agriculturalists in the province and ranged from 668 to 240 persons per square mile between the Kikuyu-Star Grass zone and the impeded drainage sub-zones. In both provinces Brown suggested that the population figures could be substantially increased allowing for full development of trades and other rural employment. Writing some ten years later Brown recognized the implications of the rapidly growing population when the holding capacity of the land was recalculated§ in terms of mere subsistence. He thus abandoned the Swynnerton Plan's hopes of 666,000 families with gross incomes of about £100 per annum. Brown's new calculations were based on reasonable yields above the present general

---

* 'Revised and Consolidated Agricultural Policy, Central Province', December 1952, and 'Draft Agricultural Policy, Nyanza Province', October 1954. Mimeographed reports by L. H. Brown (Provincial Agricultural Offices).

† *A Plan to Intensify the Development of African Agriculture in Kenya* compiled by R. T. M. Swynnerton, Assistant Director of Agriculture (Government Printer, Nairobi, 1955).

‡ *Ibid.*, p. 12, the words in brackets are mine.

§ *A National Cash Crops Policy for Kenya* by L. H. Brown, Chief Agriculturist/ Regions and Acting Director of Agriculture (Government Printer, Nairobi, May 1963).

level of production.* They allow each family 3·5 acres of class A(i) land,† thus allowing some 1,328 persons per square mile. Similar calculations for other grades of land enable one to obtain some idea of the absolute maximum numbers that could be held by the different provinces.

Table 5 and its footnotes give the Land Use Categories for the provinces of Kenya. These categories, based on rainfall regimes, conform basically with the major ecological zones and are the only available indication of land availability.

Table 4. *Estimates of population capacities* 1948 *and* 1962 *census figures, selected districts*

Region	District	Brown's estimates		1948 Census population '000	1962 Census population '000	1970 Estimate '000
		Mini-mum '000	Maxi-mum '000			
Central	Kiambu	252	283	263	407(353)[1]	(423)[1]
	Fort Hall	326	385	304	345(408)[1]	(488)[1]
	Nyeri	198	232	183	255(245)[1]	(306)[1]
Eastern	Embu	400	468	202	293	383
	Meru	857	1,005	313	469	708
	Kitui	562	616	356	551	853
	Machakos	600	605	211	285	342

Sources: *Revised and Consolidated Agricultural Policy.* Central Province. Mimeographed report by L. G. Brown, December 1952. Appendix II.
Kenya Population Census 1962 (Government Printer, Nairobi, July 1964).
[1] Estimates contained in brackets assume constant boundaries as when Brown did his analysis—these same boundaries are used for the 1970 projection. The boundary changes in the districts of Eastern Region would not materially alter the figures presented here.

It will be noted that Kenya's agricultural land (categories A and B) is limited to about 17 per cent of her 220,000 square miles of land area. This is due to the limitations imposed by rainfall, temperature, soils, slope and tsetse fly. The area available for agriculture can be expanded only marginally by the elimination of tsetse fly or by the development of irrigation schemes.

The use of Brown's 1963 estimates of population capacities and the application of them to the land use categories in Table 5 assumes

* *Ibid.,* p. 41.
† See footnotes to Table 5.

Table 5. *Land use categories by provinces*[1] (*in square miles*)

Land usage Class[2]	Coast	Eastern	Central	Rift	Nyanza	Western	Total
A (i)	445	1,455	1,064	5,046	1,023	1,907	10,540
A (ii)	—	10	—	1,625	—	—	1,635
A (iii)	474	—	234	2,698	—	256	3,662
A (iv)	643	103	104	2,220	1,110	531	4,711
Total 'A' 35 inches or more	1,562	1,568	1,402	11,589	2,133	2,694	20,948
B (i)	425	1,676	1,451	2,168	621	—	6,341
B (ii)	601	1,227	156	876	559	—	3,419
B (iii)	679	1,342	42	4,874	536	—	7,473
Total 'B' 25–35 inches	1,705	4,245	1,649	7,918	1,716	—	17,233
'C' & 'D' Class— less than 25 inches	23,586	46,293	—	47,497	—	—	165,644

[1] Excluding the North East Province.
[2] A. High potential with adequate rainfall (35″ and above).
    (i) Very High Potential Land, with adequate rainfall, good deep soils and moderate temperatures (Kikuyu-Star Grass Zones).
    (ii) High Potential Land as above, but too cold to grow two crops per year.
    (iii) Land with adequate rainfall and deep soil but with a soil fertility problem or poor drainage.
    (iv) Land with adequate rainfall but with shallow soil unsuited to arable agriculture.
 B. Medium potential (25″–35″ rainfall).
    (i) With good deep soil suited to agriculture.
    (ii) With soil fertility problem or with poor drainage.
    (iii) With shallow soil unsuited to arable agriculture but suited to grazing.
 C. Low potential (20″–25″ rainfall)—suited only to ranching except under irrigation.
 D. Nomadic pastoral (less than 20″ rainfall)—suitable only to poor quality ranching or wild life exploitations (latter probably best).

Sources: *A National Cash Crops Policy for Kenya* (Govt. Printer, Nairobi). *Kenya Agricultural Sample Census* 1960–61 (Govt. Printer, Nairobi, May 1962, p. 2).

(and it is a very big assumption indeed) the complete use of under-utilized or unutilized land and a completely rational land policy within each province allowing for a normal distribution of land. To the extent that this is not possible because of rigid tribal or clan land rights within a province these calculations are unrealistic.* For

* E.g. such gross figures are particularly misleading in the Eastern Province where the land with the capacity to hold more people is mainly in the Embu and Meru area, not in Ukambani where population pressure is greatest, cf. Table 4.

195

this reason, it would probably be more realistic to consider 'maximum populations' within a range, with Brown's estimates as the upper limit. A subtraction of 25 per cent gives a range from about 1,000 to 1,328 persons per square mile on grade A(i) land. Considering the fact that provincial boundaries tend to incorporate similar tribal groups the problem may here be looked at on a provincial basis. The redistribution of land rights may occur (or may have to occur) on a non-tribal, trans-provincial, basis in the future. This paper points out where the pressures for such reform are likely to be felt most acutely.

On the basis of population densities of between 1,000 and 1,328 persons per square mile on A(i) land, and the appropriate figures for the other grades of land, the maximum agricultural populations that could be held by each province are:

Coast	Between	1,534 and	2,045	thousand
Central	„	1,847 „	2,463	„
Eastern	„	3,217 „	4,289	„
Rift	„	10,336 „	13,782	„
Nyanza	„	1,752 „	2,336	„
Western	„	2,171 „	2,894	„

... It must be appreciated that these figures can only be regarded as guidelines indicating the possible extent of population pressures. The problem is in need of analysis on a much more local level than is possible here. In the time period we are considering it will be noticed that Nyanza Province is the only one where the projected population will exceed the upper limit of the range Western, Central and Eastern Provinces will be within the 'danger' range and pressing close upon the maximum.

As far as Nyanza Province is concerned there is considerable potential for irrigation schemes in the Yala swamp area and on the Kano plains. The World Bank Report* and the Kenya Development Plan† estimate that some 50,000 acres could be irrigated. This would settle about 17,000 families with 3 acres each (assuming that the high yields and returns obtained on the Mwea Tabere irrigation scheme will lead to a reassessment of that scheme's allocation of 4 acres per settler). Assuming a previous population density of 200 per square mile for these areas, the net additional population that could be settled would be about 134,000 persons.

* *The Economic Development of Kenya*, IBRD Report (Government Printer, 1962).
† *The Kenya Development Plan (1964–70)* (Government Printer, Nairobi, 1964).

The other major irrigation scheme which will have some effect on population is that proposed for the Lower Tana River. Provided that a dam site can be found and that there are sufficient areas of suitable soil it is estimated that some 200,000 acres could be irrigated, thus potentially allowing the settlement of 400,000 people. It would be necessary for all the settlers to come from Nyanza if the situation there were to be alleviated to any extent.

Similar, but much smaller-scale, irrigation projects using the Athi River Basin, Lumi (Taveta) basin, the Ewaso Nyiro, Perkerra and Upper Tana would total 350,000 acres at best. Consequently, in spite of the very large capital outlay required, the effect on population pressure would be little better than marginal over the time period in question.

Resettlement projects will undoubtedly continue, but if tribal land rights are safeguarded, they will be concentrated in the Rift Valley Province where the problem is least acute. In any case, their effects on population pressure are likely to be marginal.

It must therefore be to the main area of present peasant farming land that major efforts are directed. The rural areas will have to absorb these large increases in population, that is to say that the peasant farmer will have to produce at least the same amount from less land. In addition, increased production will be necessary to feed a growing urban population. If the terms of trade follow an adverse trend and/or if the value of imports must be increased, then also the quantity of exports will have to increase. In addition the peasant farmer may be called upon to provide increased tax revenues.

If one adds the expectation (and aim) of increased *per capita* incomes, that is to say that the increased population will have to be fed, clothed and housed better, then the potential seriousness, on health, welfare, and political grounds, of the population problem begins to be seen.

It will require the proverbial tenacity of the Japanese farmer for the agricultural sector to measure up to these requirements. In the forthcoming years there must be a greatly expanded programme of 'extensive' public investment in land consolidation; in agricultural research in both food and cash crops and in livestock production; in the training and increase of extension staff; in the promotion of fertilizers and pesticides and in the provision of adequate credit facilities. The Kenya peasant farmer must be given the requisite tools, services and technical assistance if his utilization of limited land and water resources is to reach the necessary high levels of productivity.

Conclusions

The conclusions that emerge from the above are serious. Kenya's population is growing very rapidly. The proportion of the population in the agricultural sector and the rate of growth of the urban areas necessitate a large increase in the rural population. The limited land resources of the country suggest that there will be severe population pressures in some provinces within the next two or three decades, if present rates of population growth continue.

The general economist who makes it his business to be interested in low income countries which have large proportions of their populations in agriculture cannot afford to consider the agricultural sector and its problems, or population growth, as being the exclusive preserves of small groups of specialists. Unlike the high income countries, or even India for that matter, the countries of middle Africa are facing rapid rates of population growth before any significant industrialization has taken place. The solution of the problems thus presented demand much more research and analysis of the agricultural sector, particularly so as to enable optimum use to be made of land resources that are currently being used at very low levels of productivity. This is a central problem in development economies so far as many African countries are concerned.

31. ECONOMIC DEVELOPMENT, EMPLOYMENT AND PUBLIC WORKS IN AFRICAN COUNTRIES

THE INTERNATIONAL LABOUR OFFICE

The dual purpose of public works in Africa

. . . Generally speaking, the purposes of public works in African countries are twofold: one is to contribute to economic development and the other is to provide employment and incomes to the currently unemployed and underemployed.

The first purpose—contribution to economic development—requires no emphasis. Practically all African countries have a great task on hand to build up the economic and social infrastructure, without which economic development can hardly proceed. The infrastructure includes such productive capital assets as transport and communications systems (e.g. railways, roads, waterways and harbours), dams, power-generating facilities, irrigation, drainage and soil-conservation works, housing, water-supply facilities, schools, hospitals and many other things. In these countries, as in most others, investments undertaken in this sphere are mainly in the public realm; the construction and other works carried out under these investment projects are public works, which are planned and administered by public authorities and on which the workers employed are paid out of public budgets. To promote economic development, governments of many African countries in recent years have allocated considerable shares of public capital expenditure to public works on infrastructure projects of various kinds. Although detailed breakdowns of such allocations are not readily available a high priority appears to have been commonly accorded to the development of transport systems, which are generally regarded as a necessary condition for the expansion of production in these countries.* Hence improving the productivity of public works can

* For sectoral distribution of government capital expenditure in the development programmes of African countries, see United Nations, *Economic Bulletin for Africa* (Addis Ababa), vol. 2, 2, June 1962, p. 22.

increase the effective level of real investment obtained with limited government funds in a major sector of the economy and can make an important contribution to economic development.

The second purpose—provision of productive jobs to the unemployed and underemployed—is important in view of the employment needs of a great many African countries. In countries of North Africa such as Morocco, Tunisia and Algeria there is serious unemployment among the working population and the situation is likely to deteriorate further in the absence of effective remedial action. In Morocco, for example, it is estimated that despite the 400,000 new jobs expected to be created under the Five-Year Plan (1960–4) the number seeking jobs will increase to some 2·3 million in 1965 (460,000 due to population growth, 1,640,000 to underemployment in agriculture and 220,000 to unemployment in the towns).* South of the Sahara the employment situation is more diverse and also less clear owing to lack of adequate information. Nevertheless, there are certain features which indicate substantial unemployment and underemployment prevailing in these countries. First, there has been a constant flow of young people from the countryside to the towns seeking regular jobs which the towns cannot provide. A second and related feature is acute unemployment among primary-school leavers, who possess no particular skills but do not want to go back to traditional agriculture. Third, in agriculture not only are productivity and incomes exceedingly low but there is also pronounced seasonal unemployment especially in savannah and semi-arid zones.

Thus in both North Africa and tropical Africa public works on development projects can be a powerful instrument both of development policy and of employment policy designed specifically to meet the employment and income needs of the unemployed unskilled manpower. Indeed, many governments are adopting or planning to adopt this line of policy. Improving the productivity of public works contributes substantially not only to economic development but also to the expansion of employment, since it reduces the cost of creating new jobs. It does this by reducing both labour costs and the amount of capital equipment required to maintain output at an acceptable level of efficiency.

---

* Ministère de l'économie nationale, Morocco, *Plan quinquennal 1960–1964* (Rabat, 1960), p. 54.

The range of techniques

In public works, more especially in earthmoving operations, a wide range of techniques from wholly manual to highly mechanized is often available. The criterion for the choice of technology in public works differs according to the purpose or objective of public works policy. For development objectives the methods to be used need to be as cheap as possible, whereas for employment objectives they need to be as labour-intensive as possible. When the same technique is the least costly and also provides the most jobs it will be the obvious one to choose. But in the more usual cases where the cost criterion does not point to the same choice of techniques as the employment criterion, two important questions arise:

(1) Can the conflict between cost considerations and employment considerations be eliminated or diminished by reducing the costs of labour-intensive techniques?

(2) To the extent that this is not possible, what principles should govern the choice that will have to be made between these considerations? . . .

From various studies it appears that in the developing countries generally the productivity of manual labour using traditional methods of earthmoving could be increased markedly by simple productivity improvements requiring little additional capital. One significant finding of the case studies in India and in Nigeria and Tanganyika (reproduced in the Appendix) is the feasibility of doubling the productivity of manual labour by introducing improvements within the general framework of the traditional methods and thereby reducing the unit money cost under such methods by nearly half. In the Nigeria and Tanganyika study it is observed that a 100 per cent increase in the productivity of manual labour makes it a practical possibility for manual labour to begin to compete with machines at middle rates of utilization and to compete effectively at lower rates of utilization even with the most efficient machines. This possibility of doubling productivity by simple improvements perhaps also exists in many other African countries. In Tunisia, for instance, some cost data have shown that earthmoving work on certain secondary canals cost 160 millimes/cu. m. by machines as against 250 millimes/cu. m. by manual labour at an output per worker of 1 to 1·2 cu. m. per day and a daily wage of 300 millimes.* Thus with a doubling of

* Figures from Benzineb, *Programmes of public works in the fight against under-employment and unemployment.* D/36/1963.

201

productivity the unit cost by manual labour, which was formerly much higher, becomes considerably lower than by mechanized methods.

The most effective manner of raising the productivity of manual labour would be to introduce simultaneous, and not isolated, improvements bearing on each and every aspect of manual operations including the following:

(*a*) the organization of the work unit;
(*b*) tools;
(*c*) methods of using tools;
(*d*) the ratio of productive work to ancillary work;
(*e*) incentives;
(*f*) food;
(*g*) supporting services, e.g. temporary housing, medical facilities, amenities, arrangements for essential provisions and for tool and appliance maintenance.

In applying this general principle the various specific measures to be introduced and the degree of importance to be assigned to each measure will have to be decided on the spot after a thorough study of the actual situation. In the Indian earthmoving study it was discovered that beyond the 100 per cent increase referred to above, further substantial increases in the productivity of manual labour will require the introduction of more efficient implements, particularly the replacement of 'mumtys' by shovels and of headbaskets by either wheelbarrows or tipping trucks. The shovel-wheelbarrow combination would increase the over-all output per worker by from 30 to 100 per cent and the shovel-tipping-truck combination by from three and a half to four and a half times, depending on the length of the lead. Other far-reaching measures suggested in this Indian study are communal eating arrangements to improve the diet and hence the strength of the workers, organization of labour co-operatives to obviate the exploitation of workers by petty contractors, and payment of wages in such a way that the major share of savings produced by productivity improvements goes direct to the workers.

The Nigeria and Tanganyika study also sets forth suggested measures based on the observed conditions. These measures include the correction of lack of balance between digging, loading and carrying and the use of improved tools (pick-point instead of chisel-end for certain earths, shorter-hafted shovel with a special handle design and the redesign of the headpan)—all calculated to bring the increase in productivity of manual labour up to the 100 per cent target. One interesting finding of this study concerns the attitudes to work: the workers on the construction site are mostly seasonally unemployed subsistence farmers, who are unused to disciplined work for regular hours, and the only kind of work to which such a man reacts favourably is some form of task work, either on the paid task basis or 'finish-and-go' or a combination of both, under which he feels that he is working for himself. It was suggested that the application of this basic incentive principle would not only increase the output per worker but also reduce the number of supervisors needed on the site as compared with payment by flat time-rates.

These studies show that though each improved measure appears simple, the designing of the right kind of measures to redress particular defects in the methods of working and the choice of the best combination of measures in a given situation demand a great deal of ingenuity on the part of the productivity experts. The spreading of improved methods discovered in demonstration projects requires, furthermore, a considerable amount of training, which calls for separate measures to be carried out. The suggestion made in the Indian study that vocational training centres should be set up by the labour co-operatives themselves merits wide attention.

Productivity may be improved and costs reduced not only by techniques designed primarily to have this effect but as a result of improvements of a more general character in the management of the labour force. The importance of paying attention to nutrition and to incentives has been emphasized above.

In addition to the need to raise the productivity of manual labour on normal public works of a large or medium scale in which there is a choice between manual labour and machines, there is also a need to raise it in small rural development works (which, almost by definition, preclude the use of highly mechanized methods) in order to increase the economic returns on the labour invested in these small projects. Here the main approach is perhaps to expand rapidly the facilities for training rural labour and, as a first step, for training project supervisors. One observer, stressing the importance of raising productivity in such projects, wrote:

> Of course there is nothing to be lost by starting to teach them the rudiments. For example, there is no need to do without technicians when there are technicians available; and simple techniques for organiz-

ing work and improving working methods must be brought within the grasp of the people. Now in this respect there is a great deal to be done. The man working with a shovel without having really learnt to use it often makes efforts out of all proportion to the results. In Africa qualified observers have estimated that suitable training would double or treble the productivity of unskilled workers. Like many others, I was struck by the time wasted using baskets on men's backs instead of wheelbarrows. This was in Tunisia, but it could have been anywhere in Africa.

Similar observations have been made by René Dumont, the agronomist, who considered that the African peasant's efficiency would be quadrupled if the all-purpose cutting instrument was replaced by an axe and a saw. As a start improved hand tools could be made in workshops which themselves occupy some of the surplus manpower.*

The problem of developing the most effective ways of training the rural people in simple methods of productivity improvement thus seems to be one of high priority in the organization of rural development works programmes.

The choice of techniques

If, when all feasible measures to reduce the costs of labour-intensive techniques have been taken, it is found that public works carried out with much labour and little machinery still cost more than the same work carried out with little labour and much machinery, what should be done? Should the possibility of providing more jobs be sacrificed to the need for having the work done as cheaply as possible? Or should somewhat higher costs be considered acceptable if this enables many more people to be provided with jobs?

If techniques other than the cheapest in terms of money cost are selected, one of two consequences will result. Either a smaller volume of public works will be completed than could have been completed for the same amount of money, or the government will have to raise additional funds from some source—presumably by imposing additional taxes or by cutting down other public expenditure.

If public works have been selected because of the need for them and the importance of the contribution they can make to economic development it will be very undesirable and bad for economic growth to accept a smaller public works programme than could have been financed for the same money. Most African governments find themselves short of money for a great many very urgent purposes. They cannot spend as much as they would like to do on schools,

* Gabriel Ardant, *A plan for full employment in the developing countries. Employment and Economic Growth, Studies and Reports. New Series No.* 67 (Geneva, 1964), p. 30; see also *Employment and Economic Growth,* loc. cit.

hospitals, agricultural extension work and many other desirable things. They will find it difficult either to divert money to a public works programme from other types of expenditure or to raise additional revenue.

These are arguments in favour of choosing the cheapest techniques in public works even if this means leaving many people without work who badly need it.

There are, however, arguments on the other side. It is very undesirable to leave people idle when they want to work and when their work could contribute to economic growth and development. And the question arises whether money costs of alternative methods of work do in fact reflect costs in a more fundamental sense. Many authorities take the view that the rate of interest payable on the capital used in many projects in developing countries understates the real cost of using the capital, while the rate of wages payable overstates the real cost of using labour. The point was explained in a recent I.L.O. report in the following terms:

> There can hardly be said to be an organized market or a market price for capital in many developing countries. Finance may be made available from public sources or with a government guarantee for some privileged types of investment in the modern sector at rates of interest lower than would have had to be paid in an open market, while usurious rates may be payable in the traditional sector. While rates of interest for certain types of borrowing may fail to reflect the true scarcity of capital, wage rates on the other hand may fail to reflect an abundance of unskilled labour. Wages have to be looked at from two points of view—as an income and as a cost. As an income, wages in developing countries are often barely, if at all, sufficient to enable even urgent needs to be met. . . .
>
> But if there is much unemployment or underemployment even very low wages may overstate the real cost of employing labour, in the sense of the value of the alternative production there would have been if the worker had not been employed where he is. The value of the alternative production forgone, so far as the activities of the worker himself are concerned, will be nil if the worker was wholly unemployed, and may be very low if he was greatly underemployed.*

* I.L.O.: *Employment and Economic growth, op. cit.*, pp. 137–8. The report points out, in addition, that there may be other elements in costs to society that cannot be neglected. Unless wage-earning employment can be provided on the spot, workers will have to move in order to take it up and this will involve costs of transport. If they move to towns, they will have to be provided with somewhere to live, and other forms of social capital. They may also need various forms of training which, however desirable, cannot be provided without costs. All these things will make demands on resources which will constitute real costs to society.

Economists who find this argument convincing, as most do, believe that in countries with 'surplus' labour it will be advantageous to choose methods of production, in public works as in other sectors of the economy, that use more labour and less capital than the methods that are cheapest in terms of money. How much allowance should be made for the underpricing of capital and the overpricing (from the point of view of real costs) of labour is another question, and one on which the data required for making a scientifically acceptable calculation are scarcely ever available. A decision by the government of a country with surplus labour to choose labour-intensive methods in public works so long as the money costs exceed the money costs of more capital-intensive methods by not more than a certain percentage could be supported by respectable arguments, but the choice of the particular percentage would be a matter of judgment.

It seems reasonable, in any case, that techniques selected in public works as in other types of production should reflect the degree of scarcity or abundance of different productive resources. In African countries capital is very scarce and labour relatively abundant, as compared with the situation in industrially advanced countries. This suggests that African countries should, at least for the present, try to use more labour-intensive techniques than are usual in industrially advanced countries, so as to provide more jobs for their people, and reserve scarce capital so far as possible for other uses in which labour cannot be substituted for it.

But governments that decide to give a preference to labour-intensive techniques in public works even at the expense of accepting some increase in money costs will have to find some way of raising additional revenue if they want to maintain the volume of their public works programmes. While in most developing countries there probably are ways of raising additional revenue by methods that do not impede economic growth and do not make excessive demands on the country's machinery for assessing and collecting taxes, such methods are seldom easy to find.

Labour-intensive public works and expansion of consumption

One other consequence of a decision to favour labour-intensive public works should also be noted. This is the problem of meeting the additional consumption by the newly employed workers on public works. These workers are engaged in the production of additional capital goods (e.g. dams, roads, etc.) but not additional consumer goods. But those of them who are drawn from the ranks of the formerly unemployed or heavily underemployed will be earning more than before and will be able to consume more than before.*

The sources from which the additional consumption might be met are, briefly, as follows:

(a) concurrent increase in the output of consumer goods consequent on the fruition of previous investments or on greater incentives to produce, especially in agriculture, provided by the demand stimulus or due to other favourable factors;

(b) redistribution of consumption from the rest of the community to the newly employed workers on public works (e.g. replacement of imports of luxuries by food imports, tax policy, rationing, etc.);

(c) transfer of resources from other uses to those which can increase immediately the supply of consumer goods (e.g. using the foreign exchange which would otherwise be spent on construction machinery for additional food imports);

(d) financing by foreign aid such as bilateral food aid or the World Food Programme.

Economic planners preparing for a wide extension of labour-intensive public works will therefore need to devise appropriate policy measures through mutual adjustment of the various elements mentioned above to prevent too great a lack of balance between the additional demand for consumer goods (which will, to a large extent, consist of foodstuffs) and the additional supply of these goods to

* For the economy as a whole the net additional consumption thus generated varies directly with—

(a) the number of unemployed and underemployed persons put to work on public works projects; and

(b) the level of wages earned by these workers;

and inversely with—

(c) the amount of savings set aside by those workers out of their newly earned incomes (e.g. for repayment of debts incurred during unemployment or accumulating a minimal cash balance for precautionary motives, etc.); and

(d) the amount of savings set aside by the former supporters of these workers.

The last two factors are probably much less important. The decisive factor is the additional wage bill, which is the product of wages and additional employment.

meet this demand. Otherwise, an inflationary situation may arise. One important consideration in meeting this demand is to avoid diversion of resources from uses for other productive investments, since this would affect adversely the rate of economic growth.

In certain types of labour-intensive public works projects which are designed to bring the workers direct and immediate benefits, the unemployed and underemployed may be willing to contribute their labour voluntarily without earning wages. Under such arrangements the problem of financing additional consumption by these workers during the construction phase will hardly arise. . . .

Appendix: Nigeria and Tanganyika

The object of the earthmoving survey, undertaken by two I.L.O. experts between January and October 1963, was to determine by work studies and examination of local conditions whether the productivity of manual labour could be improved and if so by what means, related to the following possibilities:

(a) the undertaking of public works more cheaply;
(b) the creation of extended employment by enabling manual labour to compete better with machines;
(c) the saving of foreign exchange used for the purchase of imported machinery.

The survey consisted of an examination of the output, productivity and cost of manual labour and of general purpose machines operated by contractors on roads and railway embankments, and was confined to work which could be performed either by machines or by man (or man assisted by animal or tip-truck transport). Since no cases of manual work on roads or railway embankments were found it was necessary to study manual digging in quarries, river beds, borrow pits and drainage channels, and the transport of the material to the placement area on head-pans, tip-trucks or donkeys. The data were then applied to a standard construction layout of uniform measurements and quantities based on average conditions encountered, as also were those of machine operation, to enable a direct comparison of the two methods to be made.

The manual tools were pick, round-nosed shovel and metal head-pan. The machines were dragline, mechanical shovel and scraper.

Manual labour: * *productivity, method of payment and earnings*

The varying level of productivity of a manual worker may be likened to the walking rates of a man, say two, three or four miles per hour, the latter being a rate he can maintain, given adequate rest periods, without undue fatigue. If we call four miles per hour 100 per cent, the normal walking rate of three miles per hour will be 75 per cent and the 'strolling' rate of two miles per hour will be 50 per cent. A man walking for short spells at four miles per hour—100 per cent—and having disproportionate rest periods, or idle time, could finish up with an average of two miles per hour—50 per cent— or less.

The average level of productivity observed in the work studied was of the order of 50 per cent; the national over-all level for this type of work is considered to be below 50 per cent.

The three basic methods of payment encountered were—

(a) Flat rate. Workers were paid the statutory rates for the locality. The amount of their output depended mainly on the effectiveness of the supervisors, who represented some 20 per cent of the workforce.

(b) Finish-and-go. A fairly easy set task was usually completed in four to five hours, after which the worker was free to leave; for this he received the local statutory flat rate. This was a form of direct incentive, with free time as the premium. Supervision was 4 to 5 per cent of the workforce.

(c) Paid task. Workers were paid by unit of work produced and were usually free to come and go as they chose. This was piece-work with a direct financial incentive. Supervision varied from 4 per cent to zero.

The highest productivity observed was under the paid-task system at 60 per cent or more, while for flat rate and finish-and-go the range observed was from 45 to 53 per cent. The figure depended noticeably, in the case of flat rate, on the quality of supervision.

The daily level of earnings varied with the locality, sometimes markedly. The range of earnings per eight-hour day at the seven work sites for which statistics were available was 3·4 to 6·7 shillings (48 to 96 U.S. cents), an average of 5·1 shillings (73 U.S. cents).

---

* The manual workers were all males, with an isolated exception in the Nigerian tin mines, where women from the families of men on task work assisted with the carrying of material dug.

Of the three methods of payment described, evident advantages lie with the last two, since they are related to productivity and cheapness of supervision. The cost of paid-task work in the cases observed in Nigeria, however, was inflated because the system was operated only through independent petty contractors. Where the direct labour cost per cubic yard was over the range 1·1 to 1·2 shillings, middlemen were being paid from 2·1 to 5 shillings, without bearing transport expenses. This is an increase over the direct cost of from 70 per cent to 350 per cent.

Social factors

The social factors observed on moving sites like roads and railways relate mainly to subsistence farmers recruited from scattered villages over a wide area and available seasonally only outside planting and harvesting times.

The following arrangements by a large road contractor illustrate the general customs applying to itinerant labour:

(1) Quarters were provided for labour brought to the main camp but not for that engaged locally. The cost of a lateritic soil round-house of 10 feet diameter with grass roof was £15 to £17 (43 to 49 U.S. dollars): rebuilding occurred each year.

(2) Labour was transported to and from the work site in lorries.

(3) Food was not provided: drinking and cooking water were taken to the work site in lorries.

(4) A monthly shopping trip to town (thirty miles) in lorries was provided for all labour.

In the one case observed where food was given, this consisted variously of yams, beans, garry, rice, cooking oil, green vegetables and peppers. A communal meat-stock soup was also provided daily.

Permanent labour was difficult to obtain. One site manager claimed to have engaged some 2,000 labourers over three years in order to establish a permanent workforce of 200. The important factor is the attitude of the subsistence farmer to paid work, which he usually takes periodically to fulfil some particular financial need or obligation.

Effects of quantity, distance and time on productivity

Three of the most important conditions influencing productivity in manual earthmoving are the quantity of material transported at a time, the distance it is transported and the speed of transport. The average headload carried was observed to be 56 lb. This would be transported at some two to three miles per hour over a varying distance depending on the relative locations of the digging and the placement areas.

If the cost of digging 56 lb. of average soil, loading it on to the headpan and placing it on the head is expressed as one unit, then transporting it 120 feet and returning to the digging site is also one unit, and so is every additional 120 feet travelled between the digging and the placement areas.

It will thus be seen that any increase in the journey distance rapidly increases the cost of labour. It is therefore evident that some alternative form of transport, which either carries a greater load per trip or carries it faster (or both), warrants serious consideration: tip-trucks and donkeys have been considered for this purpose.

Improving productivity in manual earthmoving

The sort of situation that has to be dealt with is well illustrated by the following example.

A minor Nigerian contractor was asked to supply sand, to be paid for on the basis of lorry-loads delivered. He contacted a senior worker in a nearby village whom he knew and asked him to assemble a gang of labourers to carry out the work, at an agreed rate to be paid daily and shared among the group *pro rata* to the work performed by each. Over a period of six days the following points were observed: the daily attendance at work varied from twelve to twenty-five men; the daily working hours varied inconsistently between five and ten; the daily lorry-loads delivered —from six to thirty-eight—were not in proportion to attendance or hours worked.

In spite of these variations, however, the over-all output averaged one lorry-load per man per day, a not inconsiderable performance of 65 per cent—equivalent in the analogy of walking rate to 2·6 miles per hour.

The example shows the attitude towards work of the villagers from among whom most of the labourers are recruited in the Northern Province of Nigeria, and inquiries and observations in other parts of both countries visited have indicated an identical outlook. Brought up in the communal village life and nurtured in its tradition, the villager is unused to artificial curbs, will work when he has the need or inclination, and likes to take his leisure or conduct his private life at his own convenience. It is not in his nature to attend work for regular hours on six days a week all the year round.

Given, however, the opportunity to work in his own way, he can show an output that not only matches but outstrips that of the regular labourer on flat rate. The one kind of work to which he reacts favourably is some form of task work, under which he feels he is working for himself. This is a very natural reaction in a man of his temperament and upbringing.

The effect on productivity of increasing the load transported and reducing its transport time was discussed in the previous section. Increasing the load carried by using donkeys for transport increases productivity over distances of 100, 500 and 1,000 feet by 20, 110 and 190 per cent respectively, while the use of the tip-truck over the same distances increases productivity by 100, 360 and 670 per cent. These and other transport devices suited to particular localities and terrain are worth fully investigating as aids to productivity.

It is also evident that the worker will respond favourably to some form of incentive, such as paid task work. In the example of the Nigerian contractor productivity was at least 30 per cent higher than the average. It is conditions such as these that may have to be accepted as a starting-point of a reorganization, a process made easier if the workers have a direct interest in the results. The correction of the work balance on this site, for instance, would alone have improved productivity by a further 20 per cent.

Public bodies find themselves restricted in the use of any form of paid task work, although petty contractors freely (and expensively for the public bodies employing them) practise the system. If a country is to make the best of its manpower resources such restrictions must be reviewed.

An examination of the efficiency of different types of pick, shovel and carrying vessel for various earths would certainly yield useful results, as also would an investigation into the normal load that a worker can carry without undue fatigue. It is considered that the improvement of tools and methods of work and the elimination of idle time could lead to an increase in productivity of some 80 per cent, rising gradually to 100 per cent or over.

Observations on earthmoving machinery

The groups of machines studied and costed were the following:

(*a*) mechanical shovel with bulldozer for digging and piling soil, and tip-truck for transport;

(*b*) dragline with ripper for breaking up earth, and grader for levelling after piling.

(*c*) large, medium and small scrapers (14, 7 and 4½ cu. yd) with bulldozer as pusher (the times for the medium and small scrapers were estimated).

There are probably as many ways of calculating the hourly cost of machines as there are machine users. The method adopted was to estimate the life of the machine in working hours according to the working conditions encountered, and to spread its landed cost over the hours worked according to its utilization; for instance, if it worked for six hours in a working day of twelve hours, its hourly cost would be double that for working the full twelve hours. To the hours actually worked were then added the relatively constant operating costs of maintenance, spares, fuel, lubricants and labour.

The vital factors, then, are the landed cost of a machine in the country and the degree to which it is utilized. It is true to say that the best use of a machine is its greatest possible continuous use over as long a period as is economically feasible. A machine standing idle is costing money.

The degree of utilization is crucial to any comparison of the cost of manual labour with that of machines, because machine utilization is machine productivity, which must be contrasted with the productivity of manual labour in any comparison. For instance, manual labour even at its present admittedly low level of productivity can, if assisted by donkey or tip-truck transport, compete with the mechanical shovel unit in the lower and middle utilizations; but if its productivity were increased by from 80 to 100 per cent, it would be in direct competition with the shovel unit and become competitive with the scraper unit in the lower utilizations. It is not easy to assess the real degree of utilization of machines because accurate records are seldom kept. Large contractors on roads and railways, who must make machine operation pay, had a utilization range of some 50 to 85 per cent. On the other hand, estimates by some public works bodies indicated a range of 10 to 50 per cent; others considered that they could operate at 75 to 80 per cent if they were not restricted by the non-availability of funds.

Among the chief reasons for a reduction in utilization are lack of work due to lack of forward planning; time for maintenance, breakdown or stand-by; travel to the work site; and the weather. It is by no means a simple matter even for practised hands to keep machine operation in the middle or higher utilizations and in the absence of strict controls it can quickly fall to a grossly uneconomic level. Another factor vitally affecting the use made of machines is the manner in which they are operated. It cannot be too strongly emphasized that specialized skills are required for their effective use and maintenance, particularly as they become more complex. To invest in a complex earthmoving machine and expect it to work to maker's specifications in unskilled hands and without proper care and attention could prove financially disastrous. Skills are properly acquired only through a sound technical training and extended practical experience, and developing countries would be well advised to consider what skills are available locally and the best means to employ for developing them to the required standard.

32. INFLATION AND GROWTH

A. J. KILLICK

The fragile economy

'If we were forced to sum up the Gold Coast economy in one word, the word we would choose would be "Fragile".' So ran the opening sentence of the 1952 *Seers–Ross Report* on problems of development.* They were, as we will see, preoccupied with the proneness of the economy to inflationary forces, but we may adopt their term for a rather more general usage, to draw attention to the general tendency of the economy towards instability.

In the course of this book we have drawn attention to a number of sources of instability in the economy. First and foremost, there are the large fluctuations in the earnings that Ghana derives from her cocoa exports. Given the present tax system and Cocoa Marketing Board price policy, the fluctuations in export earnings from cocoa give rise to even larger variations in government revenues and in the aggregate incomes received by the cocoa farmers. Partly as a result of the unreliability of cocoa tax revenues, the general government budgetary balance is unpredictable. Other exporting industries are also subject to widely fluctuating earnings, most notably the diamond, manganese and logging industries.

As is the case in most economies with a large private sector, the volume of private investment is also a volatile element. . . . Then there is the instability that stems from the very great importance in the domestic flow of goods and services of local foodstuffs, which comprises over 40 per cent of total private consumption. In the northern part of the country the output of foodstuffs is much affected by the vagaries of the weather, and the efficiency of the distributive system may also be affected by the weather factor.

The effects of these destabilizing forces show up in a number of ways. For one thing they affect the price level. A study of month-

---

* *Report on Financial and Physical Problems of Development in the Gold Coast*, by Dudley Seers and C. R. Ross (Government Printer, Accra, July 1952).

by-month price changes for the last ten years indicates a seasonal variation superimposed on the general upward trend, with prices generally reaching a peak around the turn of the year as a result of payments to the cocoa farmers and the influence of Christmas spending and falling to lower levels by the second quarter of the year, thereafter tending to rise again.*

Instability is reflected also in the rather drastic changes that are liable to occur in the balance of payments from one year to the next, in the substantial changes that occur in the numbers of unemployed from one month to the next and in the erratic pattern of growth of the Gross Domestic Product. The annual year-to-year rate of growth in the Gross Domestic Product (at 1960 prices) was as follows:

Year	Growth per cent	Year	Growth per cent
1956	5·9	1960	8·3
1957	3·2	1961	1·5
1958	−1·5	1962	3·4
1959	13·4		

An economy which can suffer a contraction of 1·5 per cent in one year and enjoy an expansion of 13·4 per cent in the next is indeed an erratic one.

Seers and Ross were concerned about the susceptibility of the economy to a particular type of instability—inflation—but enough has already been said to establish the great difficulty that must be experienced in exercising control over Ghana's economy, especially since most of the sources of instability are external, or, in the case of the weather, quite outside the control of the authorities. With many of the crucial variables so subject to short-term change, long-term economic policy will be both more difficult to formulate and to enforce.

Inflation and growth

The general upward movement after the war in the domestic price level, with the Accra retail price index at the end of 1963 160 per cent above the level existing at the end of 1945, on the face of it lends support to the *Seers–Ross Report*'s stress on the susceptibility of the economy to inflationary forces.

In essence, their contention was that development spending, that is capital formation, was inflationary because it created additional demands for goods, such as local foods, which were in inelastic supply, and that once an inflationary wave of spending got under way there

* See *Statistical Year Book, 1961*, table 110.

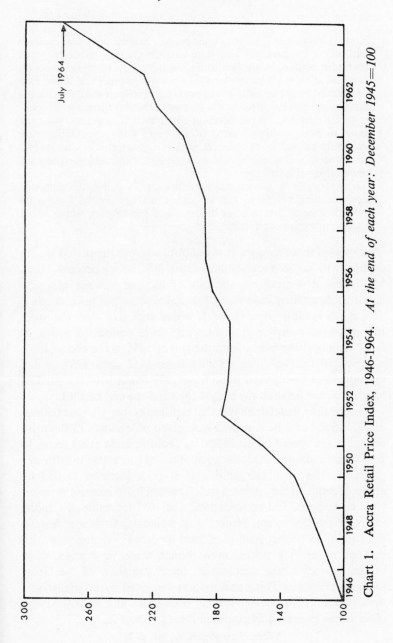

Chart 1. Accra Retail Price Index, 1946-1964. *At the end of each year: December 1945=100*

were very few checks in the economy to a continuation of the process:

> Direct taxation hardly touches most people; indirect taxes are relatively light, stocks are generally very thin, virtually the only goods produced locally for consumers are foodstuffs and the supply of these cannot be increased at short notice; imports take months to order and in any case are checked by the inability of the ports and transport system to handle much more; price control is not very effective and there are few conventional restraints on profiteering; communications are too poor for goods to flow readily to areas of shortage; savings institutions are practically unused by the general public; and largely for this reason, there is no capital market in which the Government could use monetary instruments—if it had any.
>
> A sudden rise in incomes can therefore rapidly outrun the supply of goods, causing people to bid for goods in short supply, forcing up prices, leading to demands for higher wages and salaries, which would in turn push prices up further. . . .*

In spite of these dangers, it is doubtful whether the period we are dealing with has seen a truly cumulative inflationary process. Prices have risen, it is true, but the rate of increase has not generally accelerated and there have been appreciable periods of price stability. This much is clear from Chart 1, which indicates that the price history of the post-war years falls into three periods: a period of fairly rapidly rising prices from the end of 1945 to the end of 1951, a period of relative price stability from 1952 until 1959, and a resumption of the upward trend from 1959 onwards with a particularly rapid rise between the end of 1962 and the end of 1963.

It is certainly understandable that writing, as they were, at the end of 1951, Seers and Ross should have given prominence to the price issue, but the record of the following seven or eight years seems to belie their pessimism about the possibilities of containing inflationary pressures. The main safeguard against price increases caused by excess demand, as they pointed out, is the ability to increase expenditures on imports, and between 1952 and 1959 the value of imports increased by 75 per cent. Moreover, it would appear that at least in the later fifties the production of local foods was keeping pace with demand at existing prices, even though these were years when capital formation was claiming an increasing share of the Gross Domestic Product. This conclusion is suggested by an analysis of the components of the Accra retail price index into local food and other items, presented in graphical form in Chart 2.

* *Seers–Ross Report, op. cit.*, p. 2.

This shows that while the rise in local food prices far outstripped
the prices of the other items of expenditure between 1948 and 1956
(an increase of 117 per cent as against 30 per cent), they then remained virtually constant for the next four years.

Our present interest, however, is in the nature of the economy as
it was in the early sixties and it is interesting to try to apply the
arguments of Seers and Ross to the contemporary Ghanaian
economy. Some of their specific arguments would clearly need to be
modified or abandoned. There is now adequate port capacity. The
tax structure has been substantially improved. The system of transport and communications is certainly better. There has been a major
expansion of the banking system.

But there are also some striking parallels with the situation as they
saw it. For instance, the capacity to import can no longer be relied
upon to absorb excess purchasing power. Then, they argued, the
capacity to import was subject to the physical limitations of the ports.
Now the capacity to import is limited by financial constraints. For
while the country's international reserves stood at £G145 million at
the end of 1952, and £G208 million three years later, by the end of
1962 they were down to £G72 million and were further reduced
during 1963. Hence the import and exchange controls. The large
international reserves of the '50s constituted the best guarantee
against cumulative inflation and this protection no longer exists.
Moreover, the level of inventories—another cushion against the
inflationary effect of a sudden spurt of spending—must be even lower
today (mid-1964) than it was in 1951, in relation to the volume of
transactions. For one of the effects of the import controls was to
bring about a sharp fall in stock ratios of imported goods.

Superimposed on this situation there is another important factor
which was not present in the earlier fifties. We refer to the emergence
of persistent and growing budget deficits,* which first appeared in the

* The record of budgetary balances since the war was as follows (£G million):

1946–7	+0·9	1952–3	+4·2	1958–9	−11·3
1947–8	−0·7	1953–4	+0·6	1959–60	−17·8
1948–9	+0·2	1954–5	+33·1	1960–1	−30·2
1949–50	+4·0	1955–6	−6·7	1961–2	−41·0
1950–1	+3·0	1956–7	−10·8	1962–3	−34·4
1951–2	+13·9	1957–8	−3·5		

Sources: *Economic Survey 1962*; *Financial Statement, 1963–4*.
Note: For a commentary on the growth of deficit financing in the sixties see
the *Annual Reports* of the Bank of Ghana, 1961–2 and 1962–3.

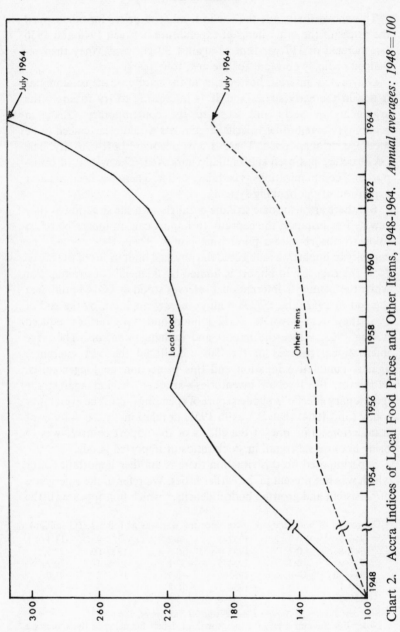

Chart 2. Accra Indices of Local Food Prices and Other Items, 1948-1964. *Annual averages: 1948=100*

mid-fifties and which in the early sixties were substantially financed by such inflationary means as Ways and Means advances from the central bank. Added to this was an increase in bank credit to the private sector of the economy. It is not clear that the resulting expansion in the money supply had had much inflationary impact even as late as 1962, since there had probably accumulated in the fifties a considerable unsatisfied demand for money balances, but it is quite certain that a continuation of this injection of money into the system would be inflationary and would occur in conditions that placed the economy in a weak position to absorb any such strain.

As the mid-sixties approached there was yet a further consideration which added to the possibility of cumulative inflation: the fact that there had been in operation since mid-1960 a 'wage freeze' in conditions of rising prices. As we saw in Table 6.12 of Chapter 6, the index of real wages for unskilled workers had fallen from 119 in July 1960 to 89 in December 1963. It is true that even though wage rates had been not allowed to increase, actual earnings did rise. But prices rose faster, so that by the end of 1963 real earnings were probably back to their 1959 levels.

Thus, although the 'wage freeze' itself was an important disinflationary influence during the early sixties, there must have been a great deal of pressure building up inside the trade unions and elsewhere for a suspension of this policy—the more so as local food prices had begun a fairly sharp upward trend beginning in 1960 (see Chart 2). A major relaxation of the wage freeze would introduce a real possibility of a cumulative wage-price spiral.

As the mid-sixties approached, therefore, the economy was experiencing substantial price increases, was in a weak position to absorb further inflationary pressures, and appeared to be in real danger of a wage-price inflationary spiral.

But did this matter? Would inflation necessarily be a bad thing? In a sense, inflation as such is always undesirable because of its social consequences and it is perfectly legitimate to argue that because of these consequences inflation should always be avoided. Inflation in Ghana is also undesirable in the sense that it conflicts with the Government's objective of a stable internal value of the Ghana pound. But what if inflation promoted the pre-eminent objective of economic growth? Would it not then be desirable? If we now make the judgment that inflation would be justified if it promoted the growth of the economy, the question that must be investigated is whether inflation would actually have this effect. It is this that we now investigate.*

There is, of course, an enormous literature on inflation and growth in the conditions of the developing countries, and although this has not yet resulted in any generally accepted set of conclusions it has at least isolated with some precision the points at issue. These we will simply state dogmatically and then apply them to the economic circumstances of Ghana.

For inflation to be successful and efficient in promoting a higher level of capital formation and a faster rate of economic growth, the following minimum conditions must be satisfied:

(1) There must be a redistribution of income away from those with a low marginal propensity to save (the poor) in favour of those with higher marginal propensities to save (the rich and the Government).

(2) The additional savings created in this way should be capable of obtaining command over a larger volume of capital goods than would have been possible without inflation and should be devoted to types of capital formation which lead to genuine growth in the productive capacity of the economy.

(3) The supply of goods and services should be elastic with respect to capital inputs; that is to say, a shortage of savings must constitute the major bottleneck holding back the growth of the economy.

(4) The institutional framework of the economy should be such that the authorities have the power to hold the inflation sufficiently in check to prevent such rapid price increases that the public loses confidence in money as a means of exchange.

Taking first the distributive effects, who in Ghana would be the likely losers from an inflation and who the gainers? The most clear-cut case is that of the export industries which would certainly be hit.

* Curiously enough, there is no discussion of this in the *Seers–Ross Report*, which simply takes it for granted that inflation is undesirable. There was, however, an implicit argument that inflation would hamper development because it would increase consumer-good imports at the expense of capital goods. The validity of this depends upon the hypothesis that imports really were limited by the capacity of the ports and that import controls to prevent such a substitution would be unworkable.

The prices of Ghana's exports are determined on the world markets and would not be influenced by the domestic inflation. The costs of domestic materials, services and probably labour, on the other hand, would be rising. The profit margins of the mining companies and the timber exporters would be squeezed, and this would hardly be conducive to an increase in the volume of domestic capital formation. The cocoa industry would be affected by the same factors. If the Cocoa Marketing Board did not increase the producers' price the burden would fall on the real incomes of the cocoa farmers with the probable consequence of a transfer of labour time from cocoa farming to food farming. Since the country's cocoa is a part of its capital stock, such a shift would imply a reduction in capital formation, although admittedly of a special type. If, on the other hand, the producer price were increased, then the squeeze would fall on the fiscal authorities (taking the Marketing Board as one of these for our present purposes).

A second group of probable losers would be the wage-earning class, because of the very close links between the Government and the trade union movement. Although by 1963–4 there existed pressure for a relaxation of the wage freeze, and although it is certainly a mistake to regard the T.U.C. as purely and simply an arm of Government, the Government is in a generally strong position to see that wages do not rise to the full extent that prices rise. Indeed, there would be no point whatever in embarking on a deliberately inflationary policy unless the Government were both willing and able to see a fall in real wages. For, unlike the losers mentioned in the previous paragraph, the wage-earners almost certainly do have low marginal propensities to save.

Who would be the gainers from a process of inflation?

Given the existing balance of payments position of the country and the unlikelihood of any great improvement in it in the near future, the operation of import licensing is likely to render the supply of imported consumer goods almost completely inelastic (we defer for a moment consideration of the effects of inflation on the balance of payments itself). The increases in the internal prices of these goods are therefore likely to be particularly large and the gainers from this process would be the distributors of these goods. Alternatively, it may be possible to restrict the increases by price controls, since these are the goods most easy to reach by such controls. In this case the profit margins of the distributive system would not be swollen, or not to the same extent (except those of black marketeers), and the redistribution of income from the low-savers to the high-savers would be retarded.

If we make the usual assumption that the elasticity of supply of local foodstuffs is low, food prices would also rise rapidly and the farmers would gain from this process. It is very doubtful whether this distribution effect would lead to any net increase in the real value of saving in the economy. But the inelasticity of food supply could be reduced by two factors: output might be attracted from subsistence consumption to the market, which would have a dis-inflationary effect;* and farmers might switch from cocoa and other export crops to local food production.

Local food (including the distribution costs) and imported goods make up nearly two-thirds of total consumption in Ghana. The rest is made up of services and locally processed goods. Thus the profit margins of both the services sector and the various industries producing for the local market would tend to rise.

There is finally the possibility that the Government would itself be able to obtain command over a larger share of the country's resources as a result of inflation. The issue here is the ability of the tax system to take a relatively large share of marginal increases in money incomes. The position in this respect is certainly better than it used to be, with the emergence of the income tax as an important source of revenue, although it still falls far short of the marginal tax capacity of the tax systems of industrial countries. To be specific, the Government would be able to take a large proportion of the increased profits of private industry. The rates of taxation on profits in the 1963–4 budget were 45 per cent plus a further 20 per cent on the repatriated profits of foreign concerns. The Government would also be able to share in the extra profits obtainable from the sale of imported consumer goods by the levying of suitable purchase taxes, always assuming the existence of price controls. It would, on the other hand, be in a very weak position to take in taxes the large increments that are likely to accrue to the distributive system and to the farmers, both groups being notoriously difficult to tax. And if in the course of the inflation it were found necessary to increase the producers' price of cocoa, revenue from the taxation of cocoa would have to go down.

* Cf. S. P. Schatz, 'Inflation in Underdeveloped Areas', *American Economic Review*, September 1957.

Assuming that the State would be one of the beneficiaries of the income-distribution effect of price increases, would this lead to a net increase in the volume of saving? The mere accrual of extra revenue to the State exchequer does not establish the answer because it could all be spent on additional consumption expenditures by the Government.

It is a fact that the share of consumption expenditures in the budget has risen in recent years. Capital expenditure fell from a peak of 39 per cent of the total in 1959–60 to 34 per cent in 1963–4. There would be little point in a deliberately inflationary policy unless the Government were willing and able to devote its increased real revenue to capital formation.

Our discussion of the likely income distribution effects of inflation in Ghana and its impact on the volume of real saving in the economy is therefore rather inconclusive. One of the main losers, the export industries, which produce about 20 per cent of the Gross Domestic Product, is a relatively high-saving group; and some of the gainers may be low-savers, such as the food farmers, the indigenous element of the distributive system, and perhaps even the Government itself. Moreover, not all the extra capital formation that may result from inflation would necessarily be an economically desirable use of scarce resources. It is more than likely that a good proportion of any extra savings in the distributive and agricultural sectors would be devoted to speculative or semi-speculative investment in inventories and urban private housing.

But there is a more fundamental doubt. Assuming that additional real savings were created, would these savings give command over an increased volume of capital goods? In the Ghanaian context this question can be rephrased to ask whether the country's capacity to import capital goods would be increased in the same proportion as the addition to domestic savings. To answer this, we must look at the probable impact of inflation on the balance of payments.*

If we make the realistic assumption that the policy of deliberate inflation would be operated in conjunction with a régime of import controls and exchange regulations, the effect of inflation on the value of the country's imports would relate to its impact on the ability of the restrictions to keep down imports and the export of capital.

---

* The literature usually abstracts from this by assuming a closed economy. This is a pity, for it is a characteristic of the developing countries that they have excessively 'open' economies.

Inflation would, of course, greatly increase the pressure on the system of controls. There would be a more than proportionate increase in the demand for imports because their prices would be increasingly favourable in relation to the prices of domestically produced goods. Moreover, the pursuit of the objective of growth by means of inflation would create an enormous tension between itself and the objective of maintaining a stable external value of the Ghana pound. The possibilities of devaluation would increase, giving rise to a strong desire to get capital out of the country which the exchange controls may find it difficult to contain. Another likelihood would be a reduction of capital inflows.

But it is for exports that inflation would have the most serious consequences. Inflation would have to go a long way before the cost of producing cocoa became greater than the world price, but the same is not true of some of the country's other exports. The gold-mining industry is very likely to be hard hit since its financial position is extremely sensitive to increasing domestic costs. The other extractive industries and the timber and sawmilling industry may be similarly affected, although to a lesser extent. Of course, it would be possible to keep these industries going by a resort to public subsidies,* but that would much reduce the capacity of the Government to finance additional capital formation out of the extra receipts we envisage it to obtain as a result of inflation.

It might be replied that devaluation would overcome at least part of this difficulty. There is, however, a general agreement that devaluation can only be successful in improving a country's balance of payments if it is undertaken in conjunction with a policy of restraint at home. At best, devaluation to facilitate a policy of domestic inflation could only cut some of the losses and to do that would have to be periodic.

In short, inflation would make it increasingly difficult to hold down consumer-goods imports, would jeopardize the competitive position of some of the country's main exports, would reduce the possibilities of obtaining private foreign capital and would increase the risk of an outflow of capital. And all this would happen in a situation where the country is already finding it difficult to meet her import requirements for development. Far from increasing the country's command

---

* Increased public subsidies in the case of the State Mining Corporation. For an account of the financial condition of the gold-mining industry see Chapter 11.

over capital-good imports in proportion to the increase in domestic saving, inflation would be very much more likely to reduce it, and thus reduce the country's capacity for capital formation as well. If for no other reason, a policy of inflation would not succeed in raising the rate of economic growth in Ghana because of its effects on the availability of imported capital goods.

To allow the argument to proceed, however, let us assume that inflation does permit a greater rate of capital formation. We then come to the elasticity of domestic production with respect to capital inputs. On this it is difficult to get beyond generalities, except to point out that some stress has been placed in this book on the shortage of high-level manpower as a constraint to growth in the Ghanaian economy with production meeting a manpower bottleneck.

We have also to consider the ability of the Government to ensure that inflation would not go so far as to cause a breakdown of the whole monetary system. This relates to the general range and effectiveness of economic policies available to the Government—a subject we discuss later in this chapter. We confine ourselves here to the point that Government control over the T.U.C. is favourable for the exercise of this degree of restraint over inflation, if the process of inflation does not impair it. What happened to food prices would probably be crucial in this respect, for if they were rising very rapidly it might prove politically impossible to hold down wages and an uncontrollable spiral might set in. Hence the elasticity of the supply of food would be of particular importance.*

The argument of this section could be summarized as follows: as it approached the mid-sixties, the economy was experiencing substantial increases in the general price level, was in a weak position to absorb further inflationary pressures, and appeared to be in real danger of wage-price spiral.

To the question of whether such a spiral would not in fact promote the growth of the economy we have answered in the negative.† While the balance of probability is that inflation would raise the

---

* See Geoffrey Maynard, *Economic Development and the Price Level*, London, 1962, Chapter III.
† We have not appealed to the historical record to test this conclusion, since usable national income figures only begin in 1955. For what it is worth, the record since then gives a general support to the conclusion. Growth was relatively rapid in 1955–60 and this was a period of relative price stability. The rate of growth was considerably lower in 1961–3 and these were years of rising prices.

economy's savings ratio, inflation would fail to promote economic growth because domestic savings are not the crucial bottleneck holding back the growth of the economy of Ghana. The availability of foreign exchange for capital goods is certainly more important and the short supply of high-level manpower also constitutes an important constraint. Inflation would worsen the former and be irrelevant to the latter.

The policy objectives of the maximum sustainable rate of growth and of a stable internal and external value of the Ghana pound are thus seen as being essentially complementary. . . .